Embracing the Past— Forging the Future

Embracing the Past—
Forging the Future

A New Generation of Wesleyan Theology

Edited by
Wm. Andrew Schwartz
and
John M. Bechtold

Afterword by
Michael Lodahl

ᏔPICKWICK *Publications* · Eugene, Oregon

EMBRACING THE PAST—FORGING THE FUTURE
A New Generation of Wesleyan Theology

Pickwick Publications
An Imprint of Wipf and Stock Publishers
199 W. 8th Ave., Suite 3
Eugene, OR 97401

www.wipfandstock.com

ISBN 13: 978-1-4982-0843-7

Cataloguing-in-Publication Data

Embracing the past—forging the future : a new generation of Wesleyan theology / edited by John M. Bechtold and Wm. Andrew Schwartz ; afterword by Michael Lodahl.

xii + 176 p. ; 23 cm. Includes bibliographical references.

ISBN 13: 978-1-4982-0843-7

1. Wesley, John, 1703–1791. 2. Methodist Church—Doctrines. 3. Holiness churches—Doctrines. I. Bechtold, John M. II. Schwartz, Wm. Andrew. III. Lodahl, Michael E., 1955–.

BX8332 .E52 2015

Manufactured in the U.S.A.   09/16/2015

Contents

Part 2—Wesleyanism in a Pluralistic Context

Part 3—Renewing Classical Wesleyanism

Contributors

Edward Antonio (PhD, University of Cambridge) is Harvey H. Potthoff Associate Professor of Christian Theology and Social Theory, Associate Dean of Diversities, and Director of Justice & Peace Programs at Iliff School of Theology. Before going to Iliff he taught at the University of the Witwatersrand in Johannesburg, South Africa where he also served as the treasurer of the South African Academy of Religion and as a Consultant for the World Council of Churches Project on Ecumenical Hermeneutics. In 2009, he was appointed an American Academy of Religion (AAR) Luce Fellowship in Theologies of Religious Pluralism and Comparative Theology. In 2010, the Center for Interfaith Action on Global Poverty (CIFA) named Antonio to lead a process in Nigeria for theological reflection and evaluation of the experience of Muslim and Christian faith leaders mutually engaged in interfaith action on malaria prevention throughout the country.

John M. Bechtold is a PhD candidate at the University of Denver/ Iliff School of Theology Joint Doctoral Program in Theology, Philosophy, and Cultural Theory. His work focuses on the interplay between Christian theology and German Idealist philosophy. He also serves as Youth Pastor at Gracia y Vida Iglesia del Nazareno. He is a frequent contributor to scholastic societies including the Wesleyan Theological Society, the Wesleyan Philosophical Society, and the American Academy of Religion.

Ben Boeckel is a PhD student in Old Testament at Southern Methodist University where his dissertation will examine the concept of covenant in Genesis–Kings. Ben is an adjunct professor of Biblical Languages at Nazarene Theological Seminary where he earned his M.Div. His other academic publications include two forthcoming dictionary articles, a review essay, and several book reviews. He is a minister in the Church of the Nazarene and has published several articles in WordAction Press' *Illustrated Bible Life* and *Adult Faith Connections*.

Rusty E. Brian (PhD, Garrett Evangelical Theological Seminary) is Senior Pastor at Renton Church of the Nazarene, and Adjunct Professor at Northwest Nazarene University. He received a BA in Bible & Christian Ministries from Point Loma Nazarene University (2002), M.Div. from Nazarene Theological Seminary (2005), and a Ph.D. in Theology & Ethics from Garrett Evangelical Theological Seminary (2011). His Ph.D. Dissertation, *Covering Up Luther: How Barth's Christology Challenged the Deus Absconditus That Haunts Modernity*, was published by Cascade Books in 2013.

John B. Cobb, Jr. (PhD, University of Chicago) is Emeritus Professor, Claremont School of Theology and Claremont Graduate University. Additional teaching posts include, Fullbright Professor at the University of Mainz, Visiting Professor at Vanderbilt, Harvard, and Chicago Divinity Schools. He is a founding Co-Director of the Center for Process Studies and accomplished author with over 700 articles and over 40 books. He is the co-author with Herman Daly of *For the Common Good* which was co-winner of the Grawemeyer Award for Ideas Improving World Order. In 2014 Cobb was elected to the prestigious American Academy of Arts & Sciences.

Dick O. Eugenio (PhD, Manchester University) is Instructor in Theology, at Asia-Pacific Nazarene Theological Seminary, Philippines. Dick teaches theology courses and serves as the Director of the Master of Science in Theology program and the Dean of Chapel. His main theological interest lies in the doctrine of the Trinity and the implications of Trinitarian thinking to the church's theological formulation, worship and mission. Dick's doctoral thesis has been published as *Communion with the Triune God: The Trinitarian Soteriology of Thomas F. Torrance* (Pickwick Publications, 2014).

Michael Lodahl (PhD, Emory University) is Professor of Theology and World Religions at Point Loma Nazarene University in San Diego, California, and has studied extensively in Israel and Jordan. He is an ordained elder in the Church of the Nazarene and has served congregations in three states. Lodahl is the author of several books, including *The Story of God: A Narrative Theology*, and *Claiming Abraham: Reading the Bible and the Qur'an Side by Side*.

Tamara E. Lewis (PhD, Vanderbilt University) is Assistant Professor of the History of Christianity at Southern Methodist University. Her research examines the ways Protestant doctrine was used in the development of racial ideologies in early modern England. This involves tracing how theological beliefs were applied to and shaped emerging discourses and practices regarding skin color differences in the late sixteenth and seventeenth centuries. Moreover, she analyzes early modern perspectives about theological anthropology and somatic difference in relation to England's burgeoning participation in the transatlantic human trade, slavery, and colonialism.

Wm. Andrew Schwartz is a PhD candidate in Philosophy of Religion and Theology at Claremont Graduate University, and Managing Director of the Center for Process Studies. He holds an MA in Philosophy from CGU and an MA in Theology from Nazarene Theological Seminary. An active member of the Wesleyan Theological Society, Andrew's academic interests include comparative philosophy and theology, Wesleyan theology, and religious pluralism.

Orlando R. Serrano, Jr. is a PhD candidate in the department of American Studies & Ethnicity (ASE) at University of Southern California, and Dornsife College of Letters, Arts, and Sciences Fellow. He was a Ford Predoctoral Fellow from 2008-2011. He received a BA in Philosophy and Theology from Point Loma Nazarene University (PLNU). He also earned an MA in American Studies from California State University Fullerton (CSUF) and an MA in American Studies & Ethnicity from the University of Southern California. Orlando has served as managing editor of *American Quarterly*; research assistant to Dr. Laura Puildo.

Susie C. Stanley (PhD, University of Denver/Iliff School of Theology) is Emeritus Professor of Historical Theology, Messiah College. She is a passionate advocate for women in ministry. Her Women in Ministry Initiative, headquartered on the Messiah College's Grantham campus, provides abundant opportunities for women students to live their faith and follow their own ministerial calling. Among her many publications include: *Holy Boldness: Women Preachers' Autobiographies and the Sanctified Self* (University of Tennessee Press 2002), and *Feminist Pillar of Fire: the Life of Alma White* (Wipf & Stock Publishers, 2007).

Nell Becker Sweeden (PhD, Boston University) is Richard B. Parker Co-chair of Wesleyan Theology, and Assistant Professor of Theology at George Fox Evangelical Seminary. Her passion in research and teaching lies at the intersection between theology and culture. She is enlivened by how the life of the church and theological reflection take shape and are re-appropriated anew in different cultures, times, and spaces. Of particular interest for her teaching and writing is introducing non-western and two-thirds world perspectives into theological reflections and worldviews. Additionally, she finds that themes involving margins, in-between spaces, border crossings, and interdisciplinarity continually come to light in her theological explorations.

Andrew J. Wood is a PhD candidate in American History at Auburn University. He received an MA in Religion from Trevecca Nazarene University, and an M.A.T.S. in History of Christianity from the Divinity School of Vanderbilt University. Andy has interests in the religious and social history of the American South, especially the history of Methodism and the holiness movement. His dissertation explores aspects of this history in the late 19th and early 20th century through the life of B. F. Haynes.

John M. Bechtold and
Wm. Andrew Schwartz

The times they are a-changin'. As such, our theology needs to adapt—to be responsive to the changing landscape. The idea for *Embracing the Past—Forging the Future: A New Generation of Wesleyan Theology*, came from our assessment that Wesleyan theology has yet to fully adapt to this changing landscape, and that the future of Wesleyan theology requires the bringing together of old and new voices.

The difficult task of balancing between continuity and change—keeping up with the developments of our culture, and staying true to the roots of our tradition—requires the dual focus of looking forward and backward simultaneously.

In this volume, we have brought together contributions by young Wesleyan scholars (graduate students and junior faculty), as a way of illustrating and articulating a new generation of Wesleyan theology. These younger voices demonstrate the desire to push Wesleyan theology in new directions. Additionally, we have included contributions from senior scholars who have been doing important work and who have already made significant contributions to Wesleyan theology. This is not simply the 'old guard', but the voices of scholars who continue to make a profound impact on Wesleyan theology.

We hope that this text will find a readership among Wesleyan-Holiness theologians, students of Wesleyan, Holiness, Methodist, Pietist, and

Pentecostal theology, as well as pastors and interested lay persons from across Evangelical Christianity.

For a number of decades, both in academia and in culture at large, it has been commonplace to speak of the current generation of thinkers as somehow "post-." We have used terms like "post-modern," "post-colonial," and even "post-Christian" to describe the movement from one way of thinking to another. Evangelical Christianity has often reacted to these descriptions with trepidation. Part 1 of this book opens up the possibility to speak of a "post-" generation that remains closely tied and indebted to its own past.

Another aspect of this changing landscape is the pluralistic context in which we increasingly find ourselves. What does it mean to do Wesleyan theology in the face of religious multiplicity? What does it mean to be Wesleyan in an era of globalization? How should diversity influence the way we do Wesleyan theology? Can there be a single Wesleyan theology or hermeneutic? These sorts of questions rest at the heart of Part 2.

As important as it is to look to the future, we must not forget our past. In the spirit of finding a balance between continuity and change, Part 3 focuses on new interpretations of Wesleyan history and classical Wesleyan theological discussions. We are grateful for those who have gone before, and seek not a departure but an evolution of classical Wesleyan theology, thinking from a Wesleyan framework about issues that matter deeply to a new generation of Wesleyan theologians.

We want to thank Mark Mann for all his work in the early stages of this project. His insights have been truly helpful in crafting this volume. We want to thank our spouses (Audrey and Reanna) for being supportive during this process. We would also like to thank you, our readers, for engaging in this dialogue with us.

Part 1

Wesleyanism and the "Post" Generation

Alter-Methodist Global Identity

———— Edward Antonio ————

A *lter* in the title of this essay gestures in two different directions. First it gestures towards otherness, as in *alter*ity. Second it points in the direction of an *alter*native way of being Methodist. The otherness and difference of global Methodism represents an alternative way of being Christian. This fact is often lost on us because of the prevalent and rather uncritical assumption that Methodist identity is unproblematically continuous. This otherness and difference exists in its most pronounced form in the Global South. It is there that ordinary men, women and youth are appropriating and re-configuring Methodist identity in disruptive and discontinuous ways. Discontinuity and disruption does not mean rejection of Methodism. Rather I use these terms to signal the spaces of difference and change that characterize the evolution of Methodism from being a western driven global movement to being a movement of alter-Methodism. Discontinuity and disruption are rhetorical or heuristic tools for raising important questions about theological identity. In this essay I make four propositions about alter-Methodism. These propositions are tentative and represent a possible agenda for theological research. However, beyond that, I use them to claim that the difference and otherness of Global Methodist identity is a difference between what I call popular Methodism and Official Methodism. I should say a word about the term Methodism. I am uneasy with this term because of its tendency to imply that Methodism is an *ism*, a kind of ideological posture. I use the term Methodist identity in addition to Methodism to suggest that what we are talking about here is a cluster of traditions that share certain fundamental things in common.

Like many other expressions of Christianity in the world today Methodism is part of the global reality in which it participates as a basic constituent of religious and theological pluralism. And like other forms of modern Christianity, Methodism is characterized by a deep consciousness of the importance of context, time, and place.

These three things: pluralism, context, and globalization are at the heart of how the people called Methodists have always, more or less, understood themselves. In this brief essay I offer four tentative propositions on how these things are represented in "global Methodism." The latter is a phenomenon with many complex dimensions. I shall argue that from its inception Methodism was always global in intent, doctrine, and practice. I shall also argue that this commitment to the global "fated" Methodism to become a non-western faith. To put it another way, the global nature of Methodism has resulted in the radical de-centering of Methodist Christianity. This de-centering does not mean loss of context but rather re-contextualization, it does not mean loss of particularity but re-particularization. However, it means loss of universality or claims to universality. The globality of Methodism (its condition of being global) is a function of its re-contextualization, that is, of how it is encountered and appropriated by different people in different countries around the world. I write about global Methodist identity not from outside of history or from some context-less vantage point that transcends all expressions of Methodist identity. I write rather as an African Methodist, a member of the United Methodist Church from Zimbabwe, teaching at a United Methodist related School of Theology. I write as an African Methodist who has had experience of the complexity of Methodist identity in at least three different registers. I have actively experienced Methodism in its American, British and African expressions. I have experienced the first two both in their national contexts and the last in two distinct ways: 1) as missionary presence in Zimbabwe (the coming of missionaries), and 2) as the active appropriation of Methodist missionary Christianity by Zimbabweans.

As is well known, there are many varieties and expressions of Methodist identity such as United Methodist, Free Methodist, African Methodist Episcopal, African Methodist Episcopal Zion, and The Methodist Church of Great Britain, to name just some. What is significant about this variety of expression is how it is embodied both contextually and globally. This means that these expressions of Methodist identity are present all over the world. The mode of their global presence is invariably local and particular. This variety and theological pluralism implicates race and nationality, theology and ideology, culture and history, politics and polity, gender and sexuality as well as doctrine and liturgy. Thus Methodist identity as a global phenomenon is the outgrowth of how all these differences are contextually mapped onto Methodist self-understanding. It is exactly this which resists homogeneity and false universalism. The differences are crosscutting and mark the limits and possibilities of creating connectional alliances on a global scale. Given all this variety how do we explain that these different movements and expressions continue to call themselves "Methodist?" Is there an underlying identity which they all share? What is it that they each generically repeat in common that allows them to collectively avail themselves of this identity?

The second proposition pertains to the identity of global Methodism as both a product of colonial missionary activity as well as the creation and re-creation of local and indigenous reception. The colonial dimension is obvious from the fact Methodism originated in a country that was driven by imperial interests which it sought to secure through, among other things, the spread of British inflected forms of Christianity and in which, whatever other motives they had, Methodist missionaries played a key role. In its initial missionary moments colonial Christianity was characterized by a desire to evangelize, Christianize and civilize. It is old news that it tended to conflate the message of the gospel with European cultural practices. Old news, but not irrelevant to the form and shape Christianity has taken in the global world. I do not mean to impugn the intentions of *all* Methodist missionaries of the colonial period. My point is simply that wherever Methodism exists today it is in one way or another marked by the history of colonialism. Indeed, it is directly or indirectly, the product of that history. At least in its spread outward from England Methodism arose as an imperial church. To name ourselves as Methodist, even as we vernacularize the name, to avail ourselves of inherited ecclesial structures, modes of organization, discipline and polity (even as we sometimes culturally modify them) and to accept and ratify western theological commitments (even as we strive to inculturate them) is to participate in the historical drama of colonialism. This point becomes even more significant if we take seriously the fact that the centers of decision-making, finance, power, resources and theological articulation remain firmly located in the Global North. The colonial legacy of Methodism, like that of many other churches, places us in a situation in which we must deal with both the possibility and the reality that the powerful churches of the north can and often do impose their will on the poorer churches of the Global South, sometimes directly and sometimes by co-opting its clergy and leaders. Again, in my strand of Methodism, one can see this at work in politicking that goes on at General Conference. Methodism is thus about the politics of identity, power, and ideology.

The third proposition is that there is a distinction between popular and official Methodism, at least in the Global South. Official Methodism is codified in documents such as, in my strand of it, the Book of Discipline, it is defined by officially ordained clergy and exists as doctrinal formulation, it is largely literate, and consciously organized around boards, agencies, and conferences. It is presided over by bishops and their staff. At the other end of the spectrum lies popular Methodism. I first encountered this in my parents who with little education consistently and proudly (albeit also unconsciously) mis-pronounced the identity of their chosen tradition as Whisiri (meaning Wesleyan). However, the term is a Shona transliteration of whistle (thus one who whistles). What they found appealing in the Methodist identity were the hymns, the colorful uniforms, the weekly women's and men's meetings accompanied by drinking tea served with bread at the end of each gathering. They consciously knew little, if anything, about the Wesleyan quadrilateral, at least not in its standard formulation; they knew or had little deliberative understanding of the creeds of the church and its dogmas. Popular Methodism is simultaneously a religious way of articulating a social identity in a society in which community or social belonging is central to life, and a social way of expressing religious commitment in a society in which religion is regulative. It is the way most uneducated and non-literate, poor and marginalized Christians in the Global South experience and live their faith. It takes the forms of grassroots expression in which ordinary men, women, and youth reimagine and rework Christian faith in terms of everyday cultural practices. Although it does not reject official Methodist identity, (and indeed explicitly validates itself officially by locating itself within the authority of Official Methodism) it, nevertheless, represents an important theological distance between its popular consciousness and official identity. Methodist theologians from the Global South or the Two-Thirds World must rethink Methodist identity in the space opened up by this "critical" distance. It is in that space that some of the most exciting and challenging theological questions and problems are emerging. Here we face questions about the continuity of the identity of Methodism across time and space, about the continuity of history and tradition. We face questions about how a church of predominantly non-literate peoples with little historical knowledge of western Christianity can stand in authentic continuity with its western source(s)?

I want to build on this notion of popular Methodism to say something about the Wesleyan Quadrilateral from the standpoint of alter global Methodism. Let us start with reason. There are at least four forms of rationality operative in popular Methodism. These are: 1) indigenous rationality; In Africa, Asia, and Latin America the majority of Methodists live in and do reflect upon their faith in relation to their traditional cultures; 2) there is non-literate rationality. This is rationality based upon and informed by oral modes of communication; 3) communal rationality whereby knowledge, standards of interpretation, and cognitive content are communally determined (i.e. are a matter of shared worldviews). Communal knowledge is rooted in the belief that knowledge is not authored by an individual *qua* individual but is a function of the individual's cognitive activity as shaped and informed by the communal arrangements of his or her social context; and, 4) experiential or pragmatic rationality. This latter is derived from experience and is molded by concern for and attention to outcomes: does this work, and in what way? This is reasoning out of the structures of one's immediate social and Methodist *habitus*.

Next I shall remark on experience. Experience is a process of *living out* one's life in, through, and out of some reality. It has at least three dimensions: content, process and outcome or impact. Experience is about how we are caught up in something (the content); it pertains to both the manner of how we are caught up (affects, feelings and emotions) and the sense we make of being so caught up (cognitive processing) and the outcomes of our being so caught up (the impact on us). It is on the one hand, both the affective and cognitive process in, through, and out of which we live the reality of being existentially involved in something, and on the other, the impact of such a process on some aspect of or on the overall structure of our life.

The objective or raw content of experience for the majority Two-Thirds World Christians is twofold: the concrete reality of social marginality, violence and poverty as well as the reality of their faith. Experience here is not experience of wealth, privilege, and progress conjoined to faith but rather mostly experience of engaging faith in the face of pain and suffering.

This is the medium in which alter Methodism does its theology. Vulnerability and insecurity are important sources of theological reflection.

Let us now address tradition, another aspect of the quadrilateral. Often when Methodists speak of tradition in relation to the quadrilateral they tend to be vague and unspecific. Let me specify four kinds of tradition out of which much of alter-Methodism operates. First, and rather obviously are the Traditions of Christian faith: its creeds and dogmas, and the historic declarations of its councils. The Wesleyan theological commitments of alter-Methodism are located here. Second, then, tradition describes the legacy of John and Charles Wesley, the teachings of George Whitefield, and the formalized, collective, and historic practices of Methodist churches since the eighteenth century. Third, tradition refers to the indigenous structures of belief, culture and practice that have sustained non-western peoples across the world for centuries. The point of interest in this is that these traditions have come to inform and shape how these people have received and reshaped Christianity, including Methodist identity. In other words, the Traditions of Christian faith have been received and mediated through these other non-Christian traditions. The interface between the two and its undoubtedly transformative impact on Methodism is consequential for global Methodist identity in ways yet to be figure out. Fourth, our understanding of tradition would not be adequate if it failed to include the "civilizing" effects of colonial domination which came with the intention to transform cultures and lives in the name of European superiority. Alter-Methodism is saddled with the legacy of colonialism. The languages in which it thinks theologically are western, its hymns are largely western, the sources and authorities to which it appeals are western and the modes within which it operates administratively are western. These are its colonial traditions. The irony in all of this is also how all these western legacies are subjected to a logic of ongoing indigenous re-contextualization in which their power is both intentionally and unintentionally disrupted, discontinued, called into question, transformed, and even subverted. It is in this process of re-contextualization and subversion that *an other* Methodism, an alternative Methodism, is being born, sometimes away from the expectations of official identity, sometimes in its face, and sometimes in collaboration.

The final aspect of the quadrilateral on which I will comment is scripture. The Bible is obviously a source of authority for many Christians. This is also the case in the Christianities of the Two-Thirds World. However, there it is not just a book attesting to God's revelation but a veritable source of social, political, and cultural contestation. It is a book that came with and as part of the colonial project. In this sense it is tied to the colonial identity of Methodism in many parts of the world. Its authority is thus, again and again, threatened by its role in the history of colonialism. It is a book that inaugurated literacy and thus confronted and challenged cultures that were traditionally regulated through orality rather than literacy. In this sense it participated in the re-organization of knowledge and conscious-ness in those cultures. It is a book that introduced new moral codes and religious ideas mediated through western cultural frameworks in which it was used to condemn indigenous cultures and to demand the conversion of indigenous peoples to new ways of being. The Bible has been central to Christianity in the non-western world in deeply transformative ways. This is somewhat ironic if we consider that the majority of people in many parts of the world are "illiterate" or non-literate. Indeed, it is through the Bible that education and literacy were introduced. The point here is that the way in which scripture functions in the Wesleyan Quadrilateral for alter-Meth-odism is socially, culturally and politically complex in ways that require re-working the question of the role and authority of scripture in a myriad of directions bounded at all ends by a profound search for an alternative way of being human and being Christian. The reception of Methodism in the Global South represents this quest. It is a quest in which for better or for ill scripture plays an important role.

My fourth proposition is that there is an intrinsic connection between Methodism and social justice which defines an active theological institu-tionalization of care and service. In the Global South this is most evident in many projects that variously cluster around relief work, development projects, the building of schools, universities, hospitals, providing clean water and of course, evangelism itself. It is hard to overestimate the ex-tent to which the relevance of Methodism in the Global South is tied to its manifestation in these activities as a social fact as distinct from being just a religious presence. In other words, the institutionalization of care and service defines a theological humanism which provides Methodism with a social face in terms of which its religious presence is judged. This is especially important because alter-Methodism is taking place in contexts marred by profound social anguish and suffering precipitated by violence, poverty, and various forms of social insecurity. This means that Methodism is an eminently practical affair for many of its followers.

I have made four basic propositions in the foregoing description. My goal was to draw attention to several important points. First, there is another Methodism. I have called it popular Methodism. It represents historical, cultural and political differences which have been operative in how Methodism has been received and is being reconfigured in the Global South. Official Methodism has been slow to recognize these differences and their power in reshaping Methodist identity. Where it has taken them seriously it has done so in a politically manipulative way to achieve and bolster its ideological goals.

Second, I have suggested that Methodism in the Global South is a practical affair defined by its social face in the arenas of care and service. To be sure, this is reminiscent of the social principles of Methodism.

Third I have tried to re-read the Wesleyan Quadrilateral in ways that illustrate not the coherence of its historically pre-established categorical structure but its dynamic appropriation in terms of the logic of the everyday. Here Methodism emerges not as the result of the interpretation of doctrines, the analysis of texts, or the conscious critical appropriation of a prescribed tradition but rather largely as the "organic" transformative power of a grassroots church in the process of self-making and remaking.

Fourth, I have raised the question of continuity because Methodists in different parts of the world need to figure out what unites and what differentiates them; they must do so in terms of their local contexts, in terms of their colonial inheritances and in terms if their relationship to the history of Christianity more generally. The limitations and possibility of difference, the determination of points of continuity and discontinuity circumscribe the forms and practices in virtue of which a globally shared Methodist identity is describable as such in the first place.

Fifth, I have hinted at several points that the identity of alter-Methodism is characterized by insecurity, violence, vulnerability, anguish and suffering. This presents the possibility of two contradictory imaginaries: despair and hope. The imaginary of despair is encouraged by the conditions of utter desperation in which many Christians in the Global South find themselves. Zimbabwe, my own country, is an important example. The imaginary of hope is encouraged by the social face of Methodism I described earlier.

Wesleyan Theology beyond the Wesleys

A "Post-modern" Proposal

John M. Bechtold

John Wesley was a man of "modernity." This statement is not made as a matter of judgment, for, in many ways, it could not be otherwise. The historical socio-cultural setting in which Wesley lived and worked was an Enlightenment setting which was thoroughly "modern." What it means to speak of the "modern" will be addressed in greater detail, but for the purposes of this essay, the notion of "modernity" should be understood primarily as that structure of thinking by which the rationally autonomous individual is the primary focus. This is easily evidenced in Descartes' famous *cogito*. The proclamation, "I think, therefore, I am," is the perfect entry point into modernity. Methodological skepticism led Descartes to question how knowledge could be possible. Descartes came to believe that whatever knowledge might be possible could only begin with the "I"—the autonomous individual. Modernity, simplistically conceived, is found in the claim that the seat of reason, or at least of the practice of reason, is found in the autonomous individual. Reason can be conceived, practiced, and worked out all in one's own mind. Indeed, insofar as "modernity" understands reason to be the structuring principle of reality, in some ways even prior to the *cogito* itself, it is fair to say that, for the modernist, an autonomous individual can come very close to properly conceiving of all reality. This is the general epistemological location in which John Wesley lived and worked. While Wesley, a particularly well-read individual, certainly had nuanced understandings of modernist philosophy, he did put a great deal of emphasis and reliance upon a modernist conception of reason.

One must be careful, however, not to paint with too broad of a brush. "Modernity," however it is described, is a complex and multifaceted concept which cannot be defined, nor easily described. Jean-François Lyotard allows room for this complexity while still offering a reasonable description of "modernity." He describes the "modern" as "any science that legitimates itself . . . [by] making an explicit appeal to some grand narrative."[1] Using individually accessible "reason" as just this sort of grand narrative is a hallmark of what is here meant by modernity. To say that John Wesley was a man of modernity, then, would imply that Wesley's thought is, at least in part, rationally self-legitimating. This does not in any way discount the activity of God in the world, but it does imply that God's salvific activities are best understood individualistically.[2] Inherent to Wesley's theology is the claim that humanity, in its "original" state, was created in the image of God, by which he meant that each individual is "a spiritual being, endued with understanding, freedom of will, and various affections."[3] Wesley's theology was necessarily individualistic because he believed that the image of God is lost through human sinfulness. The image of God is only restored when "we are renewed in the image of our mind." By tying the image of God directly to the human mind, Wesley demonstrated that salvation, and the gift of holiness, are gifts of God which are given to an individual. Of course, Wesley also mediated this claim by speaking not of a solitary individual, but of a "we," of individuals in community. An interesting aspect to Wesley's modernism is that in its important nuances, it seeks to be self-correcting.

Wesley's modernism runs much deeper than his references to the *imago Dei*. Indeed, Wesley's entire theological methodology was, in many ways, profoundly "modern." It was important to Wesley to be able to describe

---

1. Lyotard, *Postmodern Condition*, xxiii.

2. Wesley was certainly not oblivious to this problem. The very fact that he placed such an emphasis on the class meetings demonstrates Wesley's understanding that there were corporate issues to sin. However, even in the communal situation of a class meeting the primary purpose was individualistic. Each member of the class participated fully in order to personally be moved forward with their own sanctification. Thus, even when Wesley attempted to speak of soteriology corporately, he did so from within a concept of hamartiological individualism.

3. Wesley, "Sermon 45," 188.

how any sort of knowledge of God could be possible. Wesley, as a theologian, denied hard scientific materialism, but in doing so he was unwilling to leave the door open to a free-for-all claim that knowledge of God was unmediated and utterly unique. It was important that Wesley reject the charges of "enthusiasm," like those which Wesley's contemporary Immanuel Kant leveled so strongly against Emanuel Swedenborg.[4] Wesley often took a particularly strong stand against such charges. Wesley's thought sought to make rational sense of the world without denying the reality and efficacy of a divine Creator. Numerous times throughout his writings, Wesley described himself as a *homo unius libri* to denote that Christian scripture was at the heart of all of his theological writings. Yet, Wesley was apt to note that scripture can never stand on its own. Thus, Wesley recognized that even as a *homo unius libri* he was likewise bound to reason, for his reading of this one book could not be contradictory to reason.

Reason is an essential element to Wesley's Christian faith because it helps to avoid the problem of "asserting propositions ever so full of absurdity and blasphemy."[5] Reason was one tool which disallowed the type of fanciful readings of scripture which Wesley would have seen as having no basis in reality. Of course, Wesley did see the reach of reason to be limited. Indeed, reason, Wesley contended, could only reach to the point of human fallenness. Here, Wesley differed sharply from many of his modernist contemporaries. Wesley recognizes that, for those who fail to recognize the reality of personal grace, "An outside religion without any godliness at all would suffice to all rational intents and purposes. It does accordingly suffice, in the judgment of those who deny this corruption of our nature. They make very little . . . of religion."[6] Wesley also speaks of "Heathens" as those "who are guided in their researches by little more than the dim light of reason."[7] Even the "dim light of reason," however, is capable of giving knowledge of the existence of God, but with reason alone "we had no acquaintance with [God]."[8] Thus, reason, for Wesley, is in a tenuous state of being strong enough to conceive of God, but religiously insufficient. Reason comes to fallen humanity as grace, which is how it can lead to knowledge about God, but is not itself the entirety of grace.

4. Kant, "Dreams of a Spirit-Seer."

5. Wesley, "*Sermon 70*," 587.

6. John Wesley, "Sermon 44," 184.

7. Ibid.

8. Ibid.

Wesley was adamant that he came to this understanding through a careful reading of scripture. As an empiricist, Wesley gave epistemological weight to experience as well.[9] Experience, for Wesley, did not counteract either reason or scripture, but served as a lens through which both could be better understood. Experience, like reason, functions properly only when bestowed by grace, for otherwise experience would only serve to reify the brokenness of fallen humanity.[10] This insistence on grace certainly sets Wesley apart from many of the great thinkers of modernity. Yet, while there is no reason to believe that there is any sort of causal connection, the claim that Wesley was a man of modernity is strengthened by Wesley's similarity to the religio-theological position held by Immanuel Kant. Kant claimed, "There is, therefore, no norm of ecclesiastical faith except Scripture, and no other expositor of it except the *religion of reason* . . . [which] alone is *authentic* and valid for the whole world."[11] Both Wesley and Kant believed that the reading of Christian scripture, or certainly its proclamation, was an empty practice without a strong rationality undergirding it.

As men of modernity, both Wesley and Kant were appealing to reason as a legitimating grand narrative. That is to say, in their thought, reason served as an ordering principle—as an intellectual undergirding which structured the way that both thought and knowledge could occur. While Kant, as a fairly non-religious philosopher, was unapologetic about his reliance on this grand narrative, Wesley, the theologian, was less forthright because of his insistence on the complementary role of the Holy Spirit. While Wesley was quick to point out what he saw to be the limitations of reason, he did not argue that the witness of the Holy Spirit, or any other sort of divine inspiration, can or does run contrary to properly ordered reason. Wesley declared, "Is it not reason (assisted by the Holy Ghost) which enables us to understand what the Holy Scriptures declare concerning the being and attributes of God—concerning his eternity and immensity; his

---

9. It is important to understand that Wesley's understanding of 'experience' differs from the psychologically receptive conceptuality that is commonly understood today. Wesley conceived of experience as profoundly individual, but as externally and actively focused. This understanding of experience fit well into the modernist conception of an autonomous human individual who refused to merely be a receptacle of data, but instead, at the least, one who internally structured external stimuli into a sensible whole. For an excellent discussion of Wesley's empiricism see: Crutcher, *Crucible of Life*.

10. Wesley, "Sermon 45."

11. Kant, *Religion and Rational Theology*, 145.

power, wisdom, and holiness."[12] In this particular sentence, reason seems to stand in an epistemological state that is roughly equivalent to that of God. Certainly reason comes after grace, but Wesley's claim is that it is reason (assisted by the Holy Ghost), not the Holy Ghost (using the tool of reason) which enables understanding. Neither, it would seem, operates without the other. Reason is a necessary co-actor, alongside the divine, that inspires the understanding of Christian scriptures, in the encounter with knowledge of the divine itself. Depending on one's reading of the creation narratives in particular, reason is itself an attribute of the divine, if not, in the form of the Holy Spirit, the divine itself. It is interesting that Wesley spoke of reason as the locus of divine activity. It is not our understanding which is assisted by the Holy Spirit, but reason. Reason, then, is encountered as always already divinely inspired. It cannot in actuality be equivalent to God, but holds a place of high esteem in the development of Wesley's epistemology. Where Kant spoke of "pure" reason, Wesley very well might have spoken of "inspired" reason, and certainly of "inspiring reason," which would be the ultimate form of reason's own purity. Wesley went on to say, "It is by [reason] we understand (his Spirit opening and enlightening the eyes of our understanding)."[13] Again, it appears to be the case that divine activity takes place prior to human cognition. "We never reside simply under our natural, or fallen conditions because God's grace is continually and universally available to us making possible our knowledge of God."[14] Reason comes to human cognition already fully formed and functional, divinely inspired, and therefore universally valid. Reason comes to an individual as "a faculty of the human soul."[15] As a faculty of the human soul, reason is demonstrated to be both universal and individual. The universality of reason is always to be experienced by the individual. This is again evidence of the modernist grand narrative under which Wesley worked. The rational individual is the primary focus of Wesley's thought because it is the rational individual which is most fully and properly a recipient of divine inspiration.

This sort of modernism is not a hard materialism which rejects the divine, but an empiricist materialism which sees the natural as already and continually being fulfilled by the divine. In an increasingly globalized world, this sort of modernism becomes more and more problematic because it is

12. Wesley, "*Sermon 70*," 592.

13. Ibid., 590.

14. Mann, "Pragmatic Wesleyanism."

15. Ibid., 589.

incapable of recognizing its own contextuality. Even the title of Wesley's sermon, "The Case of Reason Impartially Considered," makes it clear that Wesley's notion of rationality is distinctly modern. Oddly, this sermon was Wesley's attempt to explore the philosophical concept of reason by using the tool of reason which he saw as a faculty of his own soul. By exploring reason rationally, Wesley intended to demonstrate that this rational faculty is universally valid even if individually conceived. Wesley was able to describe exactly what reason can and cannot do because he envisioned that any rational human being would have equal and equivalent access to reason. The universal accessibility of reason is demonstrated by the fact that reason appears in the empirical world as always already divinely inspired. Wesley genuinely believed himself to be practicing an impartial consideration of reason because he believed that universally available reason, as grace, allowed for the possibility of impartial consideration. This claim to impartiality is another side to the legitimating grand narrative of "modernity." Impartiality is only a viable possibility when one conceives of a universally applicable *a priori* knowledge which is available to an individual. As *a priori*, this knowledge is beyond interpretation—it simply is.

This *a priori* nature of knowledge is the result of the legitimating grand narrative of "modernity" that has been described here. Thus *a priori* knowledge is also at the heart of the modernist problem that this essay is addressing. Of course, even if one argues that Wesleyan theology ought to be much broader than a theology which seems incapable of escaping "modernity," one should yet ask why a "post-modern" development of Wesleyanism is important. It is certainly in vogue, if not already demode, to speak of any topic in terms of the "postmodern," but this does not mean that doing so is always a productive endeavor. However, it is not only important, but essential to speak of "post-modern" Wesleyanism because of the modernist context in which John Wesley lived and worked. To speak of "post-modern" Wesleyanism is not merely to claim that there is a distinct contextual difference between Wesley's writing and the writing of this text. While this is so, "modernity" does not only represent a historical time period, but also an intellectual and cultural *modus operandi* which is still very much operative in, at least, the Western world today. "Post-modern" Wesleyanism cannot simply leave Wesley behind, although neither does it need to offer an unflinching reverence for his work, but seeks to recognize the complexities in Wesley's work, and to read Wesley and historical Wesleyanism against themselves.

It is important for Wesleyan theology to intentionally consider its modernist roots, and the modernity in which it still often lives, in order to move beyond the potentially damaging claims of impartial absolute knowledge. Wesleyan theology needs to consider the "post-modern" as a way by which to reject hegemonic universalizing trends. "Post-modern" Wesleyan theology, then, is a sublation[16] that upholds the import of Wesley's own thought by using Wesley against himself. The goal of such a "post-modern" practice is to reject the pseudo-universality of a "modern" particularity. Only by rejecting this pseudo-universality of the particular, can Wesleyanism celebrate the true universality found in global diversity. "Post-modern" Wesleyanism does not impose, but inquires. As Wesleyanism has and continues to expand beyond its Anglo-American context, a "post-modern" consideration will allow it to learn and grow in ways which were previously unavailable.

Since it is Lyotard's description of "modernity" that was used to frame the beginning of this chapter, his description of "post-modernity" will also be quite helpful. Lyotard describes the "post-modern" as, "Incredulity toward metanarratives."[17] With continued globalization, the modernist grand narrative falls under suspicion because of its claims to holding an *a priori* status. Wesleyan thinkers ought to approach this grand narrative, if not all grand narratives, with incredulity. This does not mean that the whole metanarrative and all that stems from it ought to be simply discarded. The "post" in post-modern does not mean that modernity has died and been replaced with a new "post-modern" epoch. "Post-modernity," to the contrary, recognizes that there is continued value in much of what was, and continues to be, built by modernity. The incredulity of the "post-modern" leads to re-description more than it does to outright rejection. As John Stanley has noted, "We can positively appreciate modernity's emphases: rationality, the worth of the individual, scientific inquiry. At the same time, we abhor its arrogance."[18] "Post-modernity" doesn't fix "modernity," but builds upon it. There is a distinctly dialectical practice taking place in the interactions of the "modern" with the "post-modern." "Post-modernity" is not simply

---

16 Sublation should not be confused with rejection. Sublation is a negativizing moment, but, unlike rejection, it is not an outright proclamation of wrongness. Rather, sublation recognizes great value in a concept, but also proclaims something more. Whereas rejection is often a proclamation of, "No," sublation is more along the lines of a, "Yes, but . . . " Sublation simultaneously embraces and questions a given proposition.

17. Lyotard, *Postmodern Condition*, xxiv.

18. Stanley, "Elements of a Postmodern Holiness Hermeneutic," 37.

more correct or truthful than modernity, but by refusing to make totalizing claims it allows a greater possibility of learning. It names the particularity of the language of the "modern," and seeks to re-energize this language by using it for dialogue rather than demand. That is to say, a "post-modern" Wesleyan theology approaches God with a particular humility.

In the case of the particular grand narrative which this essay has been describing, the incredulity stems from the fact that claims to an abundance of a rational *a priori* knowledge are generally followed by hegemonic attacks, both subtle and aggressive, against competing metanarratives. The metanarrative of "modernity" claims a special transcendent knowledge which is unaffected by history, personal prejudice, or cultural mores. The knowledge to which Wesley's "modernity" lays claim is all-inclusive, even if imperfect, by nature of having been recognized through a divinely inspired reason. "Unless you wilfully shut your eyes, you cannot but see of what service [reason] is both in laying the foundation of true religion, under the guidance of the Spirit of God, and in raising the superstructure. You see it directs us in every point both of faith and practice: It guides us with regard to every branch both of inward and outward holiness."[19] Reason, in other words, is at the heart of all knowledge—both empirical and spiritual.

One needs to be careful, however, not to fully align Wesley with other "modern" philosophers. For Wesley, knowledge of God is always a soteriological proposition. While it is true that "Wesley believed that true knowledge of God is universally available in a limited fashion through prevenient grace,"[20] such grace was aimed, not at perfect comprehension, but at salvation. The problem here, due in part to ambiguity in Wesley's writings, is that even if the motivation of rational inspiration is salvation, it is often difficult to distinguish between a reason which has been inspired, and that which has inspired it in the first place. For Wesley, rational knowledge is always the result of spiritual inspiration, but this inspiration, as prevenient, has also been viewed as inherent to any given individual. Even though Wesley does admit that reason cannot bring forth faith, hope, or love, this hardly seems important when the knowledge of what these things are does arise from reason. Reason defines them, even if it cannot inspire them.

Such an ambiguity as to the role of reason in individual epistemology opens the door to problematic theological positions which are simultaneously both of and not-of Wesley. For example, when even the fruit of the

19. Wesley, "Sermon 70," 590.
20. Mann, "Pragmatic Wesleyanism."

Spirit are defined according to a reason that is defined contextually but proclaimed universally, then a particular contextual morality is demanded across cultures and settings. Morality was of paramount importance to Wesley's program. Because both moral philosophy and theology were swept up in the practice of rational inquiry, all parts of the Christian experience struggled to assimilate any notion of contextuality. As such, some of the history of the expansion of Methodism then became a history of oppression and subjugation. Because the Gospel was often interwoven with a modernist conception of reason, any sort of missionary work or proselytization often took place through the enforcement of the values of Methodism's founding.[21] These contextual values were both conceived of and preached as universally applicable, regardless of the particular circumstances in which they were being practiced. This rigid enforcement held profound implications for the cultures upon which they were imposed. While the spread of, at least, early Methodism also had political and cultural colonialistic motivations, the influence of Wesley's own theology on this sort of theological imperialism ought not to be underrepresented.

It is certainly not a given that "post-modern" thinking is important to the theological task in general, much less to the Wesleyan theological task in particular. In fact, in various sectors of the Wesleyan world it would not be a surprise to hear it claimed that the "rejection of all metanarratives [is] inimical to the Wesleyan tradition . . . [and] represents an unsustainable loss which must be countered."[22] Wesleyan theology should not overlook such critiques, for they are valuable. However, we must recognize that such critiques fail to escape from the very "modernity" which "post-modernity" finds incredulous. Unless Wesleyan theology is willing to question the assumptions (the grand narratives) of Wesley's modernity, it will move ever further toward being a fruitless endeavor. A theology which cannot

21. An interesting study of the moralizing character of Methodist missions can be found in, Eves, "Colonialism, Corporeality, and Character," 85–138. Here, Eves argues, "The texts of the Methodist missionaries in Papua and New Guinea reveal a particular strategy, a technology of power which sought to reconstitute the indigenous people's bodies and through this their moral constitution." A fascinating article on the ways in which Methodist missionaries carefully crafted a message of the importance of homogeneity is, Nicholas Thomas, "Colonial Conversions," 366–89. Looking specifically at missions in the Solomon Islands, Thomas argues, "The Methodists' representations were thus not motivated exclusively by the project of knowing the other and representing a certain relation of alterity, but arose as well from the mission's competitive interest in justifying its specific programme and orientation."

22. Creaseman, "Loss of Metanarrative," 170.

allow for incredulity toward Wesley's modernist metanarrative will remain a tool for the intellectual (and perhaps cultural) oppression of those on the borders. The "post-modern" proposal of this essay is not to reject all metanarratives, nor, perhaps, even to reject any metanarratives. A "post-modern" practice of theology need not reject the notion of transcendental truth. However, the incredulity toward the metanarratives of modernity will bring about the rejection of the notion that transcendental truth can be known or prescribed. What is being rejected is not truth itself, but a modernist claim that reason is a divinely inspired faculty of the individual human soul.

It is probably true that the sort of "post-modern" practices of theology described in this essay are inimical to much of Wesley's tradition, and so, in order to profitably move forward, an important distinction will have to be made between two methods of theology. The first method, which here will be called "Wesleyistic" holds a particularly hierarchical stance. One's theology is judged based upon its proximity to the actual work of John Wesley, or perhaps, in rare circumstances, Charles Wesley. The Wesleys are seen as theological teachers, who have to offer a particular extraordinary enlightenment. The work of John Wesley, which was far from comprehensive, is ruled to be a primary arbiter of theological truth. Wesleyist theology is primarily concerned with the backwards looking question, "What did Wesley have to say?" At its best, although certainly not all the time, Wesleyist theology will also ask, "How can the thought of Wesley be translated for a contemporary audience in ways which are contextually relevant?" There is nothing inherently wrong with Wesleyist theology. This practice has been a great asset to Arminian-Wesleyan churches for a long time. Even so, it is important to recognize a distinction between this practice and the "post-modern" practice which here will be called "Wesleyan" theology.

It is to the detriment of Wesleyist theology that the modernity in which John Wesley worked is often uncritically accepted as, in some way, prescriptive for continued theological discourse. To accept the importance of Wesley's theological contributions ought not to require that Wesley himself be held up as a paragon of theological practice. Indeed, failure to properly characterize Wesley's own writings as culturally and historically conditioned is to give these writings a transcendent canonical quality. [23] To

---

23. This is roughly equivalent to the move which William J. Abraham sees occurring throughout the history of Christianity with the biblical text moving "from ecclesial canonicity to epistemic normativity." See Abraham, *Canon and Criterion in Christian Theology*. While Wesleyan theologians would not equate Wesley's works with the Bible, there is a strong tendency to recognize in them an only slightly secondary epistemic normativity.

unwittingly offer the Wesleyist corpus this sort of canonicity is a common practice. In counter-practice, a primary distinction of Wesleyan theology is that it is much less hierarchical than Wesleyist theology. Wesleyan theology does not need to continually look backward to the work of John Wesley. Wesleyan theology is more egalitarian, recognizing the work of the Holy Spirit in all people. While Wesley's influence is important, it is no more valid than the panoply of voices which have been speaking for centuries since Wesley. Wesleyans need not to revere Wesley in order to respect him. Whereas Wesleyists see in John Wesley a leader, Wesleyans only need to see a common heritage. This distinction is fundamentally important, because Wesleyist theology will always be a theology which remains mired in modernity. This is not, by any means, to say that Wesleyist theology is without value, however. The transition from "modern" to "post-modern," from "Wesleyist" to "Wesleyan" is not a distinct break. Wesleyan theology is built upon generations of Wesleyist thinkers, and the contributions of those thinkers are foundational to the continuing practice of Wesleyan theology. Whatever is meant by "post-modern" theology cannot be viewed as, in any way, autonomous if it is to avoid the hubris which it recognizes in the "modern." "Post-modernity" is an inherently dialectical process. This dialectic does not guarantee, nor even seek after, progress, but is simply the attempt to distill the truths of modernity.

If Wesleyan theology stands a chance of distilling the truths of Wesleyistic theology it needs to proceed through the recognition of common linguistic practices. Wesleyan theology, at its heart, is a language game. However, in distinction to Wesleyistic theology, it recognizes that the rules of this game are fluid. To say that theology is a language game is not to denigrate it as a practice, much less to imply that it is anything but serious. To say that Wesleyan theology is a language game simply means that it is a practice which is contingent on the theologians own contextuality. We attempt to describe God, rather than define God, and the ways in which this description take place require a believing community as a "home-base" of sorts. It is within that community that Wesleyan theology properly takes place.

Wesleyanism should be, to a certain extent, a logical practice. This is the recognition of rule-governance within the language game. However, in order to refuse to continue the "modern" practices of intellectual hegemony which privilege a certain Anglo-American/European conceptuality of autonomously available universal reason, logic is understood differently.

This is not the strict Aristotelian logic which was so strongly emphasized at Wesley's Oxford.[24] A "post-modern" logic needs to recognize what Gilles Deleuze calls the particular relations of any propositions. "[Manifestation] concerns the relation of the proposition to the person who speaks and expresses himself."[25] In addition to manifestation, the other two relations are "designation," which is a proposition's relation to external states of affairs, and "signification," which is the recognition that a proposition gains sense only from within a logical web of similar propositions. Although Deleuze would not utilize the terminology, this third relation, signification, is the overarching Wesleyan language game which is being described. Within that signifying language game, however, the manifestation of an individual is equally important. The regulations of the language game cannot be fixed precisely because the game involves individual speakers who are giving a sense of sense to propositions simply by speaking them. Things don't merely "make sense" *in se*, but "sense" itself is conditioned by the community.

A "post-modern" Wesleyan logic simply cannot judge theological propositions using a logician's truth tables because logical sense is equally derived from matters of personal (manifestation) and communal (signification) context. The "modern" metanarratives are viewed with incredulity because, upon closer examination, they are clearly shown not to be "meta" at all. They are simply narratives. Whereas Wesleyistic theology often understood experience to be shaped by logic, Wesleyanism must actually see that this is reversed. Wesleyans are united through a common linguistic heritage, but the sense that is made from this linguistic practice is contextually derived. Wesleyan theological discourse rejects the universal validity of theological propositions not as an embrace of relativity, but out of a sense of humility.[26]

24. It is often assumed that Wesley was primarily influenced by Aristotelian logic during his time at Cambridge. See, e.g., Maddox, *Responsible Grace*. An interesting counter-argument that Wesley was actually more strongly influenced by Ramist logic can be found in Crutcher, *Crucible of Life*.

25. Deleuze, *Logic of Sense*, 17.

26. In his seminal work, *Word and Object*, W. V. O. Quine argued for the indeterminacy of translation. Quine believed that there could be no singular translation from one language to another, but that a number of contradictory translations could logically result from a single statement. While this essay is not speaking of the translation from one language to another, Quine's contention offers an important critique to any sort of unistic rationality. The underlying claim is not the 'anything goes' of utter relativism, but rather that the complexity of language disallows the possibility of unmediated truth claims.

"Post-modern" theological discourse celebrates the family resemblance of competing theological claims rather than being suspicious of anything short of univocity. In rejecting univocity, therefore, Wesleyanism moves the primary locus of theological engagement away from the autonomous individual to the church. This, in turn, allows Wesleyanism to maintain a unique identity based upon theological foci and ecclesiological polities, while simultaneously questioning the hard line distinctions of denominationalism. Wesleyistic theology, with its focus on the salvation and sanctification of the autonomous individual, ultimately requires little by way of ecclesiology.[27] Wesleyanism, to the contrary, by rejecting the universality of the grand narratives of "modernity," is invigorated by Cyprian's third century claim that the church is a necessary parent for the Christian family.[28] Broadly understood, Wesleyanism should embrace the historic Christian statement, *extra ecclesiam nulla salus*. In this claim, the church is not the arbiter of salvation, but that community which is saved.

It would be unfair to the theology of John Wesley not to point out that he does, in many ways, open up this very same door. Wesley seems to have recognized that there was a problem with the modernist focus on the autonomous individual. Even if Wesley didn't solve the problem, which is certainly the case, he made an effort to draw autonomous individual's into a particular learning and growing community. This is the heart of Wesley's Methodism—individuals gathering together, both in the parish and in small groups, to together work toward their (yet individual) salvation and spiritual growth. One of the problems with Wesleyist theology is that it fails to fully live into the method of Wesley's Methodism. Philip R. Meadows makes a similar point when he speaks of, "the failure of disciplined discipleship in the Church."[29] Meadows argues that Wesleyan theology needs "to recover its true identity as a fruit of disciplined discipleship."[30]

A "post-modern" use of language, from the outside, looks almost identical to the theological language of "modernity." Yet, upon closer examination, it functions quite differently. A "post-modern" Wesleyan language is used as a sublation of the hegemony of "modernity." One particular

27. Peterson, "Post-Wesleyan Eucharistic Ecclesiology." Peterson speaks of the need for 'Post-Wesleyan' practices which are "faithful to the past, while not being enslaved to it," in order that the Wesleyans can (re)claim a profound ecclesiology which is often lacking in the tradition.

28. Cyprian, "Treatise 1: On the Unity of the Church."

29. Meadows, "The 'Discipline' of Theology."

30. Ibid.

example of how this sublation functions can be seen in a renewed understanding of the *imago Dei*, a term which has a long and important history in Wesleyist theology. At its heart, a theology centered upon the *imago Dei* can easily become an individualistic theology. The notion of monotheism is at the heart of orthodox Christianity. Thus, to speak of the image of God is already to make a profoundly particularistic claim. Even a trinitarian God is one God.

Given John Wesley's writings regarding the *imago Dei*, Wesleyist theology has little choice but to recognize the *imago Dei* as an individual personal gift. The image of God was given to Adam as the representative of all humankind. However, even while the ramifications of Adam's initial sin, the loss of the *imago Dei*, are universal, they are also profoundly particularistic. "Every one descended from [Adam] comes into the world spiritually dead, dead to God, wholly dead in sin; entirely void of the life of God; void of the image of God."[31] The consequences belong to "every one," not merely to humanity as a whole. According to Wesley, because each individual is born into the world void of the image of God, it is also the individual who therefore needs to have the image of God restored through "being born of the Spirit of God."[32] This "new birth," even if communal, is also individualistic. Even as Wesley sought transformation in community, the language that he had to describe that transformation always came back to a transformation of the individual.

Such a conception of being "born again" is hardly unique to Wesley, but it is one of the cornerstones of Wesleyist theology. As this theological notion is strongly derived from Wesley's understanding of the *imago Dei*, in Wesleyist usage it becomes inextricably tied to a modernist notion of autonomous reason. The danger in this is that the distinction between the image and that which is imaged begins to become less and less clear. If reason is a divinely inspired faculty of the individual soul, then a rational human being would, in some sense, have direct access to knowledge of the divine. There is, however, an important distinction within Wesley's own thought that Wesleyist theology often overlooks. For Wesley, the quest for knowledge of God is often primarily a soteriological endeavor. Knowledge of God brings relationship with God. "If any need further light, he may receive it . . . by the reason or understanding that God has given him, which

31. Wesley, "*Sermon 45*," 190.
32. Ibid.

religion was designed not to extinguish, but to perfect."[33] Wesley's concern here is less about inerrant knowledge of God's very being, but about perfect knowledge of one's own relationship to God. Here, Wesley hedges away from a strongly rationalist understanding of reason, and speaks of reason also as "reflection on what we feel in our own souls."[34] Wesley's rationalism was heavily influenced by empiricism of a special variety. The empiricism which flavored reason for Wesley was not merely physical, but spiritual as well. However, such empiricism also strengthened the inherent individualism of Wesley's thought. Particular experiences, whether come to through the physical or the "spiritual" senses, might be considered in community, but were experiences of the individual.

For a Wesleyist theology which puts a strong focus on the autonomous individual, then, the rational human being would image God in a very particularistic way, and the image of God would tend to be described, or worse yet, defined, using ideals which are socially and communally derived, without acknowledgment or even recognition of the contextuality of this image. When the *imago Dei* is defined by "my" personal experiences, it very quickly becomes the *imago hominis*. Not surprisingly, "my God" tends to look a lot like me. Such a lack of contextual self-awareness rings quite true to Feuerbach's claim that "theology is anthropology, that there is no distinction between the *predicates* of the divine and human nature, and, consequently, no distinction between the divine and human *subject*."[35] The absolutist undertones to such Wesleyist claims ultimately can lead to the subjugation and degradation of those whose own contextual representations of God differ with the majority. So long as God is defined by the majority, the majority alone is God.

This is the great danger of Wesleyist theology, and it is potentially very damaging for those who are not in the majority. It is easy to conflate my image, as a child of God, with the image of God toward which another might strive. Discipleship and evangelism can both quickly revert into the claim, "Be like me, and so be like God." Even so, in order to reject the deification of the majority the concept of the *imago Dei* must be embraced, not rejected. This is the nature of sublation, which is both the questioning and upholding of a proposition. Wesleyanism ought to embrace the language of the *imago Dei*, as both scripturally and historically important, but it can only

33. Wesley, "Sermon 10," 271.

34. Wesley, "Sermon 11," 287.

35. Feuerbach, *Essence of Christianity*, xi.

do so by questioning the modernist grand narrative which claims that the autonomous individual is the seat of this image. The image of God is not repeatedly made manifest with the birth (or new birth) of each individual. To the contrary, the image of God is made manifest once, in the church - the body of Christ. Individuals, who may or may not be as autonomous as they would like to believe, each serve as a microcosm of this singular image, but each portrays the image differently. No singular portrayal is more or less adequate than another, but, brought together, they give a more meaningful understanding of the God which is imaged. This maintains the Wesleyist claim that God inspires each individual, but denies that this inspiration takes the form of a universal reason. It is not reason, therefore, which unites the church, nor even a common dedication to Christian scriptures. Rather, the church is united by the enactment of the (both subjective and objective) love of God which most perfectly images God. A trinitarian theology claims that unity is found not in unicity but in diversity. The rationality of this contention is judged pragmatically rather than mathematically. Such a reconceptualization of the historical doctrine of the *imago Dei* serves the important role of bringing together multiple voices, without preconceived judgments of validity, in order to more fully celebrate Wesleyanism as a global community of faith. Such a reading of the *imago Dei* is but one example of what "post-modern" Wesleyanism might look like.

The beauty of "post-modern" Wesleyanism is that it does not really exist in any meaningful way. It is an idea, a goal, perhaps a practice. It is simply the recognition that, while John Wesley was a man of "modernity," Wesleyanism does not have to remain mired there as well. Wesleyanism ought to look critically at its own history in order to recognize the sinful ways in which it has, and continues to, oppress those who do not fit cleanly into the modernist conception of autonomous rationality. Wesleyanism, moving forward, cannot productively continue to practice theology as though it is descriptive only of a relationship between individuals and a transcendent God. The "modernity" of Wesleyistic theology cannot fully acknowledge the importance of the church, an acknowledgment that Wesley made repeatedly, which is one reason that there is a dearth of meaningful literature regarding Wesleyan ecclesiology. "Post-modern" Wesleyanism is by no means a celebration of relativism, but is, to the contrary, a recognition of the profoundly communal embodiedness of theological truth. The sublation of Wesley, and consequently of Wesleyistic theology, makes possible a future in which Wesleyanism can embrace continued globalization without simultaneously serving as the enforcer of the Enlightenment ideals of universal rationality and autonomous morality. With the shift to Wesleyanism, the work of John (and Charles) Wesley can still be fully embraced as an important moment in ecclesial history without thereby giving that work an undeserved canonical status. Only with the shift from Wesleyistic theology to Wesleyanism can the status quo by which the church is subservient to the individual be overcome. With a renewed focus on the church will come theological discourse which is based on love, not power. A focus on the church, as a global and diverse community, cannot accept demands for theological univocity. Demonstrated in Eucharist, the church is a community of servanthood and openness (both spiritually and interpersonally), not of condemnation and forced belief. The church is not the army of God, but a growing, seeking, hoping community of faith. With such an understanding of the church, and of the individual's place within it, Wesleyanism can come creatively come back to the foundation upon which it began. "This is the sum of Christian perfection: It is all comprised in that one word, Love."[36]

Bibliography

Abraham, William J. *Canon and Criterion in Christian Theology*. New York: Oxford University Press, 1998.

Creaseman, Ron. "The Loss of Metanarrative: Resources for Formulating a Wesleyan Response." *Wesleyan Theological Journal* 35 (2000) 165–81.

Crutcher, Timothy. *The Crucible of Life: The Role of Experience in John Wesley's Theological Method*. Lexington: Emeth, 2010.

Cyprian, "Treatise 1: On the Unity of the Church." In *Ante-Nicene Fathers*, edited by Alexander Roberts and James Donaldson, vol. 5. Reprint, Peabody, MA: Hendrickson, 1994.

Deleuze, Gilles. *The Logic of Sense*. Translated by Mark Lester. London: Continuum, 2004.

Eves, Richard. "Colonialism, Corporeality, and Character: Methodist Missions and the Refashioning of Bodies in the Pacific." *History and Anthropology* 10 (1996) 85–138.

Feuerbach, Ludwig. *The Essence of Christianity*. New York: Harper, 1957.

Kant, Immanuel. "Dreams of a Spirit-Seer." In *Kant on Swedenborg: Dreams of a Spirit-Seer and Other Writings*, translated by Gregory R. Johnson and Glenn Alexander Magee. West Chester, PA: Swedenborg Foundation, 2003. Kindle Edition.

———. "Religion Within the Boundaries of Mere Reason." In *Religion and Rational Theology*, edited by Allen W. Wood and George Di Giovanni, 39–216. New York: Cambridge University Press, 1996.

36. Wesley, "Sermon 76," 74.

Lyotard, Jean-François. *The Postmodern Condition: A Report on Knowledge*. Translated by Geoff Bennington and Brian Massumi. Minneapolis: University of Minnesota Press, 1984.

Maddox, Randy. *Responsible Grace: John Wesley's Practical Theology*. Nashville: Abingdon, 1994.

Mann, Mark Grear. "A Pragmatic Wesleyanism: Peirce, Wesley, and a Nonfoundational Religious Epistemology." *The Wesleyan Philosophical Society Online Journal* (2002). http://home.snu.edu/~brint/wpsjnl/Mann01.htm.

Meadows, Philip R. "The 'Discipline' of Theology: Making Methodism Less Methodological." *Wesleyan Theological Journal* 36 (2001) 50–87.

Peterson, Brent D. "A Post-Wesleyan Eucharistic Ecclesiology: The Renewal of the Church as the Body of Christ to be Doxologically Broken and Spilled out for the World." PhD diss., Garrett-Evangelical Theological Seminary, 2009.

Quine, W. V. O. *Word and Object*. Cambridge: MIT Press, 2013.

Stanley, John E. "Elements of a Postmodern Holiness Hermeneutic Illustrated by Way of the Book of Revelation." *Wesleyan Theological Journal* 28 (1993) 23–33.

Thomas, Nicholas. "Colonial Conversions: Difference, Hierarchy, and History in Early Twentieth-Century Evangelical Propaganda." *Comparatives Studies in Society and History* 34 (1992) 366–89.

Wesley, John. "Sermon 10: The Witness of the Spirit: Discourse One." In *The Works of John Wesley*, edited by Albert C. Outler, vol. 1. Nashville: Abingdon, 1985.

———. "Sermon 11: The Witness of the Spirit: Discourse Two." In *The Works of John Wesley*, edited by Albert C. Outler, vol. 1. Nashville: Abingdon, 1985.

———. "Sermon 44: Original Sin." In *The Works of John Wesley*, edited by Albert C. Outler, vol. 2. Nashville: Abingdon, 1985.

———. "Sermon 45: The New Birth." In *The Works of John Wesley*, edited by Albert C. Outler, vol. 2. Nashville: Abingdon, 1985.

———. "Sermon 70: The Case For Reason Impartially Considered." In *The Works of John Wesley*, edited by Albert C. Outler, vol. 2. Nashville: Abingdon, 1985.

———. "Sermon 76: On Perfection." In *The Works of John Wesley*, edited by Albert C. Outler, vol. 3. Nashville: Abingdon, 1985.

Blues Conversion as Third Act of Grace

Towards Post-Colonial Ministerial Practices

─────── Orlando R. Serrano, Jr. ───────

The blues are the cries of a new society being born.

—CLYDE WOODS[1]

In 1819, John Overton, James Winchester, and future president Andrew Jackson founded Memphis, TN.[2] Situated on the banks of the Mississippi River, the founders named the city after the capital of Egypt that sat on the Nile River five thousand years prior. They hoped to replicate the prosperity its namesake enjoyed and use the Mississippi River as an artery to carry goods throughout the growing U.S. south region. When the Memphis and Charleston Railroad was completed in 1857, the region was successfully linked to the Atlantic Ocean.[3] Agricultural products dominated the local economy. One stood out in particular. Memphis became the capital of a

---

1. Woods, *Development Arrested*, 39.
2. Memphis History, 2013.
3. Ibid.

quickly growing cotton empire. History did indeed repeat itself as the empire was built in large part on the backs of slaves and on appropriated land. The international slave trade that began in the colonial U.S. was outlawed in 1808, but the internal trade continued until the Thirteenth Amendment's ratification in 1865. The Treaty of Doak's Stand, in conjunction with the Indian Removal Act of 1930, forced the removal of the region's indigenous peoples.[4] It was in this context that the Black communities of the U.S. south worked to create a new world. The blues, borne of an exploitative past and present, pointed toward a different present and a future forged in the encounter across difference. The blues, an art form and epistemology constructed on notes played in a specific way, when slaves squeezed African scales into European ones, provide a way to reconceptualize Christianity in the service of developing post-colonial ministerial practices.[5]

Colonial Difference, Coloniality, and Colonialism

In order to hold the ideological terrain steady enough to discuss what post-colonial ministry can mean and how it can be practiced, a few working definitions are in order: colonial difference, coloniality, and colonialism.

At its simplest, *colonial difference* is the space between worldviews. As the peoples of Europe began traveling further from their continent, they increasingly encountered alternative political, economic, and ideological structures and institutions. In other words, they encountered peoples with different beliefs and different ways of seeing the world. This is called colonial difference because of the European and Arawak encounter of 1492 that resulted in the colonial period.[6] In and of itself, *difference* is apolitical. Difference is neither "good" nor "bad;" ends and means co-define each other. Each moment has the potential for power and difference to combine for either productive or fatal ends.[7] The possible outcomes created by these

4. Woods, *Development Arrested*, 43–45.

5. Ibid., 35.

6. It is important to note that this chapter works with scholarship developed across the Américas because there are intellectual traditions that have grown in different contexts; ie. African, Asian, and Pacific. Although there are similarities, there are differences significant enough to merit this disclaimer. I use "the Américas" and not "the Americas" because the work in this chapter is coming from theoretical, academic, and activist traditions that are both taking back the term to signify the Western Hemisphere—not just the U.S.—and reimaging what the region can be.

7. Gilmore, "Fatal Couplings of Power and Difference," 15–24. Historically, power

encounters are exponential.[8] This is precisely why the space of colonial difference is so vital—it retains the capacity for immeasurable good and evil.[9]
Unfortunately, for the peoples of the Américas, the crises that began in 1492
and continued thereafter resulted in their near complete obliteration.[10]

Coloniality is a reaction to colonial difference. At its core, the logic
of coloniality seeks to control through domination—resolving conflict by
imposing one's own worldview on others. This mindset has undergirded
most of the interactions between Europeans and their descendants with
non-Europeans since the late 15th century, as the Spanish, Dutch, and British sought control of the Atlantic economy and politics, "and from there the
control and management of the entire planet."[11] Such is the *modus operandi*
of coloniality.

Colonialism occurs when the logic of coloniality is deployed to resolve
colonial difference. Colonialism is not a moment in time, but the process
that employs the logic of coloniality to establish hegemony. Mignolo points
to Spain, Holland, Britain, and the U.S. as the line of succession for global
hegemony. He writes, "The logic of coloniality has been in place from the
conquest of Mexico and Peru until and beyond the war in Iraq, despite
superficial changes in the scale and agents of exploitation/control in the

---

has been, and currently is, combined along various axes of difference to fatal ends. For
instance, in *Golden Gulag: Prisons, Surplus, and Opposition in Globalizing California*,
Gilmore defines racism as "the state-sanctioned and/or extralegal production and exploitation of group-differentiated vulnerability to premature death" (27). Race, class,
sexuality, and gender are all axes of difference that have resulted in premature death.

8. For instance, the indigenous peoples could have obliterated the European travelers. Or, the European peoples could have regarded the indigenous peoples as equal
and not killed them and/or settled and stolen their land. Taken together, the three possibilities outlined in the footnote and text comprise the extreme and middle points on
a spectrum of possible resolutions to the crises created by the repeated encounters of
worldviews that began with Christopher Columbus meeting with the Arawak.

9. Space must be understood as produced by the interaction of humans, non-hu-
mans, and the environment. Space is not absolute. Doreen Massey's conceptualization
of space/space-time is key here. She argues that space has a topographic and temporal
component, *For Space*. In the context of the Américas, European *telos* and topography
crushed Arawak, Maya, Aztec, and Inca *telos* and topography through colonialism. This
was one of many possible outcomes.

10. For instance, the Taíno people of what is now Puerto Rico and the Lucayan people
of the Bahamas—both members of the Arawak tribe—were completely destroyed. Williams, *From Columbus to Castro*.

11. Mignolo, *The Idea of Latin America*, 7.

past five hundred years in history."[12] While these are classical examples of colonialism on a national/international scale, anytime a dominant group attempts to assert hegemonic authority over another's way of life, colonialism is present.

Aníbal Quijano and Mignolo argue that colonial difference, coloniality, and colonialism remain today because they are the underside of modernity; what modernity defines and constructs itself against. Stated otherwise, the project of modernity simultaneously produces and depends on colonial difference, coloniality, and colonialism. The fact that modernity and coloniality are inseparable and can be profoundly debilitating for the marginalized. Colonialism and modernity form a binary structure that does not allow for shades of difference and creates an us/them dichotomy. Throughout history, and continuing into the present, Christianity has often become entangled within the modernity/coloniality binary. When this happens, the church becomes a handmaiden to colonialism. "Blues Conversation as Third Act of Grace," calls the church to divorce itself from a modern worldview that is grounded in a colonialism that objectifies, marginalizes, and seeks to dominate others. In this way, the church must learn to embrace colonial difference if it is to love its neighbor.

Coloniality/Modernity

The history of Christianity in the Américas is rife with examples of forced conversions which are often theorized as cultural genocide by post-colonial theologians.[13] Missions, boarding schools, and adoption programs, while well intentioned ministries, have (at times) been used to establish hegemony and destroy colonial difference. In fact, any ministerial practice that does not work from the space of colonial difference participates in the processes of colonialism by virtue of forcing a particular and preconceived prescriptive Christianity (i.e. one's own notion of Christianity) onto those being ministered to. Most Wesleyan ministerial practice, like most Evangelical ministerial practices, are structured in this way—rooted in the framework of a modern/colonial binary. What results is a Christianity conflated with our own dominant cultural notions. As such, Christian conversion has historically been more than simply becoming "Christian," but involved chang-

12. Ibid., 11.

13. Deloria, *Custer Died for Your Sins*; Cone, *Black Theology of Liberation*; Smith, *Conquest*; and Smith, *Native Americans and the Christian Right*.

ing dress, educational structures, diets, and even social/political structures. This is further seen in the us/them mentality so prevalent in the church. "We" feel responsible to preach to "Them." "We" want to invite "Them" into our church, to share with them our God. Modern/Colonial Christianity erases difference by "converting to" rather than "growing with."

The purpose here is not to criticize the good work that many well-intentioned Christians do to bring the kingdom of God to bear on earth. Rather, the purpose is to critique the modern/colonial framework adopted by the Wesleyan-Holiness tradition, and encourage us to think about how we are replicating the violent binary structure of the very power dynamics Scripture calls us to unmake. Quite often, in our zeal to share the grace of God with a suffering and oppressed world, we unknowingly participate in the reproduction of coloniality/modernity by deploying an oppressive church structure and ministerial practice. Blues Conversation as Third Act of Grace calls us to rethink ministerial practices in a way that embraces colonial difference and avoids, as best we can, participation in the reproduction of oppressive structures framed by coloniality/modernity.

I have grown up in the Church of the Nazarene. I believe this Wesleyan-Holiness denomination is trying to model and continue the ministry of Christ. However, I also believe that this endeavor often fails before it begins. By replicating modern/colonial binary in which power is centralized and controlled, it continues practicing a colonial and colonized ministry. As such, the good intentions are dead on arrival when applied in practices informed by a colonial/modern framework. The Church of the Nazarene proclaims itself to be an international denomination because it has a presence in over 150 nations across the globe. Yet, denominationally, much of the strategizing, and most of the decisions and doctrinal statements arise from a central power structure which is heavily white, male, and U.S.-centric. As a centralized structure, the Church of the Nazarene often fails to learn from the difference which thrives throughout its diverse body. We embrace this centralized structure, in part, because we imagine the kingdom of God and the work of the church as becoming The Kingdom and The Church in a way that obliterates difference. However, this is not the example we see in Christ. Christ unmade the insular, binary, and centralized structures of the Pharisees and Sadducees. Paul's proclamation in Galatians 3, that there is "no longer Jew nor Greek," is not a rejection of difference *as such*. Paul's claim does not deny the reality of distinctions, but rather argues that the kingdom of God itself *rejects the inequality* of power structures based upon these distinctions. In God's encounter with humanity through Christ, the curtain that separated God and humanity was torn. This did not bring humanity to God across the line that separated secular from sacred. Instead, it marked God's encounter with humanity and the beginning of a kingdom built in the space—the life of Christ—characterized by a decentralized power practiced as solidarity. It is, again, the story of the Exodus in which God comes down to creation. The work of the church should be to replicate these encounters and build the kingdom, not merely by converting individuals but by making the world we live in more kingdom-like. The work of the church is to make the world more sacred by unmaking the partition between secular and sacred through the practice of solidarity with humanity-in-difference. In order to move towards post-colonial ministerial practices we must move away from resolving encounters with difference by imposing our own worldview. We must develop ministerial practices *in* the space of difference, not by obliterating difference. The concept of grace—which is pivotal to the theology of John Wesley and the Wesleyan tradition—is pivotal to post-colonial ministerial practices. Grace is often spoken of in terms of salvation and of sanctification, in various forms. In what follows, I propose a new way of thinking of grace: *blues conversion*. I turn to the blues to help us understand how the church can reconceptualize itself and in turn develop post-colonial ministerial practices.

The Blues and Post-colonial Ministry

Clyde Woods' *Development Arrested: The Blues and Plantation Power in the Mississippi Delta* is a study of the persistence of planter hegemony in the U.S. South during and after abolition. He theorizes the blues not simply as a folk art form, but as an epistemology—a "complex of social explanation and social action."[14] The blues, as an epistemology, influences cultural and personal development by offering a particular way of coming to the world. The blues encourages one to see the world differently. Woods added, "The blues became an alternative form of communication, analysis, moral intervention, observation, celebration . . . .the hearth of African-American consciousness."[15] In a place made by their labor and out of their bodies, the Black communities of the U.S. South turned to the blues as an alternative way of knowing and being rooted in an encounter between worlds.

14. Ibid., 29.

15. Ibid., 36–37.

Furthermore, the blues are apocalyptic, they are the blueprints for a new way of being in a new world—"The blues are the cries of a new world being born."[16] Woods' theorization of the blues provides a way for us to begin thinking about how we as Christians can be a ministering people—ontology—shaped by an alternative worldview—epistemology—that is universal yet not universalizing—teleology. The blues can speak to who we are, to how we approach the world, and to what it might look like for the world to become more like the kingdom of God. I am not in any way suggesting that the blues and the Christian tradition are equivalent. Rather, I am using the blues as a bridge between critical theory and theology to move toward post-colonial ministerial practices.

There are four ways in which Woods' conceptualization of the blues as epistemology and ontology, that is, how we approach the world and how this shapes the people that we become, is helpful in developing post-colonial ministerial practices. First, blues people are at home not in the margins of the nation-state, but outside its parameters. The Black slave abolitionists in the antebellum U.S. South and prison abolitionists of our current historical moment constitute an uninterrupted genealogy of the radical Black tradition. A common thread woven into this tradition is a lack of dependence on, and operation outside of, the dominant social structures and institutions in the U.S. to establish ways of life, social organization, and social reproduction. From the maroon societies of the Delta, repatriation movements to the Caribbean, Mexico, and Central America, Freedom City, and the Blues and Jazz clubs of Kansas City and Chicago, to the Colored Farmers Alliance, Mississippi Freedom Democratic Party (MFDP), and the Poor People's Committee of the 1960s civil rights struggles, blues people have lived outside dominant U.S. structures and institutions.[17] In each of these examples, the blues are not concerned with state recognition or participation. Even in the cases that engage the U.S. state—the MFDP and Poor People's Committee—they do so in opposition to state power and do not seek amelioration in terms between the state and Black communities. Instead, they seek a reconfiguration of the relationship between the state and Black communities that acknowledges Black existence outside the state. The blues do not seek to control, but simply to exist. They reject the inequivalency of power by refusing to recognize the societal power struc-

---

16. Woods, *Development Arrested*, 39.

17. For more information on these movements, see Duster, *Crusade for Justice*; Kelly, *Hammer and Hoe*; Lee, *For Freedom's Sake*; and Woods, *Development Arrested*.

tures. They are a tectonic footing for survival in the midst of domination, not a way to usurp power. This is something we can learn from and use to develop post-colonial ministerial practices.

In the Christian tradition, far too often we are concerned with our existence vis-à-vis the state. In other words, contemporary Christianity measures itself by the kind of relationship it has with the state: the more Christianity is favored by the state the more effective it can be. For instance, there is much angst over whether or not the president is Christian, whether or not a Christian minister prays at the presidential inauguration, or if the Bible is read in court. This has been true from the time of Kennedy's election as the first Roman Catholic president, to the 2012 election cycle in which television pundits debated repeatedly about the relationship of Mitt Romney's Mormonism to traditional Christianity. In even uglier terms this angst was displayed by the Islamaphobia expressed in concerns about Barack Obama being secretly Muslim. It is important to understand that the state is modernity's—and thus coloniality's—apparatus for institutionalized control over the four domains of human existence. Participation in the state is really participation in state-building and the domination over life required to do so, which folds Christianity into the infrastructure of colonizing western culture. In seeking state recognition, favor, and power, contemporary Christian practice and ministry misunderstands its purpose vis-à-vis the state. The Christian tradition, going back to its roots as Israel in Egypt, has always existed outside of and in opposition to dominant structures and institutions of power. In fact, Israel ceased being God's presence in the world when it ceased pointing to another way of life and began to replicate the monarchies of its day. Christianity is supposed to be the tectonic footing for an alternative form of being in the world, not the dominant form of being in the world. Ministerial practice is shaped by how Christianity sees itself in relation to dominant forms of institutionalized power: if it sees its fate tethered to that of the state it will replicate the state's forms of control over life. If it sees its fate independent of what happens to the modern state, a different Christianity—a Christianity of solidarity—takes shape.

The blues critiques oppressive and uneven social conditions and charges communities to make them better. A prevalent misunderstanding of the blues tradition is that sorrow is at its core. In actuality, radical hope is at the center. To be certain, there is sadness and sorrow in much of the blues across all iterations: music, literature, and visual art. The work of Memphis native John Lee Chatman is indicative of these characteristics. Performing as Memphis Slim, a surface level analysis of his lyrics finds familiar blues tropes. For instance, the lyrics to "Just a Dream" read,

Lord what a dream I had on my mind

What a dream, what a dream.

Lord what a dream had on my mind.

And when I woke up this morning, nothing right could I find.

. . . .

Lord what a dream I had on my mind.

When I woke up this morning, no childrens, no money, nothing could I

find.[18]

Listeners will hear sadness due to the loss of family, lack of income, and lack of power in the state apparatus. However, when analyzed in its historical context the lyrics reflect the life of a Black man who grew up in the U.S. South and whose elders were more than likely slaves. True, this reveals a sadness, but it's a sadness wrapped around hope. For a Black man in the early 1900s, a safe family with twelve children and a steady income was merely a dream because of the brutalities of sexual violence in slavery and juridical apartheid.[19] This explains why meeting the president was a nightmare. But once again, the lyrics are wrapped around hope, because "they confirmed and reaffirmed African-American working class social vision and cultural traditions in new cities and new regions."[20] Ben Harper, a contemporary heir to the blues tradition, reiterates this when he agonizingly sings, in "Better Way,"

Reality is sharp

It cuts at me like a knife

Everyone I know

18. Memphis Slim, "Just a Dream."

19. In 1965, then Assistant Secretary of Labor and future Democratic Senator for New York Daniel Patrick Moynihan wrote "The Negro Family: The Case for National Action," popularly known as the Moynihan Report. In the report, Moynihan argued that Black families without a mother and father were more likely to create unstable conditions and lead to behavior that is criminalized. However, he does not address the historical and social reasons that create familial instability. For a critique of the report, see Ferguson, *Aberrations in Black*. The report is available online at the U.S. Department of Labor's site, www.dol.gov/oasam/programs/history/webid-meynihan.htm, accessed June 17, 2013.

20. Woods, *Development Arrested*, 150.

Is in the fight of their life

Take your face out of your hands
And clear your eyes
You have a right to your dreams
And don't be denied

I believe in a better way[21]

Harper draws on the epistemology of the blues to call forward a new ontology and aurally represents the truth that the blues are more than just aesthetic expression, they "transform human consciousness by introducing the uninitiated to alternative conceptions of spirituality, time, place, individual expression, and social responsibility."[22] Contextualizing and historicizing the work of Memphis Slim and Ben Harper reframes it. What appears as sorrow at first listen is actually a hope wrapped in sadness that points to a past as proof that a better version of the present and future can be made. Within the Christian tradition there is a rough analog for this aspect of the blues. We must recover it and be emboldened by it.

Walter Brueggemann's theorization of the prophetic imagination provides a theological language and guide for how to critique and agitate for change. In *The Prophetic Imagination*, Brueggemann argued that the ministries of the Old Testament prophets and of Jesus Christ can be characterized by two tasks: 1) they radically criticized the dominant ideology of the day, and 2) they energized their communities toward an alternative consciousness. He writes, "It is the task of the prophetic imagination and ministry to bring people to engage the promise of newness that is at work in our history with God."[23] It is the job of the prophetic imagination and ministry to engage people with an alternative reality created in the encounter between God and humanity that began with Abraham, was recontextualized by Christ, and continues today. In the same way Ben Harper and other contemporary blues people are part of a long blues line, contemporary Christians can be—*and should be*—part of a long prophetic line. We must radically criticize and oppose dominant ideology, what Brueggemann called the "royal consciousness," institutionalized in forms and structures

21. Harper, "Better Way."
22. Woods, *Development Arrested*, 214.
23. Brueggemann, *Prophetic Imagination*, 59–60.

of social organization and energize our communities by creating an alternative new reality based on encounter. If the blues provide a tectonic footing and epistemology for a new ontology, then the prophetic imagination gives us a guide for how to be in the world in a way that is shaped by God's encounter with humanity. It gives us "a means to move back into the deepest memories of this community and activate those very symbols that have always been the basis for contradicting the regnant consciousness."[24]

A major reason blues people can be both critical and productive is that they do not seek state recognition or state power, but recognize that the dominant power structures are not definitive or righteous. Blues people are free of the state to make a new world. Once Christian communities understand their rightful place of existence and ministry is outside of a contemporary world structured by colonial/modern institutions and structures we will also be free to criticize and energize. To stand outside is to reject the principalities by which hegemony is imposed on certain groups of people. Hegemony cannot thrive if a community rejects its power. The hegemony of colonialism can be rejected in that space which exists outside of the regnant institution. The question then becomes one of how we form community in this liminal space. Here again the blues can be instructive.

Woods' blues epistemology and ontology are rooted in a particular shared experience, but is open to all. Although the blues spring from the Black experience of theft, slavery, and apartheid in the context of U.S. state-building, blues people can be Black, indigenous, Asian, Latino, and/or white. The subject category of "blues person" is not ascribed, it is assumed by someone seeking an alternative to the epistemological, ontological, and teleological limits of coloniality/modernity institutionalized in the state. It is possible to be a person of color *and* a white supremacist, it is possible to be white, or indigenous, or Asian, or Latino and a blues person.[25] The requirement for affiliation is solidarity with oppressed peoples and opposition to institutions and structures that create and reproduce the conditions for oppression. Blues' openness is exemplified by the improvisation, and call and response, that characterizes blues performance. The fluidity and participatory nature of Mamie Smith, Robert Johnson, Lizzie "Memphis Minnie" Douglas, Chester "Howlin' Wolf" Burnett, and countless blues artists' renderings of knowledge created in encounter and passed down

---

24. Ibid., 64.

25. On multicultural white supremacy, see Rodriguez, "Dreadful Genius of the Obama Moment."

through experience and performance are emblematic of blues openness. They also do the important work of dismantling the socially constructed wall that separates the sacred from the secular.[26]

With each blues performance and each new blues community, the secular slowly becomes sacred, or, perhaps, the blues participants begin to see the sacred in the secular. In this way, contemporary ministerial practice can learn from the blues by being both open and responsive. The blues, as a ministerial practice that transforms the secular, is much like a Sabbath practice. The Sabbath, created for enjoyment, is unsettling to a culture which thrives on order and hard work. The blues, like the Sabbath, reject both order and the need for results. The Sabbath, as described throughout scripture is misrepresented when it becomes a legalistic need for order and discipline. The story of Jesus repeatedly shows his insistence that Sabbath keeping is not an imposition on humanity, but rather that the Sabbath, like the blues, is a transformative and unsettling agent in a settled world. "The day that came to articulate social order was now transformed into an occasion for freedom."[27] The blues are a performative Sabbath practice insofar as they stand in opposition to institutions and structures that create and reproduce the conditions for oppression. Blues performance, as ministerial practice, breaks down the barrier between performer and audience. The blues require that the audience, through improvisational relationship, are themselves enactors of the dismantling of oppression. Holistically, the blues, like the Sabbath, stand as a particular form of life within a dominant and dominating culture. Just as the Sabbath stands as a distinguishing mark for Israel, so too should the blues distinguish post-colonial ministerial practice.

Post-colonial ministerial practices must be driven by solidarity leading to affiliation based on assumed participation rather than ascribed membership. Stated otherwise, post-colonial ministerial practices must begin with grace as intentional community and fellowship with the people we as the church are ministering with, not to. Can Wesleyanism embody post-colonial ministerial practices? As with the call and response which is inherent in blues performance, Christian ministry in a Wesleyan context must always already multivocal and open to a variety of practices. The Wesleyan traditions cannot deploy static programs or top down services. We must be open to improvisation based on critical listening used during

26. Woods, *Development Arrested*, 57.

27. Brueggemann, *Prophetic Imagination*, 85.

the initial call and response of an encounter. By allowing the encounter to shape the work we do in a given context, we avoid reproducing the modern/colonial binary trap of us/them as well as its uneven and hierarchical power structure. Rethinking ministry as solidarity and community forged in encounter also reconfigures the meaning of church. If ministry is what the church does, then in this context what the church is changes from a hierarchical structure to a process. We must think of church as an event. In his essay "In Solidarity With the World: The Holiness of the Missionary Community," Nathan Kerr wrote, "The church is that people whose existence is always being made new, as it responds to the call of God that goes out to it in each new moment."[28] The church is in fact an apocalyptic event.

> To say that the church is an *apocalyptic* event is to say that the church is constituted in its response to this call by the life-giving power of the Spirit, who is always at work in ever-new ways to transfigure this fallen world by liberating for freedom in Christ. And to say that the church is a *missionary* event is to say that the church lives *by* and *from* the world's transfiguration, and that it is always being made new only as it is being sent to live in solidarity with the world God loves, the world reconciled to God in Christ [emphasis in original].[29]

The church as event happens when it stands in solidarity with the world, not when people are converted to a church culture that exists in and of itself—that would only replicate the modern/colonial binary system. When God emptied God-self into the world in the person of Christ the curtain that separated the Holy of Holies (Matthew 27:51; Mark 15:38; and Luke 23:45) from humanity was torn. This signaled the outpouring of God into all the earth. All of creation is being transfigured, becoming something new. This newness is a place at which the church must practice solidarity with the world, particularly that part of the world which exists as colonized. Just as Jesus rejected the legalistic interpretation of Sabbath, the post-colonial church must stand on the side of those struggling for the recognition of humanity. The oppressive structures of the world are not overturned by a simple rejection, but by the enactment of creative alternative practice- the blues. In the torn curtain, the humanly constructed binary of secular and sacred is shattered and even ostensibly "secular" practices, such as the blues, demonstrate themselves to be sacred. In the resurrection, God began

28. Kerr, "In Solidarity With the World," 195.

29. Ibid., 195–96.

the work of making all things sacred. Commenting on the resurrection Kerr wrote, "This act encompasses *all things*. There is no longer any world as such that is to be known and related to outside of the one world that we have been given to know in its reconciliation to God that is revealed in Jesus Christ."[30] He added, "The church only exists as it continually moves out of itself and into the places where God is at work to transfigure the world in Christ; the church lives as it goes to those places and lives as a real witness to the transfiguration of the world that is happening there."[31] In this context, "Church *happens* as it stands in solidarity with the world in its confession of what Christ has done and is doing in the world."[32] When church happens anew every time and in every situation, we can develop post-colonial ministerial practices that are open, responsive, and contribute to the work of making the kingdom of God rooted in the space of encounter between God and humanity created by the life, death, and resurrection of Christ.

The church has traditionally spoken of its primarily role in the world as one of conversion. Yet, the church needs to be careful about the way that conversion is practiced. Too often, the church uses the notion of conversion to impose colonizing forces onto already oppressed people. Historically, Christian missionaries have often seen their role as one of "civilizing." Rather than continue to perpetuate oppressive colonizing structures, the blues can offer a nuanced understanding of conversion which celebrates the sacred in the secular, and which counteracts a colonial top-down worldview. Woods develops the idea of blues conversion to describe what happens when one is confronted with difference and instead of obliterating it, works from the space created by the encounter. Shortly before his assassination, Dr. Martin Luther King, Jr. visited the Mississippi Delta for the first time. His encounter with the extreme poverty and poor public health of the Black communities of the region changed him, his ministry, and his activism. King did not impose his own understanding of what the needs of others must be, but rather learned from them, and became a leader by serving from within. Key to this conversion was the realization that even though he had been struggling for social justice for many years, the communities of the delta had their own needs, as well as their own form of social explanation for their current historical context and utopic longings. Confronted with a variation on civil rights struggle, King did not impose

30. Ibid., 197.

31. Ibid.

32. Ibid., 198.

his ministry and activism on "them." Rather, a new ministry and activism with new foci took root in the space created by the encounter, informed as much by the ministered to as the minister. Instead of resolving the epistemic, ontological, and teleological crises in the encounter by subsuming the local knowledges of the delta, King resolved them by allowing a new paradigm to take shape with him and the local communities as co-laborers. King's blues conversion in the segregated U.S. South provides a demonstration of how post-colonial ministerial practices rooted in the recognition of colonial difference can begin, outside of and in opposition to dominant structures and institutions. Wesleyan-Holiness Christianity can benefit from a blues conversion that leads to post-colonial ministerial practices supple enough to respond to and include difference.

In order to move towards post-colonial Wesleyan ministerial practices, the church must unhinge itself from a modern/colonial geopolitical location that obliterates difference upon encounter. A contemporary church cannot continue to be a handmaiden to a colonial past and present that uncritically seeks power and imposes itself on others. The fact that colonialism continues should cause us pause in using the term "post-colonial ministerial practices." I am not arguing that we should not use it or strive for them. What I am arguing is that we need to understand "post" not as signifying completion, but as moving through and past colonialism in spite of its persistence. To do this, the church must allow itself to be changed by the encounter with difference—not in call or in content, but in application and meaning. Again, we have a model for what this looks like in the life of Christ.

The ministry of Christ neither broke with its Judaic past nor was it ahistorical; it was an improvisational extension and recontextualization of the covenant between God and humanity. In the same way that God's encounter with humanity as a human produced a local ministry that was open and universal but not universalizing, ministerial practices must be shaped by their location. We must not confuse the call to be co-laborers in God's universal work of reconciliation through grace with participation in universalizing modern/colonial epistemic, ontological, and teleological narratives that obliterate difference upon encounter. We must allow ourselves to be changed in the moments we meet difference in the service of post-colonial ministerial practices. If the blues are the cries of a new society being born, Christianity must become the voice of God's kingdom drawing near.

Bibliography

Brueggemann, Walter. *The Prophetic Imagination*. Minneapolis: Fortress, 2001.

Cone, James. *A Black Theology of Liberation*. 20th anniversary ed. Maryknoll, NY: Orbis, 2008.

Deloria, Vine, Jr. *Custer Died for Your Sins: An Indian Manifesto*. Norman: University of Oklahoma Press, 1988.

Duster, Alfreda M. *Crusade for Justice: The Autobiography of Ida B. Wells*. Chicago: University of Chicago Press, 1970.

Gilmore, Ruth Wilson. "Fatal Couplings of Power and Difference: Notes on Racism and Geography." *Professional Geographer* 54 (2002) 15–24.

Harper, Ben. "Better Way." *Both Sides of the Gun*. Virgin Records America. 2006.

Kelly, Robin D. G. *Hammer and Hoe: Alabama Communists during the Great Depression*. Chapel Hill: University of North Carolina Press.

Kerr, Nathan R. "In Solidarity With the World: The Holiness of the Missionary Community." In *Nurturing the Prophetic Imagination*, edited by Jamie Gates and Mark H. Mann, 189–202. San Diego: Point Loma Press, 2012.

Lee, Chana Kai. *For Freedom's Sake: The Life of Fannie Lou Hamer*. Urbana: University of Illinois Press, 2000.

"Memphis History: A Chronology." Memphis Public Library. http://www.memphislibrary.lib.tn.us/history/memphis2.htm.

Memphis Slim. "Just a Dream." *The Folkways Years: 1959-1973*. Smithsonian Folkways Recordings. 2000.

Mignolo,Walter. *The Idea of Latin America*. Malden, MA: Blackwell, 2005.

Rodriguez, Dylan. "The Dreadful Genius of the Obama Moment: Inaugurating Multicultural White Supremacy." *Colorlines*, November 10, 2008. http://colorlines.com/archives/2008/11/the_dreadful_genuis_of_the_oba.html.

Smith, Andrea. *Conquest: Sexual Violence and American Indian Genocide*. Boston: South End, 2005.

———. *Native Americans and the Christian Right: The Gendered Politics of Unlikely Alliances*. Durham: Duke University Press, 2008.

Woods, Clyde. *Development Arrested: The Blues and Plantation Power in the Mississippi Delta*. London: Verso, 1998.

3

Wesleyanism after Religion

An Exercise in Christian Ethics amidst a Social-Conscious Turn of the Post-Christian "Nones"

Nell Becker Sweeden

According to a 2012 Pew Research Center study, approximately one in five people in the United States categorizes themselves as religiously "unaffiliated," often signified by the category "None."[1] That number jumps to one in three Americans under the age of 30.[2] Furthermore, the Pew Global Religious Landscape report shows that while Christians and Muslims make up the two largest groups of religious affiliates in the world, the nones are the third largest.[3] Intrigued, concerned, and at times overwhelmed by the perplexing "post" era of Christianity, Christian leaders and authors are deliberating the current state of Christianity—both how it got here and where it is headed.[4] Understanding the rise of the nones is a point of urgency when Christian leaders consider the broad decline in membership and church attendance, especially among young people.

Utilizing the disciplines of practical theology and ecclesiology, this chapter explores potential responses of Wesleyan-Holiness churches in

1. Funk and Smith, "Nones on the Rise."

2. Ibid. See 10 and 33 of the full report: "35% of the unaffiliated are 18 to 29 years old."

3. See Pew Forum, "Global Religious Landscape."

4. For further insight into the "post" era, see chapters by John Bechtold and Orlando Serrano.

light of the "after religion" phenomenon.[5] I explore the rise of the new nones, specifically those nones who grew up in the Christian church but have since exited. In order for Wesleyan-Holiness denominations to better understand their place and mission in light of post-Christianity, it is important to uncover who these new nones are and why they prefer to self-identify as "unaffiliated" rather than "Christian." I argue that it is critical for Wesleyan-Holiness congregations and denominations to rediscover their own identity and heritage and re-appropriate their Christian story in context. In light of the "social-conscious turn" of the post-Christian nones, the Wesleyan-Holiness tradition may share some key affiliations with the "unaffiliated." I argue that a step forward is to look back to John Wesley and eighteenth- and nineteenth-century Methodism to identify important aspects of ecclesial life that sparked Christian revival. Centuries after John Wesley, something remains in his impetus for individual and social transformation and his methods for reforming the church that can inspire continued self-reflection and re-form for the Wesleyan-Holiness tradition. Accordingly, I suggest that Wesleyan-Holiness congregations and denominations renew and build authentic witness within an increasingly post-Christian culture through the avenues of Christian ethics, community formation, and collaboration.

Exactly why the nones at large are on the rise remains in question, although it is clear that no one reason explains this phenomenon. The "none" category is broadly diverse and houses a wide variety of belief and non-belief, such as "atheist," "agnostic," and "spiritual, not religious."[6] Interestingly, of the roughly 25 to 30 percent of Americans under 30 who are religiously unaffiliated, only seven percent of them identified as atheist or agnostic.[7] It is clear that the unprecedented growth of young people self-identifying as none is closely tied to other trends estimating that nearly one in five (or 18 percent) adults under 30 have left the religion of their upbringing and

5. Diana Butler Bass in her book *After Religion,* makes the case that the increase in persons who categorize themselves as religiously "unaffiliated" in the United States is linked to the turn away from organized religion and specifically the Christian church, though not necessarily a move away from new forms of spirituality. She and others have described this shift away from organized religion and organized Christianity with the language of "after religion" and "post-Christian." See her chapter, "The End of the Beginning," especially 11–18.

6. See Pew Forum, "U.S. Religious Landscape Survey," 20.

7. Stedman, "It's Time to Get to Know the Nones." Also see Curtis, "Fact Check, Please." Statistics oscillate between 25 percent in the above mentioned Pew Forum study and 35 percent in the later study by Funk and Smith, "Nones on the Rise," 10, 33.

are now unaffiliated.[8] Robert Putman and David Campbell in their 2010 publication, *American Grace: How Religion Divides and Unites Us*, offer perspective on the rise of the new nones who have appeared rather suddenly in the last two decades.[9] They affirm that most of the nones were likely raised as "somethings."[10] They add, however, that, "While the new nones are, by definition, less attached to organized religion than other Americans, they do not seem to have discarded all religious beliefs or predilections."[11] They reject organized religion specifically, while not always entirely abandoning their religious feelings.[12]

Nones on the Rise: The "Whys" as We Know Them

One way scholars have sought to understand why the nones are on the rise, is to look at trends in American Christianity from the last half of the twentieth century to the present. Putman and Campbell specifically describe the "shock" and "two aftershocks" that Christianity, and specifically evangelicalism, endured in America.[13] The first "shock" reverberates from the cultural changes of the 1960s, characterized by "sex, drugs, Rock 'N' Roll, and the God is Dead phenomenon."[14] This shock engendered a strong conservative evangelical reaction resulting in strong numerical growth throughout evangelicalism in the 1970s and 1980s.[15] These decades might be identified as the peak of evangelical churches, which have since been in decline. As a result, an "aftershock" resounds in the 1990s and 2000s characterized by young people's "disaffection from religion."[16] Since the 1990s, objection to the influence of religious leaders has been evident across all parts of the

8. See Pew Forum study on "Religion Among the Millennials," 4.

9. Putnam and Campbell summarize some of the most common findings from their own Faith Matters surveys and other scholars who have researched this phenomenon. See Putnam and Campbell, *American Grace*, 124–25.

10. Ibid., 126. They cite the 2007 Pew Survey of the American religious landscape, which found that "16 percent of American adults say they are currently unaffiliated with any particular religion, compared with only 7 percent who were raised unaffiliated" (ibid., 126–27).

11. Ibid., 126.

12. Ibid., 126.

13. Ibid., 91–133.

14. Ibid., 91.

15. Ibid., 117.

16. Ibid., 119.

religious spectrum.[17] Putnam and Campbell tie this objection largely to the alignment of religion and U.S. partisan politics in the 70s and 80s in which theological, social, moral, and political conservatism came to be identi-fied with the Religious Right.[18] By the 90s, it is clear that many Americans were tired of the "growing public presence of conservative Christians."[19] The fraction of Americans who identified as religiously "none," as well as those who said they "never" attend church, sharply increased.[20] Consider-ing generational succession, since 2000, "Cohorts of whom barely 5 percent say they have no religious affiliation are being replaced by cohorts of whom roughly 25 percent say they have no religion."[21] It appears this aftershock in American Christianity helped to provoke an increasing nationwide preva-lence of the nones.

The nones have only continued to increase in the last two decades. A 2004 study by the Barna group found that young adults outside the church came to view religion as judgmental, homophobic, hypocritical, and too political.[22] The 2010 Pew Study "'Nones' on the Rise," presents four of the commonly held theories about root causes of the rise in the unaffiliated category. The study first identifies political backlash, signified by "the turn away from organized religion" because it is perceived "as deeply entangled with conservative politics."[23] Concomitantly, the backlash is intimately tied to cultural wars regarding issues like abortion and gay rights, as well as perceptions that religious institutions are too concerned with money and power.[24] The above Pew study also references three other root causes of the

17. Ibid., 120.

18. Ibid.

19. Ibid.

20. Ibid., 122.

21. Ibid., 123.

22. See Kinnaman and Lyons, *UnChristian* for a more complete portrayal of their study. Putnam and Campbell reference this study in *American Grace* on page 121. Butler Bass offers a nice summary of the study's findings: "In a 2004 survey, the Barna organi-zation found that young adults who are outside of the church hold intensely negative views of Christianity: 91 percent think that Christianity is 'antihomosexual,' 87 percent say Christians are 'judgmental,' 85 percent accuse churchgoers of being 'hypocritical,' and 72 percent say Christianity is 'out of touch with reality.' Only 41 percent think that Christianity seems 'genuine or real' or 'makes sense,' while only 30 percent think that it is 'relevant to your life'" (Butler Bass, *After Religion*, 86).

23. Pew Forum, "Some Theories About Root Causes of the Rise of the Unaffiliated," 29–32.

24. Ibid., 30.

escalation of the nones—delays in marriage, broad social disengagement, and secularization—yet as individual factors these are less indicative of overall growth in the none category and tend to be more widely debated.[25] Additionally, the "'Nones' on the Rise" study does not appear to be alone in its findings. As other studies show, large numbers of nones say they are unaffiliated simply because "they think that religious organizations focus too much on rules and not enough on 'spirituality.'"[26]

Interestingly, Putnam and Campbell also draw attention to the trend from the 1990s onward of the younger generations of nones who hold more liberal views on homosexuality and marijuana.[27] They highlight a great distinction between younger generations' more liberal views regarding "moral and lifestyle issues," in comparison with an older generation of religious leaders who they perceived as "consumed by the political fight against gay marriage."[28] Putnam and Campbell reflect, "Just as the youngest cohort of Americans was zigging in one direction, many highly visible religious leaders zagged in another."[29] Confirming this generational disconnect, the Barna study of young adults noted that "72 percent say Christianity is 'out of touch with reality,'" while "only 41 percent think that Christianity seems 'genuine or real' or 'makes sense,'" and "only 30 percent think that it is 'relevant to your life.'"[30] In other words, studies clearly show a wide chasm between the younger nones' worldviews and perceived relevance of organized Christianity, and Christian leaders of older generations.

Christian Reaction and Response

There is a sense of urgency among Christian leaders—specifically in reference to the disconnect between the church and young adults—that has engendered various reactions and responses. In addition to the many social

25. See Putnam and Campbell's section on certain facts regarding the nones, *American Grace*, 125–27.

26. Ibid., 131. Putnam and Campbell cite the 2009 Pew Forum on Religion & Public Life's study entitled, *Faith in Flux*. Diana Butler Bass also makes this case in her book *After Religion*.

27. Putnam and Campbell, *American Grace*, 129.

28. Ibid., 130.

29. Ibid., 130.

30. Butler Bass, *After Religion*, 86. See Kinnaman and Lyons, *UnChristian* for full study.

scientists who are investigating why the nones are on the rise, there are many Christian authors writing on the subject and serving as consultants to Christian pastors and denominational leaders.[31] Some scholars advocate that the post-Christian nones and/or disaffected Christians *are* the new Christian, and the church needs to listen to them. Others push for greater relevance in the church on behalf of the nones and younger generations. Some Christian churches and leaders desperately seek to find a way to "save" the nones, while others adamantly reject anyone claiming "none" or any beliefs that remotely lean that direction. Within these varying postures toward the nones, broadly speaking there is a concerted effort to "rebrand" Christianity in light of the growing exodus of young people. Undoubtedly, new creativity and innovation of Christian practice in light of contemporary contexts is much needed. Yet, this may do little to change or slow the rise of the nones. Putnam and Campbell observe that younger generations of nones "seem unwilling or unable to distinguish the stance of the most visible, most political, and most conservative religious leaders from organized religion in general."[32] In many respects, for the nones, all organized religion has been tainted.

I have discussed thus far how the disconnect between the new nones and American Christianity is largely tied to cultural shifts and disparate worldviews in recent decades. From a practical theological perspective, moreover, the disconnect is specifically tied to how Christian communities and traditions have interpreted and enacted their Christian identity within these changing contexts. Interpreting and embodying the ways of Jesus in new contexts is an ongoing challenge for the church. The church must simultaneously look back and move forward, discovering ways to embody Christian faithfulness anew. Accordingly, Christian witness is the act of reviving, again and again, the living story of God in Jesus by the power of the Holy Spirit.

For individual Christians and Christian communities this task can be difficult. Past centuries of the church's failure to live out what it professes is no secret, and it does not take the "rise of the nones" to illuminate that fact. The church's complicity in abuse, exploitation, power, racism, violence, and the subjugation of the poor and marginalized is but a small testimony to its failure to live out the ways of Jesus. Yet, despite these continual failures

31. For example, see the work of Diana Butler Bass, Ross Douthat, David Kinnaman, Gabe Lyons, Leonard Sweet, Alan Hirsch, etc.

32. Putnam and Campbell, *American Grace*, 131.

throughout history, the church remains the *ekklesia*—those "called out"—to witness to God's reign breaking forth in each time and place. Looking back, the church can recognize and repent of its failures. Moving forward the church may discover that the best way to embody Christian faithfulness is to simply be the church, that is, to seek to be the tangible embodiment of God's reign. God's reign made incarnate in the person of Jesus is the hope—the *euangelion* that the church offers the world.

The church must discover again how to be a people who reveal and embody the strange beauty of Jesus Christ for the world. The task is no different for Wesleyan-Holiness churches seeking to faithfully respond to the rise of the nones. In particular, I believe a process of critical reflection on Christian praxis, which engages the social consciousness among new nones and post-Christians can yield unique possibilities for the church. Through parallel lenses of Wesleyan social responsibility and ethics, I will demonstrate how Wesleyan-Holiness congregations and denominations can authentically and collectively live into and out of their rich Christian heritage. In a post-Christian context, the Wesleyan-Holiness tradition is uniquely equipped to resource this rediscovery.

Spiritual (and Ethical?), Not Religious

Like "unaffiliated" or "none," the catch-all label "spiritual, not religious" is not necessarily an accurate description of the many young people disaffected with Christianity. Even Putnam and Campbell note that the nones generally do not use this language to describe themselves.[33] Even still, while a more generalized sense of appeal to the "spiritual" has come to characterize the nones, new nones also generally demonstrate a deep social consciousness, especially evidenced in forms of advocacy and responsible consumer choices.[34] Whereas the motivations and practices of the nones may remain ungrounded or at least unidentified, Christian ethics remain grounded in the church. Indeed, if the church is *itself* a social ethic, as Stanley Hauerwas claims, then it should have something valuable to contribute to a human

33. Ibid., 126.

34. It is not entirely clear which traditions "religious" or otherwise may function in a normative capacity for the new nones. The challenge, as Putnam and Campbell acknowledge, is that little research has been done on the social and moral beliefs of the new nones (See Putnam and Campbell, 127). Consequentially, even less research has been done on the social and ethical *practices* of the new nones, not to mention the motivations driving those practices.

concern for alleviating global injustice.[35] With regard to this chapter, the Wesleyan-Holiness language of social responsibility (i.e. "social holiness") is an especially pertinent example.

The social consciousness of the new nones is linked to their education and the information explosion of the twenty-first century. The new nones have a growing awareness of global injustices and a strong desire to act. Though more research needs to be done before identifying the size and scope of the social-conscious orientation, undoubtedly there is a growing market niche—from TOMS shoes, to buying Red products, to Kiva—that embraces the turn toward social responsibility at least in consumer choices and investment opportunities.[36] Even the market recognizes how working to alleviate poverty, hunger, and oppression of marginalized and vulnerable persons has captured the imagination of the new nones, including post-Christian nones.[37] If such commitments continue and momentum grows, let us hope that these efforts produce valuable fruit for social change that promotes justice, equality, and human flourishing.

Interestingly, social concern and action remains an individual endeavor for many nones. Pew studies indicate, and Putnam's and Campbell's research confirms, that generally speaking there is broad social disengagement when it comes to the collective nones. The Pew, "Rise of the 'Nones,'" notes a large "tendency among Americans to live more separate lives and engage in fewer communal activities."[38] The Pew Research Center/Religion & Ethics NewsWeekly survey also finds, "Religiously unaffiliated Americans are less inclined than Americans as a whole to feel that it is very important to belong to 'a community of people who share your values and beliefs' (28% of the unaffiliated say this is very important to them, compared with 49% of the general public)."[39] While these trends are not necessarily true

35. Hauerwas, "Reforming Christian Social Ethics," 111–15.

36. To learn more about the mission of these businesses and movements see: Toms Shoes; Product Red; and Kiva. Also see the One Campaign.

37. For an interesting description of the socially conscious orientation of younger evangelical Christians, see Lyons, *The Next Christians.*

38. Pew Forum, "The Rise of the 'Nones,'" 30. Also see, Putnam, *Bowling Alone.* See *American Grace,* 29; also see chapter 13: "Religion and Good Neighborliness," pages 369–418. Not only are the unaffiliated non-participatory just in religious communities, "but also in 'all types of volunteer and community groups, from sports leagues to arts groups, hobby clubs and alumni associations.'" (Pew, "The Rise of the 'Nones,'" 30). See the December 2011 report by the Pew Research Center's Internet & American Life Project "The civic and community engagement of religiously active Americans."

39. Pew Forum, "The Rise of the 'Nones,'" 30–31.

for all nones, the research presses the question, if the nones are generally disengaged from communities and community practices, what shapes their social consciousness and social action?

Undoubtedly, if the social engagement of nones remains primarily an individual endeavor—that is, not the action or outcome of groups or communities—then it is difficult to identify who or what is grounding these efforts.[40] In such an absence, Wesleyan-Holiness churches offer a two-fold response to the nones: first by sharing their orientation toward social consciousness and action, and second by offering a robust ecclesial tradition in which concrete notions of good can be nurtured.

That is not to say Christians, and even those of the Wesleyan-Holiness persuasion, have not failed to live into the good of their own tradition. One cannot accuse the nones of lacking a grounded understanding of the good without also acknowledging how many Christians misrepresent the church's professed beliefs. Clearly, the nones' critiques of Christianity reveal the shortcomings of the church in living out what it proclaims. The fact that younger nones find Christians hypocritical and the church irrelevant to their lives should cause the church to self-reflect and look critically at its own witness before the world. The sad reality is that few Christians would be able to identify how their own participation in congregations and denominations influences their actions toward others, much less an understanding of good grounded in God's desire for hope, justice, and restoration in a broken and suffering world.

Nevertheless, the nones' social consciousness is an invitation for Christians, and specifically those within Wesleyan-Holiness traditions, to uncover their own roots in social holiness and rediscover how to be a people

40. Influenced by the argument Alasdair MacIntyre sets up in his text, *Whose Justice and Which Rationality?* I pose the questions: "*Whose* good is one striving after?" and "*How* does one arrive at this good?" to post-Christian nones and Christians alike. If we are working toward social change, it is important to understand what change we are working toward. Additionally, many of our decisions and actions come out of a particular agenda or tradition. This is particularly important in consumer purchasing, for example. Our consumer choices are often driven by the control of certain companies with their own agendas. We are never as "free" as might think in our consumer choices. MacIntyre raises this point against the Enlightenment notion of "autonomous" rationality. He argues that bodies of tradition provide particular narratives by which rationalization, justice, and even ethics are understood. He states, "So rationality itself, whether theoretical or practical, is a concept with a history: indeed, since there are a diversity of traditions of enquiry, with histories, there are, so it will turn out, rationalities rather than rationality, just as it will turn out that there are justices rather than justice" MacIntyre, *Whose Justice? Which Rationality?*, 9.

who embody a rich tradition of social responsibility and action. While this rediscovery may or may not be enough for the nones, their exodus should provoke the church to remember, restore, and re-appropriate its manifestation of God's good news for the world.

Reviving Authentic Christian Life

The contribution of John Wesley and the Methodist movement toward revivalism in the eighteenth and nineteenth centuries offers an important lens for reflecting upon how the church continues to reform and re-appropriate the good news of God amidst great cultural shifts. Two aspects of Wesley's contribution to eighteenth and nineteenth-century revivalism—his organization of *ecclesiolae* within the *ecclesia* and his innovation in social transformation—help provide a catalyst for ecclesial innovation and commitment to Christian responsibility and ethics within a post-Christian culture. Uncovering this rich tradition of individual and social transformation is a pivotal place to start.

Differently from the social and economic instability that are often cited as fertile ground for revival, Henry Rack describes how the institutional stagnation within the seventeenth-century Anglican Church created a watered-down faith that left many common people without meaningful religious or spiritual purpose.[41] He attributes the weakness of the Church of England to the development of a civil religion that lacked vitality.[42] Several scholars have noted that a large majority of the people Wesley reached were nominal Christians with a reasonably strong Christian background; the church, however, had been unsuccessful in revitalizing their faith.[43] Wesley accomplished this, as Albert Outler describes, by preaching a new depth and dimension of Christianity that was aimed toward "the fullness of faith and the endless maturing of life in grace."[44]

---

41. Rack, *Reasonable Enthusiast*, 173.

42. Ibid., 178.

43. I am indebted to Ron Benefiel unpacking this historical perspective in his unpublished essay "John Wesley's Mission of Evangelism," 17. Also see Rack, *Reasonable Enthusiast*, 173.

44. Again Benefiel points this out in "John Wesley's Mission of Evangelism," 21. See Outler, *Evangelism and Theology in the Wesleyan Spirit*, 21.

Ecclesiolae in Ecclesia

Wesley's concern was not to create a new denomination or even a movement, but to revive the Church of England. Wesley sought to awaken new life by creatively re-appropriating the rich Christian tradition of care for persons who were trapped in poverty. Wesley's primary concern was to nurture an understanding of salvation in believers that would lead to their holistic transformation. To help guide Christians in the way of salvation, he organized a system of societies, classes, and bands and channeled those saved through his field preaching into these groups to provide accountability and growth in love and holiness of heart and life that also included their full participation in the church. The groups would come to be identified with the people called Methodist, but were meant to be an *ecclesiolae* within the *ecclesia*, that is, to reform the broader church and call Christians back to its roots of loving God and neighbor wholeheartedly.[45] Wesley's Methodist *ecclesiolae* began to revitalize individual faith and provide the structure and formation for the collective embodiment of faithfulness for participants.

Through the *ecclesiolae* within the *ecclesia,* Wesley established a program that would inspire continual growth in grace inwardly *and* outwardly so as to transform society with the good news of Christ. For Wesley, one's individual transformation would always lead to outward manifestations of social transformation.[46] Christian holiness was social in nature, or specifically, relational in perfect love of God and neighbor.[47] Individual transformation was not simply an internalization of the salvation message, but it was a simultaneous turn to others manifested in works of mercy modeled after Matthew 25:36-41. In addition to promoting Christian accountability and growth in grace, the small groups would be responsible to visit the sick and imprisoned, care for the poor, and feed the hungry. Works of mercy became a means of grace for the participants as well as the beneficiaries.

45. I am indebted to Bryan Stone for illuminating Wesley's radical ecclesial formation through *ecclesiolae* in *ecclesia* in his unpublished paper, "Wesleyan Ecclesiology." Stone draws from Colin Williams' development of these concepts in *John Wesley's Theology Today*. Also see Snyder, *The Radical Wesley and Patterns for Church Renewal*.

46. As Rebekah Miles put it: "One could no more be a Christian and refuse to love and care for a neighbor than one could be a Christian and refuse to love God. Indeed, in the end, both loves amounted to one thing—the one happiness and one religion" in "Happiness, Holiness, and the Moral Life in John Wesley," 210.

47. Again, I am indebted to Ron Benefiel for helping to illuminate these concepts in his unpublished papers, "Christian Holiness and the Wesleyan Mission of Mercy," and "John Wesley's Mission of Evangelism."

Today, new vision for establishing *ecclesiolae* in *ecclesia* is needed for reviving authentic Christian witness in the face of an increasingly post-Christian mindset. In fact, many across the Christian tradition have already been exploring primitive forms of ecclesial gathering in order to inspire renewal in the church.[48] Intentional gatherings as *ecclesiolae* are needed to nurture social responsibility and action within the church. Imagine small communities of Christian responsibility sharing a commitment to service, living simply, combating individualism, and making wise consumer choices. These small *ecclesiolae* communities would be both faithful embodiments of Christian witness and intriguing alternatives to the post-religious status quo. Furthermore, the communities would be centers for discernment and co-laboring in social holiness for each new context. Wesley's vision of *ecclesiolae* in *ecclesia* is a great contribution even for our time—an inspiration for the church to again be the church.

Innovation in Social Transformation

Wesley's contribution to social transformation was not limited to his organization of the Methodist *ecclesiolae*. He also creatively arranged ways for himself and others to care for vulnerable persons suffering from poverty in eighteenth-century England. For Wesley, the poor were those who lacked the necessities of life, while "whoever has sufficient food to eat and raiment to put on, with a place where to lay his head, and something over, [was] *rich*."[49] Wesley strictly advocated for *all people* to take responsibility in helping their neighbor no matter their own condition.[50] His approach was both personal and institutional in nature. In addition to the organization of *ecclesiolae,* Wesley modeled his own principles of earning all he could—including soliciting large contributions from the wealthy—living in extreme thrift so as to save all he could, and giving generously to all who had need.

Wesley's mission to offer holistic transformation in Christ was expansive. He addressed poverty through education, prison reform, health care, and microenterprise. Wesley organized schools for both children and

---

48. Movements such as the organic church, missional church, and house-church movements, including neo-monasticism, the emerging and emergent church movements are some examples of this.

49. Wesley, "The Danger of Riches," 453.

50. Heizenrater, *The Poor and the People Called Methodist*, 30.

adults, providing education for the underprivileged.[51] Wesley utilized public spaces for his schools—they met in residences, institutions, chapels, and school buildings. He also rallied teachers, pastors, preachers, and capable laypersons for instruction. The schooling was offered free of charge for families in need, and children were often given clothing and meals.[52]

Wesley offered further educational opportunities by providing inexpensive quality literature.[53] He made use of technological advances in printing of the late seventeenth and early eighteenth centuries to establish a "comprehensive and well-organized publishing program."[54] The goal was to provide the poor with books that would complement his preaching and provide instruction on ethical issues. Such books included many of his own writings, theological primers such as Thomas à Kempis's *Imitation of Christ*, and also a broad spectrum of literature like biographies, poetry, school books, travelogues, etc.[55] His own book *Primitive Physic*, which included home remedies for illnesses to help those who could not afford health care, was among the publications.

Wesley explored micro-loan programs to help struggling merchants and manufacturers initiate consistent earnings through small businesses. His journal entry in 1746 describes a lending system where one-time loans were given at twenty shillings, which was to be repaid after three months.[56] Though modest, this innovative program provided needed capital for securing materials, such as yarn for weavers' looms.[57] Alongside microloans, Wesley experimented with setting up work cooperatives. His 1740 journal gives indication of a women's sewing cooperative for twelve of the poorest women who worked to spin cotton for four months during winter in order to make sales in the spring.[58]

---

51. Ibid., 51–52. His first school was set up for Kingswood miners near Bristol in 1739. Heizenrater notes that Wesley followed suit with schools in Bristol, London, Newcastle upon Tyne and other places.

52. Ibid. Also see, Marquardt, *John Wesley's Social Ethics*, 83–84.

53. Ibid., 57.

54. Ibid.

55. Ibid.

56. See Jennings, *Good News to the Poor*, 61. Also see Wesley, *Journal* (January 17, 1748), *Works*, 204.

57. Heitzenrater, *The Poor and the People Called Methodist*, 34.

58. See Wesley, *Journal* (November 25, 1740), *Works*, 173. Also see previously cited works by Heitzenrater, Jennings, and Marquardt.

Committed to the biblical mandate to visit and care for those imprisoned, Wesley regularly visited prisons and advocated for better conditions for prisoners, including foreign French, Dutch, and American prisoners.[59] He encouraged Methodist societies to visit prisoners and collect money to supply proper clothing, food, and mattresses for them.[60]

Many contemporary Wesleyan scholars point out that Wesley did not go far enough in how he addressed poverty and injustice by not attacking root causes of these issues.[61] Others caution Wesleyan-Holiness Christians not to over-idealize Wesley's social transformation.[62] Unquestionably, Wesley's primary motivation throughout his life was to inspire holiness of heart and life and motivate love God and neighbor. For Wesley, social transformation arose out of individual transformation. Wesley's Methodist predecessors, however, continued to stretch his legacy in social transformation.[63] Building off the prolific revival movement that Wesley modeled and helped to organize in eighteenth-century England, there is much room for expansion as each new century of Wesleyans seeks to manifest the Christian story anew.

In the nineteenth century, Methodism in America took on new expressions as Wesleyan-Holiness denominations were established. Many of these denominations arose out of Christians' deep convictions that the church was failing to embody good news when confronted with injustices of slavery and poverty.[64] These groups split off in order to more intentionally focus on the mission of the church in the world. In light of the turn away from religion, what is needed is not new or more denominations. The contemporary context is simply demanding that Wesleyan-Holiness churches discover again their origins in care for persons who are poor and marginal-

---

59. See Wesley, *Journal* (October 15, 1759) and (October 24, 1760), *Works*, 231, 285. Also see previously cited works by Heitzenrater, Jennings, and Marquardt.

60. Marquardt, *John Wesley's Social Ethics*, 83.

61. See Míguez Bonino. "Wesley's Doctrine of Sanctification from a Liberationist Perspective," 49–63; Bonino, "Salvation as the Work of the Trinity," 69–83; Jennings, *Good News to the Poor*; Marquardt, *John Wesley's Social Ethics*; and Tamez, "Wesley as Read by the Poor," 67–84.

62. See Heitzenrater, *The Poor and the People Called Methodist*, 25. Also see Randy Maddox's chapter in this volume, entitled "Visit the Poor," 59–82.

63. The Wesleyan denomination, for example, began out of the impetus to end slavery in America and many other Wesleyan-Holiness groups followed suit. See Dayton, *Discovering an Evangelical Heritage*.

64. See Dayton, *Discovering an Evangelical Heritage* in its entirety.

ized. The new nones, those who believe themselves to be post-religious, are a reminder that there is no greater testimony of the gospel than the church embodying what it is called to be before the world.

As Wesleyan-Holiness congregations of today embrace and embody Wesley's own impetus for holistic transformation, they will demonstrate their own vitality in a world plagued by suffering and injustice. In doing so, the church offers the new nones a community where support, collaboration, and eventually formation can take place. As the church learns to be the church in each new context, it rediscovers how to participate in God's story and invite others into God's transformation that is hope and restoration for the world

Conclusion

Wesley committed his life to individual and social transformation through the development of accountability and learning communities among Christians, in schools for impoverished children and adults, in visiting the sick and imprisoned, in simple medical remedies for those who could not afford health care, and in charity for persons trapped in poverty. In the subsequent centuries, Wesley's predecessors would also carry this impetus for social transformation through their participation in abolitionism in America and concern for the urban poor. From a "people called Methodist" to the nineteenth century Methodist offshoots, Wesleyan-Holiness churches have sought to embody the life of Jesus and offer hope to those most impoverished and marginalized in society.

Today, new forms of Wesleyan ecclesial innovation are possible, and are especially evident in reform that reuses and recycles old practices and modes of gathering as the church. Wesleyan-Holiness congregations have a rich inheritance suited for ecclesial reform and innovation. What is needed now is not a new attempt at relevance in the face of declining church participation. Rather, new life in the church and a deepening of Christian formation and reflection must arrive to combat the church's own failures of complicity to power, compromise of beliefs, and institutional stagnation and ineffectiveness. New imagination and configurations of gathering the church can cut across denominational lines and draw the church to authenticity, unity, ethical integrity, and communal accountability, discernment, and formation. The rise of the nones may be a wake-up call for the church to reform yet again, and in the process rediscover what it means to be the church in embodying God's mission of peace, love, justice, and wholeness in the world.

Bibliography

"Religion Among the Millennials." Pew Research Center, Washington D.C. February 2010. Accessed 2/11/2015. http://www.pewforum.org/Age/Religion-Among-the-Millennials.aspx.

Benefiel, Ron. "John Wesley's Mission of Evangelism." Unpublished lecture, 2007.

Bonino, José Míguez. "Salvation as the Work of the Trinity: An Attempt to a Holistic Understanding from a Latin American Perspective." In *Trinity, Community, and Power: Mapping Trajectories in Wesleyan Theology*, edited by M. Douglas Meeks, 69–84. Nashville: Kingswood, 2000.

———. "Wesley's Doctrine of Sanctification from a Liberationist Perspective." In *Sanctification and Liberation*, edited by Theodore Runyon, 49-63. Nashville: Abingdon, 1981.

Butler Bass, Diana. *After Religion: The End of the Church and the Birth of a New Spiritual Awakening.* New York: HarperOne, 2012.

Dayton, Donald. *Discovering an Evangelical Heritage.* New York: Harper & Row, 1976.

Funk, Cary, and Greg Smith. "'Nones' on the Rise: One-in-Five Adults Have No Religious Affiliation." Pew Research Center, October 9, 2012. http://www.pewforum.org/Unaffiliated/nones-on-the-rise.aspx.

Hauerwas, Stanley. "Reforming Christian Social Ethics: Ten Theses." In *The Hauerwas Reader*, edited by John Berkman and Michael G. Cartwright, 111–15. Durham: Duke University Press, 2001.

Heizenrater, Richard P., ed. *The Poor and the People Called Methodists, 1729–1999.* Nashville: Kingswood, 2002.

Jennings, Theodore W., Jr. *Good News to the Poor: John Wesley's Evangelical Economics.* Nashville: Abingdon, 1990.

Kinnaman, David, and Gabe Lyons. *UnChristian: What a New Generation Really Thinks about Christianity and Why It Matters.* Grand Rapids: Baker, 2007.

Lyons, Gabe. *The Next Christians: Seven Ways You Can Live the Gospel and Restore the World.* Colorado Springs, CO: Multnomah, 2010.

MacIntyre, Alasdair. *Whose Justice? Which Rationality?* Notre Dame: University of Notre Dame Press, 1988.

Maddox, Randy L., and Jason E. Vickers, eds. *The Cambridge Companion to John Wesley.* Cambridge: Cambridge University Press, 2010.

Marquardt, Manfred. *John Wesley's Social Ethics: Praxis and Principles.* Nashville: Abingdon, 1992.

Outler, Albert C. *Evangelism and Theology in the Wesleyan Spirit.* Nashville: Discipleship Resources, 1996.

Putnam, Robert D., and David E. Campbell. *American Grace: How Religion Divides and Unites Us.* New York: Simon and Schuster, 2010.

Putnam, Robert D. *Bowling Alone: The Collapse and Revival of American Community.* New York: Simon & Schuster, 2000.

Rack, Henry D. *Reasonable Enthusiast: John Wesley and the Rise of Methodism.* 2nd ed. Nashville: Abingdon, 1993.

Snyder, Howard A. *The Radical Wesley and Patterns for Church Renewal.* Downers Grove: InterVarsity, 1980.

Tamez, Elsa. "Wesley as Read by the Poor." In *The Future of the Methodist Theological Traditions,* edited by M. Douglas Meeks, 67–84. Nashville: Abingdon, 1985.

Wesley, John. "The Danger of Riches (1781)." In *John Wesley's Sermons: An Anthology,* edited by Albert C. Outler and Richard P. Heizenrater, 451–64. Nashville: Abingdon, 1991.

Part 2

Wesleyanism in a Pluralistic Context

Rejoicing in a New Generation

John B. Cobb, Jr.

F or some time now I have been discouraged about the future of Protestant theology. This is partly because, at least in the United States, theology is being replaced by religious studies. These have much to contribute to historical understanding and expanding our information about what is going on. But they do not take the place of theology.

Theology in my view must be confessional in the sense that it expresses belief and conviction. Some theology may try to speak for a whole community and give voice to what its leaders or members believe. Other theology is more individual and personal, although individuals usually put forward their beliefs as proposals for what others might also believe.

Teaching theology has involved informing students about what various groups and individuals have believed in the past and believe now. But if one is really teaching theology, and not just teaching *about* theology, all of this is for the sake either of indoctrination or of encouraging the theological development of students. This activity cannot be carried on in "religious studies."

I observed the marginalization of theology over many years in the American Academy of Religion. For a while, there was a fairly good balance between theology and what was often called history of religions and theology. This meant that discussions among teachers of Bible could go either way. Some were purely objective and factual. But others were concerned with the normative role of scripture in the church or synagogue. The Bible could be taught by a believer who struggled with the issues it raised or by one who found it to be an interesting part of ancient literature. Meanwhile there were other places where theological issues were directly treated.

However, as time passed, the second way of treating the Bible became dominant. Intruding normative or theological questions into its teaching was no longer acceptable. Its teaching in the university was justified only in the same way as ancient Egyptian or Mesopotamian literature. Humanists were interested in all things human.

In addition, theology as such became rare. When I began going to the AAR, it was difficult to get a hearing for my kind of theology because academics were properly more interested in German theology. That faded, but for a while there were meetings on feminist theology and black theology. Other excluded groups expressed themselves theologically. Later even these tended to be replaced by women's studies, black studies, and so forth.

Liberation theology of the Latin American variety gave some new life to theology, and it held on a while at the margins. By the time I stopped going, however, almost the only meetings of theologians were among conservatives. Process theology has maintained a foothold by meeting jointly with those from a conservative evangelical background who were committed to open or relational theology.

I am glad that in more conservative circles there continues to be serious interest in theology. But this does not alleviate my general distress. I favor what in the past could be thought of as "liberal" forms of theology. Probably an element of indoctrination is inescapable. It occurs even in religious studies. But I have been particularly interested in encouraging individual students to think about important questions for themselves, understanding themselves to be shaped by a particular tradition, and seeking the truth, while knowing that one never finally finds it. This is commonly considered "liberal."

I have discovered, however, that most Christians who consider themselves "liberal" are more concerned to avoid dogmatism and indoctrination than to encourage serious thinking about theological questions. They have, accordingly, offered no resistance to the replacement of theology with religious studies. They seem not to care what future ministers believe as long as they make no attempt to impose their beliefs on others. It is enough that they be well-informed. I have come to the conclusion that a major reason for this is to be found in the role of Kant and the neo-Kantians.

Liberal Protestants were partly defined by their refusal to oppose science and scholarship. They accepted evolutionary theory and biblical criticism. Since science and scholarship were based on the assumption that the natural and human worlds should be explained without reference to anything outside them, and also the assumption that God is outside nature and history, the scholarly project is to exclude God from any explanatory role with respect to worldly events. For all practical purposes this is atheism. The liberal acceptance of scholarship was acquiescence in this project.

So what was left for Christians to believe? Kant's response was to distinguish theoretical and practical reason. God has no foothold in theoretical reason. But practical reason leads to the postulation of God. Kant's formulations are complex. His followers, especially his theological followers, simplified matters. They distinguished facts and values. Facts are the province of scholarship. God is excluded from the factual world. But we live in a world of values, and there God has importance.

Many liberal Protestants were thus brought up to think that what matters is having the right values. For them, what they understood to be "doctrines" dealt with by "theology" were okay, but unimportant. They were dangerous because they were divisive. Better call God a "mystery" and assume that nothing more need be said.

This is where my special concern about the future of Wesleyan theology comes in. The liberal spirit has flourished more easily and more naturally in Wesleyan circles than in Calvinist or Lutheran ones. Certainly, it has played a dominant role in the United Methodist Church. In my opinion, the freedom this afforded members of the denomination and its earlier component parts has often been well used. I take pride in the contribution of United Methodists to Christian thought in the United States.

While liberal thought on the continent of Europe was almost entirely Kantian, this was not so true in the United States. Wesleyans in the United States led in developing a philosophical theology that talked quite straightforwardly about God and wrestled with questions of the relation of God and human beings. However, we were shaken by the assault of neo-Orthodoxy, and its decline did not lead to the renewed flourishing of philosophical questions. In the new context, Wesley's emphasis on experience led Wesleyans more to psychology. Wesley was tolerant of those with whom he disagreed when he admired their actions and their spirit, and liberals use this as a justification for belittling theology.

In fact, of course, Wesley's sermons are theological through and through. The tolerance noted above was an outgrowth of theology, not a reason to neglect it. I fear there are very few Wesleyan congregations that are prepared to hear the sermons that Wesley preached to illiterate people in open fields. So great is our theological decline!

If the liberal spirit continues to express itself only in indifference to theological ideas, we face the end of liberal theology. This seems to be as true of the Wesleyan form of liberalism as of the neo-Kantian one. In this context, and with the marginalization of theology in academia, I had feared that intellectually active younger Wesleyans in the United Methodist Church would stop doing Wesleyan theology. Partly because of its abandonment of the theological enterprise, the only future I could see was continued decline.

For Protestant theology generally, I have seen more hope among those we have called conservative evangelicals. Especially among those who have been influenced by Wesley, there is openness among them alongside commitment and conviction. They recognize that what we believe matters, indeed, that it is of critical importance. Of course, in a hostile secular context, this can lead to a defensive fundamentalism, which I do not find promising. But it can also lead to serious reflection based on reason, scripture, tradition, and experience. I do find this encouraging. From my perspective, this is what authentic conservatives in the Wesleyan tradition *should* be doing.

Accordingly, I rejoice to find that some are truly doing it. The essays in this section are serious reflections about some of the most important issue of the 21st century: namely, Wesleyan theology and identity in the face of immense diversity—religious, cultural, and other. These issues are approached from the perspective of Christian believers who stand in the tradition shaped by the Wesleys. Hence they are engaged in authentic Wesleyan theology.

I celebrate this because I am a Wesleyan. Of course, I am a Wesleyan chiefly because I was brought up in the Methodist church. But I am an enthusiastic Wesleyan because I believe that, of the great Reformers, Wesley's theology is the most faithful to Jesus and to Paul.

I believe that Luther juxtaposed *pistis* too much to both reason and works. I believe that Paul's meaning is better captured in "faithfulness" than by "faith." I believe that Jesus' faithfulness to God and our participation in that faithfulness are different from both reason and works, but do not exclude them. And I believe that Wesley's focus on love comes closer to putting these matters into a Pauline perspective than Luther's theology.

I am also quite sure that the Calvinist emphasis on divine sovereignty is a distortion of the message of Jesus and of Paul. Jesus' *"abba"* is not well understood as a cosmic ruler. The Bible does not teach divine omnipotence and human impotence. Wesley came far closer to the New Testament message.

I say these things here because too often Wesleyans have been hesitant to take Wesley with full seriousness as a Bible-scholar and a theologian. I certainly do not recommend proof-texting Wesley. His theology forbids it. But I do want to encourage Wesleyan theologians to brag a little. I believe that the world needs Wesley's theology today. It will not have the benefit of hearing that theology if there are no Wesleyan theologians. That there *are* younger Wesleyan theologians today ready to think in the perspective that is Wesley's legacy is a fact to be deeply celebrated. May the fine work that is begun here grow and flourish and renew theological reflection in Wesleyan churches.

4

Comparative Theology

Wesleyan Theology in a Pluralistic Context

—— Wm. Andrew Schwartz ——

The reality of religious diversity is one of the greatest challenges facing Christian theology today. The religions of the world embody diverse practices and at times incompatible beliefs. What does it mean to be Christian in the face of religious plurality? What might it look like to do Wesleyan theology in the pluralistic context of our 21st century world—taking seriously both one's own faith and the faith of others? Many ways of responding to religious diversity are violent (both physically and socially), and contribute to a world at war. In the midst of division, hate, and marginalization, the need for peace and reconciliation is apparent. We must find ways to connect across our differences. One possibility for constructive and peaceful engagement with religious difference is *comparative theology*.[1]

What Is Comparative Theology?

Comparative theology is a new and growing branch of theology (alongside but not exclusive of other theological disciplines such as philosophical

1. Please note that comparative theology need not be a uniquely Christian practice. There can also be Muslim comparative theologians, or Hindu comparative theologians. Insofar as a tradition is capable of theology, it is capable of comparative theology. Throughout this chapter, however, I will use the phrase "comparative theology" to mean *Christian* comparative theology. This is done for the sake of simplicity, not imperialism.

theology, systematic theology, historical theology, etc.). Although comparative theology is constitutive of two essential components—comparison and theology—it should not be confused as simply a matter of comparing different theologians (e.g. putting Calvin and Wesley in conversation). Instead, comparative theology is "the attempt to understand the meaning of Christian faith by exploring it in the light of the teachings of other religious traditions."[2] Put another way, "Comparative theology—comparative and theological beginning to end—marks acts of faith seeking understanding which are rooted in a particular faith tradition but which, from that foundation, venture into learning from one or more other faith traditions."[3][4]

While the theological nature of comparative theology is found in faith seeking understanding, the comparative element indicates where this seeking takes place; namely, beyond the borders of one's own faith tradition. As James Fredericks notes, "Doing theology comparatively, therefore, is theology in the broadest sense of the word: the intellectually rigorous interpretation of the classic texts, doctrines and practices of one tradition."[5] But, instead of simply interpreting the texts, doctrines, and practices of one's own tradition, the comparative theologian explores the texts, doctrines, and practices of other religions as well. This faith seeking understanding, which takes place within and beyond one's own religious tradition, leads to a unique transformation involving "fresh theological insights that are indebted to the newly encountered traditions as well as the home tradition."[6]

2. Fredericks, *Faith among Faiths*, 169.

3. Clooney, *Comparative Theology*, 10.

4. It is important to note that this "definition" of comparative theology does not represent the depth and diversity of dialogue concerning the discipline itself. There are those who would challenge the notion that comparative theology must be done from within the confines of a given theological tradition or that it is a matter of "faith seeking understanding." Nevertheless, the definition of comparative theology being used in this chapter borrows from the dominant position exemplified by Francis Clooney and what is sometimes referred to as the "Boston School." My goal is not to reify this definition, but (for the sake of simplicity) to use this as a starting point for introducing comparative theology to Wesleyans.

5. Fredericks, "Introduction," xii.

6. Clooney, *Comparative Theology*, 10.

Why Do Comparative Theology?

The reasons for engaging in comparative theology are vast and varied. First, comparative theology, in so far as it is comparative, requires the theologian to learn deeply about those of other religions in a way that engenders a more peaceful and loving understanding of the other. Encountering difference is an inventible fact of life in our world, but not all engagement is positive. Comparative theology is a means of positively engaging religious difference, resulting in a deeper appreciation of the religious other. In so far as doing Christian theology in the 21st Century requires us to take seriously the multiplicity of religious experience and expression, comparative theology becomes as an important method of theological and interreligious engagement.

Second, comparative theology, in so far as it is theological, results in a deeper understanding of oneself and one's own theological tradition— helping the Christian be a better Christian. While it might be natural to ask, "What can studying non-Christian texts and traditions teach us about Christianity," the question is misguided and premature. It is premature because we can only answer the question after critically studying non-Christian traditions. After all, how can we know what Buddhism has to offer Christianity until we first do some study of Buddhism? Furthermore, the question is misguided because it implies that we can't learn from difference. On the contrary, knowledge requires difference. Contrast is that means by which distinctions can be made, and distinctions are the heart of intelligibility. What is left without right? If the whole world was blue, how could we understand color? Otherness is a mirror. In this way, studying non-Christian traditions is a means to better understand ourselves.

By reading the classic texts of another tradition, or entering into dialogue with adherents of another tradition, we face diverse perspectives which challenge us, so that our deeply held truths don't become obstacles to learning.[7] Quite simply, impetus for comparative theology may arise out of a desire to take seriously one's own theological commitment in a context of unparalleled diversity. James Fredericks calls this, the "intellectual grounds," for doing comparative theology. As Fredericks notes, "Honest thinking does not stop at boundaries, and our minds are always crossing over established borders."[8]

7. Ibid., 13.
8. Fredericks, "Introduction," xii.

Finally, religion often deals in the realm of deep mystery and paradox. As stated in the book of Job, "Can you fathom the mysteries of God? Can you probe the limits of the Almighty? They are higher than the heavens above—what can you do? They are deeper than the depths below—what can you know? Their measure is longer than the earth and wider than the sea" (Job 11:7–9). Using the resources of other faith traditions can expand our understanding of these mysteries and help shed light on our own theological convictions. Comparative theology, as a faith seeking understanding, pushes us beyond our comfort zone, and expands the search radius in our quest to comprehend the deep mysteries of life.

Wesleyan Comparative Theology

As a constructive theological discipline, comparative theology will always reflect the unique characteristics of the tradition in which the comparative theologian is rooted. Since comparative theology is done from within the framework of a particular faith perspective, Wesleyans can provide new contributions to the discipline of comparative theology, just as the practice of comparative theology can provide new insights for Wesleyan theology.

There are several elements in the Wesleyan-Holiness tradition that make it quite amenable to the practice of comparative theology. First, comparative theology requires vulnerability—a venturing out of one's comfort zone to take seriously even those ideas that run contrary to one's own. In this way, as Francis Clooney notes, "Comparative theology may purify doctrinal claims by uncovering the cultural and philosophical accretions that inevitably surround truths held over a long period of time, and by showing that most theological expressions of truth have in some form appeared elsewhere too."[9] Such cultural and philosophical accretions, when not confronted, can become crippling prejudices. Similar notions are found in the statements by John Wesley himself, who notes "Who can tell how far invincible ignorance may extend? or (that comes to the same thing) invincible prejudice?—which is often so fixed in tender minds, that it is afterwards impossible to tear up what has taken so deep a root."[10]

Second, comparative theology requires humility. We must acknowledge the limitations of our own understanding and, subsequently, our faith tradition—conceding the possibility that there is something we can learn

9. Clooney, *Comparative Theology*, 113.
10. Wesley, "Catholic Spirit," 495.

from non-Christian traditions. Such epistemic humility is prescribed by Wesley, who states, "It is an unavoidable consequence of the present weakness and shortness of human understanding, that several men will be of several minds in religion as well as in common life. So it has been from the beginning of the world, and so it will be 'till the restitution of all things.'" [11] Wesley adds, "Yet can no man be assured that all his own opinions, taken together, are true. Nay, every thinking man is assured they are not: seeing *humanum est errare et nescire*: 'To be ignorant of many things, and to mistake in some, is the necessary condition of humanity.'" [12] While, in one sense, epistemic humility is rooted in the limitations of human existence, it is also grounded in the expansiveness of God. [13]

In addition to these general principles embraced by the Wesleyan tradition, there are unique principles within Wesleyan-Holiness theology which, when interpreted in light of religious multiplicity, can provide strong inclination for comparative theological engagement. Some of these principles have been highlighted by Michael Lodahl in his book, *Claiming Abraham: Reading the Bible and the Qur'an Side by Side.*

Lodahl begins by locating the impetus for comparative engagement in the Bible, citing Leviticus 19:34, "Love your alien as yourself." [14] This call to love the 'stranger' is not an easy one. As Lodahl admits, "It is a difficult undertaking, this attempt to engage, appreciate, and even learn from the religious 'other' . . . But I [Lodahl], along with many others, have found it to be an undertaking that is inherently rewarding." [15]

In reading through the entire Qur'an for the first time, Lodahl shares that he was drawn in by the similarities and intrigued by the differences between the Bible and the Qur'an. Lodahl's experience reflects Clooney's claim that comparative theology ordinarily starts with being drawn by resemblances between one's own tradition and that of another. [16] By examining the theological assumptions in the text of the other, we confront

---

11. Ibid., 494.

12. Ibid., 495.

13. "Can you fathom the mysteries of God? Can you probe the limits of the Almighty? They are higher than the heavens above—what can you do? They are deeper than the depths below—what can you know? Their measure is longer than the earth and wider than the sea" (Job 11:7–9).

14. Lodahl, *Claiming Abraham*, 2.

15. Ibid.

16. Clooney, *Comparative Theology*, 11.

our own theological assumptions in such a way that our assumptions and religious commitments may be "challenged, chastened, or even changed."[17]

Perhaps the most uniquely Wesleyan resource for engaging in comparative theology is *prevenient grace*. As Lodahl explains, "The doctrine of prevenient grace . . . may provide the beginning point for a Christian theology of Muhammad's religious significance."[18] Although in his context prevenient grace is seen as a means of appreciating Muhammad's religious significance, Lodahl leaves open the possibility of extending prevenient grace to all humans from every religion. For, "Prevenient grace is God's active presence at work in every human."[19] From a Wesleyan perspective then, the affirmation of prevenient grace allows one to recognize the work of God in the lives of all people, Christian and non-Christian alike. As such, Wesleyans can embrace the possibility of learning from non-Christians, where God is already actively at work.

Comparative theology takes place in the tension between comparison and commitment. As Clooney notes, "Comparison retains a confessional dimension, while confession is disciplined by comparative practice, and in the process the theologian sees beyond the expectations of her tradition and changes accordingly."[20] This transformative tension "pushes us toward wider knowledge, emphasizing a freedom that is more tolerant and objective, less rooted in personal and communal views, while 'theology' drives us deeper, into a world of commitment, faith, and encounter with God."[21] Such tension is not resolved in comparative theology, but *is* the very essence of comparative theology. The Wesleyan comparative theologian must embrace this tension as a sort of purifying fire.

Wesleyan Comparative Theology: A Demonstration

In order to better demonstrate what Wesleyan comparative theology might look like, the following will be a comparative theological exercise between Zen Buddhism and Wesleyan Christianity. This example will explore a Zen understanding of *anatta* [not-self] and a Wesleyan conception of *holiness*. The goal of this exercise is a creative synthesis resulting in a transformation

17. Lodahl, *Claiming Abraham*, 3.

18. Ibid., 183.

19. Ibid.

20. Clooney, *Comparative Theology*, 45.

21. Ibid., 57.

of a Wesleyan understanding of holiness. As is typical in comparative theology, one must begin from within a given tradition; in this case, from the Wesleyan tradition.[22]

From this perspective, we will cross over into Zen Buddhism, exploring a Zen concept of *no-self*. It is important at this stage to recognize two things: 1) that we are strangers in a foreign land, and 2) as such, we must resist the desire to make hasty conclusions about the religious other. We must live with the Zen tradition a bit, in order to come to a respectful and grounded understanding of *anatta* from the Zen perspective.

Only after we have such an understanding (to the best of our ability) can we cross back into our own Wesleyan camp. Though it is impossible to shed one's own tradition in the process of comparative theology, we must do our best to temporarily bracket our own beliefs in order to "live" in the Zen perspective. By "bracketing" beliefs, I simply mean attempting to withhold judgment about the Zen perspective, in order to first understand the Zen perspective. "Bracketing" in this sense, is not a matter of abandoning one's own perspective for the sake of ascending to some sort of objectivity—as if to do so where even possible. Withholding judgment, however, is possible, though only temporarily necessary. When we have successfully accomplished this, we are able to reassume our Wesleyan perspective [unbracketing our own beliefs]—again asking Wesleyan questions from within a Wesleyan framework.

What one discovers in comparative theology is that this crossing-over was a journey that brought about a transformation. As a result of traveling across religious borders, the comparative theologian finds that the beliefs that were bracketed in the second stage of comparative theology do not look the same when unbracketed again. Instead, a transformation has occurred, in which the beliefs once held are now seen in a new light. This is not a transformation of the beliefs themselves, so much as a transformation of the one holding the beliefs. That is, the beliefs may remain the same, but they will be seen in a new light.

---

22. As an example within the context of this chapter, this exercise in Wesleyan Comparative Theology may feel both brief and rushed. If you are not familiar with Wesleyan-Holiness theology or Zen Buddhism, you may be uncomfortable and rightly feel as if certainly leaps are being taken without proper explanation or analysis. Unfortunately, the location and function of the present exercise requires certain leaps to be taken. Please keep in mind, however, that doing comparative theology should involve a serious study of both one's home tradition as well as the foreign tradition.

So, in what follows, I will present a Wesleyan perspective, specifically looking at John Wesley's doctrine of entire sanctification. I will then attempt to present a Zen perspective regarding *anatta*. Finally, I will readdress the Wesleyan view of entire sanctification, keeping in mind the Zen perspective of *anatta*. What results, whatever it may look like, will hopefully be a deeper Wesleyan understanding of sanctification—enriched by the Zen doctrine of no-self.

Stage 1: Wesleyans Are Wesleyans

In response to the question, "What is Christian perfection?" John Wesley answers, "The loving God with all our heart, mind, soul, and strength. This implies that no wrong temper, none contrary to love, remains in the soul; and that all the thoughts, words, and actions, are governed by pure love."[23]

In another place he describes being wholly sanctified as to, "Let your soul be filled with so entire a love to Him, that you may love nothing but for his sake. Have a pure intention of heart, a steadfast regard to his glory in all your actions. For then, and not til then, is that 'mind in us, which was also in Christ Jesus,' when in every motion of our heart, in every word of our tongue, in every work of our hands, we 'pursue nothing but in relation to him, and in subordination to his pleasure . . .'"[24]

Then, tying his doctrine of holiness to the rest of the Christian tradition by way of biblical sources, Wesley states, "'I am crucified with Christ; nevertheless I live; yet not I, but Christ liveth in me;'—words that manifestly describe a deliverance from inward as well as from outward sin. This is expressed both negatively, 'I live not' . . . and positively, 'Christ liveth in me.'"[25] He continues, "Indeed, both these, 'Christ liveth in me,' and, 'I live not,' are inseparably connected."[26]

From a Wesleyan perspective, as demonstrated by the perspective of Wesley himself, there is an inseparable connection between "I live not" and "Christ liveth in me." These inseparable principles are portrayed by Melvin Dieter, who states, "Negatively, entire sanctification is a cleansing of the heart, which brings healing of the remaining systemic hurts and bruises from Adam's sin . . . Positively, it is a freedom, a turning of the whole person

23. Wesley, "A Plain Account of Christian Perfection," 394.
24. Ibid., 368.
25. Ibid., 377.
26. Ibid.

toward God in love to seek and to know His will, which becomes the soul's delight."[27] The negative and positive aspects of entire sanctification are not two, but one in the same. That is, the cleansing of the heart *is* the turning of the whole person toward God in love. But what happens when one's heart is cleansed? After it is cleansed, what remains? When one dies to self, and is crucified with Christ, how is it that "I" live? In what sense is the perfected self a 'self'? How are Wesleyans to reconcile the language of being "brought to completion" and being "fully conformed to the image of the Son," with "I live not?" If I do not live, then what sort of relationship am I capable of having with God? If I have been completely conformed to the image of the Son, what distinguishes me from the Son?

We might ask, if one dies to self, and is filled with the love of God to the extent that nothing else remains, then what ultimately distinguishes the sanctified from the sanctifier? In short, how are Wesleyans to understand "self" in the process of entire sanctification? When one is crucified with Christ, and no longer lives, but only Christ lives, what happens to the "me" that Christ now lives in? Is the self transformed? If so, into what? Is the self annihilated? Does something take its place?[28]

Stage 2: Wesleyans Become Zen

In his book *Zen and Western Thought*, Masao Abe quotes a famous Zen parable given by a Chinese Zen master. According to Abe, this saying "provides a key by which we may approach Zen philosophy." It reads as follows:

> Thirty years ago, before I began the study of Zen, I said, "Mountains are mountains, waters are waters." After I got an insight into the truth of Zen through the instruction of a good master, I said, "Mountains are not mountains, waters are not waters." But now, having attained the abode of final rest [that is, Awakening], I say, "Mountains are really mountains, waters are really waters." "And

27. Dieter, "The Wesleyan Perspective," 18.

28. I realize that these questions are extremely leading and seem to presuppose an encounter with Zen before that encounter takes place. However, to cover the Wesleyan doctrine of holiness and transition into a Zen interpretation of *anatta* in only two pages is inevitably rushed and slightly awkward. Please keep in mind that this is simply a brief demonstration of comparative theology. For more complete examples of comparative theology see: Hyo-Dong Lee, *Spirit, Qi, and the Multitude* (2013); and Michelle Voss Roberts, *Tastes of the Divine* (2014).

then he asks, 'Do you think these three understandings are the same or different?'"[29]

This saying portrays three stages. The first stage is the dualistic worldview, where mountains are not waters. This dualism is representative of all dualisms, most significantly, the division between subject and object. The subject-object distinction is found at the heart of empirical experience. I, the knower, the experiencer, the subject, am having an experience of, or knowing about objects, the world. These objects are not me. How can they be? Therefore, insofar as we hold a concept of "self" as a subject standing over against objects, we are bound to the illusion of dualism, and cannot fully realize *sunyata* (emptiness). Such distinctions must be overcome in order to realize the true nature of *sunyata*, which leads to *nirvana* (the salvific extinguishing of self).

At the second stage, one embraces *sunyata* in such a way that the differentiation between mountains and waters is overcome by a monistic emptiness in which mountains are not mountains. At this stage, there is no subject. There is no object. There is only emptiness. Many Western interpreters of Zen make the mistake of stopping here, interpreting Zen as ultimately leading to an empty nihilism. But doing so is to ignore the third stage.

In the third stage, "Emptiness empties itself, becoming non-emptiness, that is, true Fullness."[30] This non-dualism is a more robust understanding of *sunyata*, which recognizes that "the true Self is realized only through the total negation of no-self, which is in turn the total negation of the ego-self."[31] In this way, the Zen doctrine of emptiness (perhaps more properly understood as a doctrine of fullness) is directly tied to the doctrine of *anatta* (not-self).

Masao Abe uses the concept of 'Suchness' to help explain Zen emptiness to a Western audience. He writes,

> Buddhists emphasize 'Emptiness' and say that everything is empty. Although this is a very important point for Buddhism in general and for Zen in particular, I am afraid that it is quite misleading, or at least very difficult to understand, particularly for the Western mind. So I think that 'everything is empty' may be more adequately rendered in this way: 'Everything is just as it is' . . . Everything

29. Abe, *Zen and Western Thought*, 4.

30. Ibid., 10.

31. Ibid.

is different from everything else. And yet, while everything and everyone retain their uniqueness and particularity, they are free from conflict because they have no self-nature. This is the meaning of the saying that everything is empty.[32]

One of the central roadblocks on the path to *nirvana* is considering the "self" as a distinct subject. To overcome this obstacle, Zen posits *anatta* or no-self. For, when the self is emptied of itself, all that remains is *sunyata*. And when emptiness is emptied of emptiness, what remains is 'Suchness', an expansive fullness that embraces the unity of what is differentiated.

Stage 3: Wesleyans Are Really Wesleyan

In light of this encounter (albeit brief) with the Zen doctrine of *anatta*, how might the Wesleyan understand entire sanctification more deeply? I believe the clearest area of enrichment is in rediscovering entire sanctification as a matter of emptying oneself of self, as to become a perfected self. Not that this notion is absent from Wesleyan thought without an encounter with Buddhism. Rather, an encounter with Buddhism can enrich this understanding, especially helping Wesleyans avoid the pitfall of interpreting "no-self" or dying to self, as emptiness instead of fullness. By understanding Zen *anatta* [the process of becoming less, which is to become more] Wesleyans can rediscover the special logic of entire sanctification—one attains fullness by becoming empty.

A Wesleyan understanding of holiness, enriched by an encounter with Zen Buddhism, no longer sees the process of dying to self and being "filled" with Christ as a something akin to cleaning the garage so the car fits. Rather, to die to self *is* to be filled with Christ. This is so, both in the sense that to die to self is to emulate the path of the crucified Christ, and in the sense that the pure nature of humanity is one created in the perfect image of God. In this way, the division between the human self and God (the dualism of stage 1) is overcome by dying to self so that there is only God (the monism of stage 2) which is overcome by the union of the self and Christ (the non-dualism of stage 3).

By crossing back over, being Wesleyan but shaped by Zen, we see that another way of interpreting Wesley's doctrine of entire sanctification is as "suchness." As Wesley proclaimed, the image of God is within humanity,

32. Ibid., 223.

though it has been distorted by sinfulness, and therefore needs to be restored. By restoring humanity to its original state, humans are really humans. They are, just as they are. In this way, to be entirely sanctified is to be fully human. Sinfulness is not a mark of human nature, but the corruption of it. Wesley's description of sanctification as the cleansing of the heart, begs the question, cleansed of what? The answer—sinfulness. But in what sense?

If Mildred Bangs Wynkoop is right, and self-centeredness is sinfulness, while God-centeredness is holiness, then to be cleansed of sinfulness is to be cleansed of self-centeredness.[33] But if sanctification is the process of being cleansed of sinful nature, which is the self-nature, then to be sanctified from this perspective, is to be emptied of self-nature. Or, in the words of Amos Yong, to be empty is to be without self-substantiality.[34] Now, since, as Masao Abe astutely notes, emptiness is more accurately understood as suchness, to be empty is not (as in the nihilistic understanding) to have a negative ontological status, but to be just as you are. So, if in being just as you are there is no self-nature, what remains? From a Wesleyan perspective, the positive articulation of emptiness, in which there is no self-nature—the fullness of perfect love, Christ-likeness, and holiness. This understanding of the relationship between emptiness and holiness directly opposes the claim of James L. Fredericks, who argues that emptiness is the "negation of holiness."[35] Instead, emptiness is the fullness of holiness!

With the marks of Zen on the comparative traveler, the Wesleyan now sees entire sanctification as a matter of emptying oneself of self—which is the fullness of the love of God. In doing so, it is not I but Christ that lives within me—which is me. The sanctified believer is brought into a union with Christ, such that Christ living in me is truly me. To be entirely sanctified, from this new Wesleyan perspective, is to be Such—to be emptied in a way that can only be described as all fullness. While we should be careful not to conflate entire sanctification with *anatta*, or *sunyata*, by engaging Zen, we Wesleyans can see our own doctrine of holiness in a new light. And perhaps this new understanding of entire sanctification is a deeper understanding—perhaps now, Wesleyans are really Wesleyans.[36]

33. Wynkoop, *A Theology of Love*, 25.

34. Yong, *The Cosmic Breath*, 100.

35. Fredericks, *Buddhist and Christians*, 85.

36. Please note that this "new" understanding of holiness is not altogether different than interpretations of holiness already found, in some form, in the Wesleyan tradition.

Bibliography

Abe, Masao. *Zen and Western Thought.* Edited by William R. LaFleur. Honolulu: University of Hawaii Press, 1985.

Clooney, Francis X. *Comparative Theology: Deep Learning across Religious Borders.* Malden, MA: Wiley-Blackwell, 2010.

Dieter, Melvin E. "The Wesleyan Perspective." In *Five Views on Sanctification,* by Melvin E. Dieter et al., 9-46. Grand Rapids: Zondervan, 1987.

Fredericks, James. *Faith among Faiths: Christian Theology and Non-Christian Religions.* New York: Paulist, 1999.

————. "Introduction." In *The New Comparative Theology: Interreligious Insights from the Next Generation,* edited by Francis X. Clooney, ix–xix. New York: Continuum, 2010.

Lee, Hyo-Dong. *Spirit, Qi, and the Multitude: A Comparative Theology for the Democracy of Creation.* New York: Fordham University Press, 2013.

Lodahl, Michael. *Claiming Abraham: Reading the Bible and the Qur'an Side by Side.* Grand Rapids: Brazos, 2010.

Voss Roberts, Michelle. *Tastes of the Divine: Hindu and Christian Theologies of Emotion.* New York: Fordham University Press, 2014.

Wesley, John. "A Plain Account of Christian Perfection." In vol 11 of *The Works of John Wesley.* Edited by Thomas Jackson. Grand Rapids: Baker, 2007.

————. "Sermon 39: Catholic Spirit." In vol. 6 of *The Works of John Wesley.* Edited by Thomas Jackson. 3rd ed. Grand Rapids: Baker, 1996.

Wynkoop, Mildred Bangs. *A Theology of Love.* Kansas City: Beacon Hill, 1972.

Yong, Amos. *The Cosmic Breath: Spirit and Nature in the Christianity-Buddhism-Science Trialogue.* Boston: Brill, 2012.

Remember, the goal of comparative theology is not to inject foreign elements into Christian theology, but to draw out and expand existing elements by tapping into outside resources. In doing so, we get the added benefit of having a constructive encounter with the religious other, resulting in a peaceful appreciation of religious difference.

5

Global Wesleyanism

Beyond Homogenity and Isolationissm

Dick O. Eugenio

❙❙ I look upon all the world as my parish," John Wesley claimed.[1] He would not have known that such a prophetic statement would find its fulfillment two centuries later through the commitment of his theological descendants. Henry Rack's conclusion that "Wesley's most obvious and measurable achievement and legacy must necessarily be the Methodist churches world-wide" is indubitable.[2] Today, Wesleyanism boasts a global presence, and through the multi-faceted undertakings of the numerous denominations under its umbrella, such a presence is incandescently visible. This is truly an age of "pan-Wesleyanism."[3] Wesleyanism is global, Donald W. Dayton argues, both literally and metaphorically: "We must think of the Wesleyan tradition globally, not only geographically, but also in the complexity and range of Wesleyan traditions in the world today." Dayton lists five Wesleyan streams in the world: (1) mainline Methodism, referring to churches that dominate the World Methodist Council, (2) renewal Methodism, referring to renewal movements carrying Wesleyan banners without becoming ac-

1. Wesley, *Journal and Dairies*, 67.

2. Quoted in Weyer, "The Early Impact of Wesleyanism on Continental Europe," 241.

3. Oden, *Doctrinal Standards in the Wesleyan Tradition*, 150.

tual denominations, (3) centers of self-conscious Wesleyan identity, which includes the early denominations that split from the Methodist Church (like the Free Methodist Church, the Wesleyan Church, and the Church of the Nazarene), (4) some Pentecostal groups,[4] and (5) various indigenous and independent churches throughout the world.[5] One might also argue that, because of the Wesleys' influence to its theology, even Anglicanism itself is "Wesleyan."

The Encyclopedia of World Methodism lists the members of "World Methodism" in 1970 as 20 million, but this figure does not include many independent churches and Pentecostal traditions whose theological heritage owes much to the Wesley's.[6] Procuring accurate statistics is always problematic, but the real challenge in identifying the members of "World Methodism," is determining guidelines of inclusion and exclusion. In light of this, Justo Gonzalez claims that "there are millions of persons who, many without knowing it, are spiritual heirs of Wesley and the Methodist movement of the eighteenth century."[7] And yet, although Wesleyanism enjoys a global audience, there is a dreadful scarcity of attention and published literature on how Wesleyanism is thriving in the non-Western parts of the world. Nearly three decades ago, Albert C. Outler wrote, "We need to learn much more about the Methodist traditions on the European Continent, in Africa, Asia, in Australasia and Latin America, and the residual influences of Methodism in the 'united churches' in which Methodists have cast their lot."[8] Yet, in the past 25 years little has been done to remedy this. We have,

---

4. Historians and theologians from the Wesleyan tradition and Pentecostal groups hold divergent positions about whether Pentecostalism really emerges from the Wesleyan movement. For those who argue that Pentecostalism is theologically rooted in the Wesleyan-holiness movement, see Dayton, *Theological Roots of Pentecostalism*; Dieter, "Wesleyan-Holiness Aspects of Pentecostal Origins," 55–80; Synan, *The Holiness-Pentecostal Movement in the United States*, and Synan, *The Century of the Holy Spirit*. Those who disagree include Menzies, "The Non–Wesleyan Origins of the Pentecostal Movement," 81–98; and Edith L. Blumhofer, who argues specifically that the Assemblies of God is non-Wesleyan, in *Restoring the Faith*. Grant A. Wacker narrates how "radical evangelicals," which includes the Wesleyan movement, responded negatively to early Pentecostalism, but acknowledges that these radical evangelicals "were the Pentecostals' spiritual and in many cases biological parents," in "Travail of a Broken Family," 23–49.

5. Dayton, "The Global Impact of the Wesleyan Traditions and their Related Movements," 7–10.

6. Oden, *Doctrinal Standards*, 155.

7. Gonzalez, *Juan Wesley*, 6;.

8. Outler, "Methodists in Search of Consensus," 36. It is beyond the scope of this essay to provide a historiography of global Wesleyanism, but for preliminary readings,

of course, many denominational histories and studies in different global locales, but they were written with little attempt to establish connections with the global Wesleyan family.

Realities and Real Challenges

John Wesley's prophetic vision for a world parish is realized, but his aspiration "that the Methodists are one people in all the world, and that it is their full determination so to continue" is far from realized today.[9] On the contrary, "there is not a single Wesleyan tradition in the world today, but a number of Wesleyan traditions which trace their origins to the movement began by John Wesley and his brother Charles (1707–1788) in the eighteenth century. As Wesleyanism has developed in different areas, nations, and cultures, variations of it have appeared."[10] Dayton thinks that this phenomenon is bound to continue, even prophesying that "Methodism will develop competing parties and denominations carrying a variety of fragments of original Methodism [and] the problem is that each of these fragments can sustain a claim to be genuinely Wesleyan, but none of them represent the full Wesley."[11] The distinction between *formal* and *material* Wesleyanism must be made.[12] While many may designate themselves as Wesleyans at the *formal* level, rightly because they find their historical-theological roots in Wesley and Methodism, the *material* content of their specific Wesleyanisms may vary. This means that although there is global Wesleyanism at the formal level, there are definite challenges in the material level. Robert Schreiter's distinction between "official religion" and "popular religion" will help here. The former refers to the overarching theological

---

with excellent bibliography, see Bundy, "The Holiness Movements in World Christianity," 21–53. The non-engagement with Wesleyans outside North America is evidenced in Bundy's earlier article, "The Historiography of the Wesleyan-Holiness Tradition," 55–77.

9. Wesley, "Letter to Ezekiel Cooper," 260.

10. Yrigoyen, "Introduction," xix.

11. Dayton, "The Global Impact of the Wesleyan Traditions," 11. Hence, the death of Wesleyanism (as movement and theological tradition) is nowhere in sight for the foreseeable future, in contrast to the thesis of Keith Drury in "The Death of the Holiness Movement," 13–15. See the pointed critique of Wright and Harrison on the designation "Wesleyan," in "The Ecclesial Practice of Reconciliation and the End of the Wesleyan," 194–214; and in Abraham, "The End of Wesleyan Theology," 7–25.

12. This phraseology is borrowed from McCormack, *Karl Barth's Critical Dialectical Theology*, 453–4.

tradition, but adherents usually live their lives in terms of the more immediate local setting.[13] Thus, although Wesleyans may recognize their affiliation to a "formal Wesleyanism," their commitments are largely devoted to the local and particular community of interpretation (denominationally and geographically) that they belong to.

Dayton rightly recognized that the problem is *identity*. Who is a true Wesleyan? Around the world, a sort of Samaritan Wesleyanism has emerged, as a result of cross-fertilizations with culture and other theological traditions. Kiyoshi Kunishige admits that the Japanese Wesleyan denomination, Immanuel Gospel Mission, has not fully accepted Wesley's theology.[14] Chongnahm Cho laments that for Wesleyan churches in Korea, the emphasis is more on power and miracles than on the life of holiness.[15] Victor A. Shepherd reports that United Church of Canada has adopted a "theological liberalism that diverges from the Methodist tradition in many respects."[16] In all these cases, and many similar others, the primary question revolves around the degree of openness to seemingly dissenting groups on matters that others take to be central. Joan A. Millard's rhetorical question bites: "Are they not Methodists too?"[17] Millard's position represents that of Wesley's: "Whoever they are that have 'one Spirit, one hope, one Lord, one faith, one God and Father of all,' I can easily bear with their holding wrong opinions, yea, and superstitious modes of worship: Nor would I, on these accounts, scruple still to include them within the pale of the catholic Church; neither would I have any objection to receive them, if they desired it, as members of the Church of England."[18]

We must first admit that no individual church/denomination represents the whole Wesleyan movement. The Wesleyan tradition has no shortage of global representatives, each with its own version of the tradition and emphasizing distinct strands of the tradition. Influenced by denominationalism, culturalism, and other variables, Wesleyanism boasts many manifestations. In this sense, a common Wesleyanism can be shared at the formal level, albeit exhibited as varied Wesleyanisms at the material level. This is a

---

13. Schreiter, *Constructing Local Theologies*, 124–6.

14. Kunishige, "Alternate Wesleyan Influence," 143–56.

15. Cho, "The Impact of John Wesley's Ministry and Theology on the Korean Church," 157–69.

16. Shepherd, *Mercy Immense and Free*, 142.

17. Millard, "Are They Not Methodists Too?," 105–17

18. Wesley, "Of the Church," 52.

humble recognition that amidst formal unity are specific divergences that do not jeopardize our interconnectedness, but actually enrich the whole body. For Wesleyanism to prosper worldwide, this inculturation is necessary. Wesley realized the ineffectiveness of a verbatim imitation of British Methodism when it was transplanted to America, and thus encouraged some sort of self-particularization in the mission fields. Max L. Stackhouse explains this in terms of flowering.

"The boundary between kernel and husk is less precise, and the emphasis is on the growth of new possibilities once the seed of the gospel is planted in a new location, inevitably in its old husk. But, once the seed is planted, it will interact with the soil into which it has been planted, and new forms of faith will spring into being."[19]

The flowering model better explains the diverse forms of Wesleyanism in the world. Firstly, as a verb in the present tense, it is open to further influences in its ongoing metamorphosis. Each glocal (global and local at the same time)[20] strand is always in the process of self-particularization, existing in the tension "between past and future, between the direction in which we are moving and the direction in which we ought to move."[21] Secondly, it allows for a more open and inclusive stance regarding groups that appear as "dissenters" because their present forms do not conform to any historically recognized manifestation of the tradition. In short, this model sanctions Wesleyanism to take on *new* and *unknown* forms. The balance is described by Outler: "At the heart of our Wesleyan legacy is an ample vision of grace . . . and this has given us the core of whatever consensus we have ever had or can hope for in the times ahead [but] any such consensus must allow for variety in formulation."[22]

We must admit, secondly, that Wesleyanism is not a disordered movement. It is bound to certain principles. It is not a swirling entropic vortex of controversies. Hence, there are legitimate questions of boundary and

---

19. Stackhouse, *Apologia*, 107.

20. An example of something *glocal* is McDonalds. It is a franchise that has a global presence and which carries the name "McDonalds" anywhere in the world. However, it is also local in that each McDonald branch is situated at a particular locale and offers menus specifically designed to cater to local appetites and tastes. For instance, McDonalds serves rice in the Philippines, precisely because rice is a staple diet in the country. In this way, McDonalds is both global and local at the same time.

21. Beck, "Prospects for Methodist Teaching and Consensus," 15.

22. Outler, "Methodists in Search of Consensus," 37.

identity.[23] Such questions are difficult to address, simply because no sanctioned canon of genuine Wesleyanism exists. Of course, there is novelty in accepting the reality of differences, but the concept of unity is equally mesmerizing.[24] Wesley himself envisioned that "that the Methodists are one people in all the world, and that it is their full determination so to continue."[25] In his lifetime, Wesley preached against schism,[26] warned against "inward disunion,"[27] and argued against separation and isolationism.[28] His concern was not only for unity in the catholic Church, but also within the Methodist movement, appealing that his followers should "avoid schism, observe every rule of the society, and of the bands, for conscience' sake."[29] Schism "is not separation *from* any church (whether general or particular, whether the catholic or any national church) but a separation *in* a church."[30] Disunity in both the catholic and local levels is something that he did not wish his followers to undertake. Furthermore, grounded in his theology of Christian perfection, Wesley was convinced that "it is the nature of love to unite us together, and the greater the love the stricter the union."[31]

Given that the Wesleyan movement inherited Wesley's theological and ecclesiological DNA, it is not surprising that there remains today an aspiration for ecumenical Wesleyanism. The question, however, is: "How can unity be achieved?" Thomas Oden proposed the first of three possible approaches to unity, appealing to "doctrinal standards" grounded in Wesley's *Sermons, Notes Upon the New Testament,* and *Articles of Religion.*[32] There are two problems with this: (1) not all Wesleyan denominations subscribe to these three, and most of them, as Dayton claims, only possess fragments of Wesley's teachings or practice; and (2) despite the existence

---

23. See Tanner for her discussions of these issues in *Theories of Culture,* 93–119.

24. Cubie, "A Wesleyan Perspective on Christian Unity," 198–229.

25. Wesley, *Letters,* 260.

26. Wesley, "On Schism," 59–69.

27. Wesley, *A Plain Account of Christian Perfection* , 102.

28. See Wesley, "Reasons Against a Separation from the Church of England," 332–49; "Farther Thoughts on Separation from the Church," 538–40; and "Ought We to Separate from the Church of England?," 567–80.

29. Wesley, *A Plain Account of Christian Perfection,* 103. His equal concern for both the catholic Church and the local congregations is again displayed in his sermon "On Zeal," 314.

30. Wesley, "On Schism," 60.

31. Ibid., 64.

32. Oden, *Doctrinal Standards,* 15–73.

of many Wesleyan denominations, the underlying sources of difference among them is not doctrinal, but social, political, and ecclesiastical.

A second standard is proposed by Albert Outler, who speaks of "the Wesleyan spirit" (although he makes no explanation as to its meaning). Outler seems to be referring to doctrines, particularly to what he considers the three pillars of Wesleyan theology: original sin, justification by faith alone, and holiness of heart and life.[33] But again, the problem of identity lies in disagreement concerning what doctrines, if any, are essential to being Wesleyan. Yeo Khiok-khng writes that "the spirit of the Wesleyan tradition can be characterized as biblical, evangelical, reformational, and missional."[34] Or could it be, in the words of William B. Lawrence, that a Wesleyan is "not an heir to a tradition that affirms a rigid doctrinal code [but] embraces theological diversity?"[35]

Finally, many propose that unity is achievable by rediscovering Wesley's theology, vision and practices, like Paul W. Chilcote, who writes: "A process of rediscovery—a reclaiming of the Wesleyan vision of Christian life—is required within our tradition if the global church community is going to chart its course successfully into the future."[36]

Scylla, Charybdis, and the Narrow Way

The three proposals above have potential, but they also have their own self-collapsing problems. The real hurdle is definition. What are "doctrinal standards?" What is "the Wesleyan spirit?" Who is "the genuine Wesley?" If, in attempting to respond to these questions we have already reached an impasse, then conversations aimed at consensus are but a shallow dream. It is no wonder that some have given up on the idea of consensus.[37] The consensus is that there is no consensus. Meeks blatantly concludes, for

33. Outler, *Theology in the Wesleyan Spirit*, 23. See also *Evangelism in the Wesleyan Spirit*.

34. Khiok-khng, "Salvation by Grace through Faith," 66.

35. Lawrence, "Introduction."

36. See Chilcote, "Preface," in which he disapprove the idea that doctrinal rediscovery is the way forward.

37. Donald G. Matthews, for instance, writes that "the goal [of meeting together] is not consensus but testimony in love," in "United Methodism and American Culture," 304. Tanner even argues that "uniformity of belief in general is overrated," and that "the fact that Christians do not agree in their interpretation of matters of common concern is the very thing that enables social solidarity among them," in *Theories of Culture*, 121.

instance, that even the Oxford Institute of Methodist Theological Studies has become "somewhat contentious [and] suspicious about these words (unity and consensus), for we know that they are political words." He adds, "We may not have a positive consensus about what to teach, but we do have a strong shared sense of a real and potential domination. . . . We are a people who do not want to be dominated and who are ready to struggle against domination."[38] But if such suspicion persists, and no consensus is ever reached, then we are forced to live in "dual systems," where we are always torn between "cosmopolitan perspectives and particular loyalties, centuries-long traditions and immediate religious excitements," and official dogmas and folk practices.[39] As long as the question of identity remains, Wesleyan churches and denominations will continue to float in the sea of confusion with no watch tower to guide them to port. Worse still, Wesleyan entities will continue to wander in the "Maybe," where they acknowledge that they are Wesleyan in one sense and also not in another sense. So what is the way forward?

Centralized Wesleyanism

Global Wesleyanism can potentially assume the shape of a global organization with centralized ruling powers. But for the institution of a centralized government to be effective, entails local churches surrendering their sovereignty to self-determine ecclesiastical and theological matters. The ruling global body will have the authoritative word, and their decisions will be imposed on local churches that do not have the capacity to make an appeal. In short, local autonomy is swallowed for the sake of the universal. There is no geographical center *per se*, but a center nevertheless would exist to adjudicate theological conundrums. Global Wesleyanism becomes like Jeremy Bentham's Panopticon, a prison organized around a central surveillance tower which sees everything but is not seen and which subjects everyone but is subject to no one. The problem with this tactic is that those who will be placed in the "policing" position are the same names found in the magisterium of the largest bodies. In this sense, as William T. Cavanaugh assessed, globalization represents the hyperextension of an already established power and not really the flattening of the world.[40]

---

38. Meeks, "Reflections and Open Tasks," 131.

39. Stackhouse, *Apologia,* 114.

40. Cavanaugh, *Theopolitical Imagination,* 4, 6.

Competing Wesleyanisms

Considering the pluralistic reality and attitude prevalent today, the establishment of an ecclesiastical-theological oligarchy will be met with angry resistance. This is to be expected from representatives of the non-Western world, but even Western theologians realize the inappropriateness of such a maneuver. Today, there is no scarcity of published literature condeming imperialism and colonialism.[41] Therefore, in moving forward, the Scylla of globalizing Wesleyanism is and must be intentionally avoided. The more pressing problem, however, is the Charybdis of pluralistic Wesleyanisms. Thomas Oden, for instance, argues that Wesleyanism must always make room for both *cultural pluralism* and *theological pluralism*, and even though he admits *doctrinal pluralism* to be problematic, it can nevertheless "be affirmed, provided it moves generally within the frame of the church's doctrinal standards."[42]

Thomas L. Friedman notes that "the forces of particularization now seem to be as strong as the forces of homogenization."[43] In World Christianity, however, it is the forces of particularization that are dominating the theological landscape, evidenced by the celebration of concepts like contextualization, indigenization, inculturation, local theologies, and the like. Even back in 1982, the Asia Theological Association Theological Consultation that met in Korea and pronounced that much Western theology is irrelevant to non-Western concerns—a pronouncement paradigmatic of the global attitude today. Christianity has a polycentric nature, the argument runs, and thus, "the task in the twenty-first century is to conceptualize theology in light of the fact that the Christian faith is global with multiple heartlands."[44]

Self-particularization is always specific. However, there is a distinction between *functional* self-particularization and *reactionary* self-particularization. The former refers to the bourgeoning number of context-specific theologies and contextually relevant theological formulations; the latter refers to members of the former group that have assumed a more reactionary and

41. See the Bechtold and Serrano chapters in the present volume.

42. See Oden's discussion in *Doctrinal Standards,* 74–77 (italics original). H. O. Tom Thomas critiques United Methodists's (and Oden's) espousal of theological pluralism as a deviation from Wesley's vision for the Methodists in "John Wesley: Concept of 'Connection' and Theological Pluralism," 88–104.

43. Friedman, *The World is Flat,* 479.

44. Shenk, "Recasting Theology of Mission, 105.

comparative stance, so that their self-particularization is not only driven by local context, but also by the desire to be isolated, distinct, independent, and even veraciously trenchant. José Míguez Bonino describes the trend of the latter group as "partisanship," or the "opting for one side, radical opposition to the existing system."[45] As in early feminist theology, we see the same Gnostic-like presupposition in many local theologies—that the West is evil and the East is essentially good. The promotion of particularization, thus, includes a disturbing bashing of existing powers, i.e. right now, the West. In order for the East and South to assert authority and dominance, many aim to anathemize the West and "write off the traditions of the North."[46] The increased awareness and acknowledgment of the demographic shift of Christianity from North to South or West to East has also ignited more aspirations toward theological freedom from "the Old World Order"[47] This fact is also employed as a platform for the crusade to abdicate the West from the throne, only to be replaced by more radical powers.

Ironically, globalization, instead of producing a common sense of accountability, has ushered an era of competition for recognition and dominance. As Cavanaugh discerns, "the compression of space in the 'global village' has not only exacerbated but produced insecurity and conflict in the late twentieth century, since global mapping brings diverse localities into competition with one another." Competition, he adds, "produces an apparent attachment to the local," because "diverse places must emphasize what is unique and advantageous to their location."[48] Geographic and cultural shifts, along with the spirit of the age hijacked by nationalism and parochialism, resulted in a plethora of unprecedented new forms and expressions of the Christian faith. Vanhoozer calls this the many's "theological ethnification."[49] Sadly, however, indigenosity is leading towards increasing isolationism. Parochialism remains challenged as "how to ensure that differences in strategies and tactics do not become the sources of permanent and bitter divisions,"[50] for if this persists, globalism "produces fragmented

---

45. Bonino, "Reflections on the Church's Authoritative Teachings on Social Questions," 67.

46. Jenkins, *The New Faces of Christianity*, 192.

47. Jenkins, *The Next Christendom*, 108.

48. Cavanaugh, *Theopolitical Imagination*, 107–8.

49. Vanhoozer, "'One Rule to Rule Them All?,'" 104.

50. Bello, *The Future in the Balance*, 229.

subjects incapable of telling a genuinely catholic story."[51] We can become uncritically engrossed with our own particular socio-political and cultural setting and become "romantic folklorists,"[52] self-engrossed and alien to all. So, in an era of globalization and theological ethnification, how does global Wesleyanism avoid homogenization, isolationism, and competition?

Eucharistic Wesleyanism

Ecclesiastical and theological politics are not immune to violence. The global nature of Wesleyanism, on the one hand, can pave the way for the existing powers to dominate the landscape. On the other hand, it can produce an overabundance of diverse bodies competing for recognition, power, and authority. Both colonialism and parochialism must be avoided,[53] but it is the latter beast that needs more taming, for it is this force which is gaining momentum. Jenkins's alarming prediction must serve as a warning: "The story of Christianity over the coming decades will be marked by new schisms that broadly follow the North-South division."[54] Schismatic Wesleyanism is certainly not the ideal shape of global Wesleyanism, but what is? I propose *Eucharistic Wesleyanism*.

In the Eucharist, everyone is gathered by a mutual participation in Christ and with one another. This participation does not necessitate symmetry or uniformity. In fact, as Ellen K. Wondra highlights, following Levinas, all earthly relationships are asymmetrical.[55] We all come to the Table with our cultural baggage, economic status, denominational bias, and reservations. And yet, in the midst of all these, there is a realization that we are one, that even in the paradoxical mixture of my superiority and inferiority, I am no better or worse than the one who sits beside me. The Eucharist transcends natural and social divisions (Gal 3:28). The members of the

---

51. Cavanaugh, *Theopolitical Imagination,* 98.

52. Stackhouse, *Apologia,* 100.

53. Hiebert, "Beyond Anticolonialism to Globalism," 263–82; and *Anthropological Reflections on Missiological Issues,* 93–103. R. Larry Shelton argues that "a fresh exposition of a Wesleyan paradigm should be biblically-centered and not encumbered by either fundamentalist leavening or an undiscriminating canonization of pluralism," in "A Wesleyan/Holiness Agenda for the Twenty-first Century," 67–100.

54. Jenkins, *The New Faces of Christianity,* 190.

55. Wondra, "Participating Persons: Reciprocity and Asymmetry," 57–73.

global Wesleyan village are not juxtaposed or compared with one another, but are simultaneously served and serving. In the words of Cavanaugh,

> Juxtaposition situates diverse localities in competition with one another. . . . In Eucharistic space, by contrast, we are not juxtaposed but identified. In the body of Christ, as Paul says, "If one member suffers, all suffer together with it; if one member is honoured, all rejoice together with it" (1 Cor 12:26). This radical collapsing of spatial barriers accomplishes not competition, but says Paul, greater honour and care for the weakest member, who is identified with oneself. At the same time the other is not merely different but wholly other, for the suffering are identified with Christ himself (Col 1:24), who nevertheless remains other to the Church.[56]

In the Eucharistic fellowship, all divisions are transcended in Christ. Thus, it reminds us that catholicity does not rest upon human endeavors and even efforts to unite (or destroy) the Church. This is what John Zizioulas, following Nicholas Afanasiev, calls "Eucharistic ecclesiology."[57] Because there is no competition, the temptation of sectarianism is diminished. Differences are treated not as avenues of schism, but as reasons for *koinonia*. In the first place, it is precisely because we are different that we have much to share with one another. In the second place, our Wesleyan community is a community of different others.

In terms of space, the locus of the Eucharist is always the local, but the local must remain as the "decentred centre."[58] This neither leads to nor promotes isolationism. Rather, it acknowledges that the celebration of the Eucharistic community is not found in the global village, for such is not tangibly existent. The local remains the center of the Eucharistic celebration, but it is a center that acknowledges the universal. "The global and the local are refracted in such a way that one becomes more united to the universal the more one is tied to the life of the particular local community."[59] It is not curved upon itself, but is always both incorporating and incorporated. It is in this sense that it becomes *glocal*, because the local and the global intersect in its existence.

In terms of time, our present Eucharistic identity incorporates both the memories of the past and the future. On the one hand, global Wesleyanism

56. Cavanaugh, *Theopolitical Imagination*, 120–1.

57. Zizioulas, *Being as Communion*, 23–25.

58. Cavanaugh, *Theopolitical Imagination*, 113.

59. Ibid., 4–5.

"not only must include dialogue partners from the broad diversity of world Christianity that exists *today* but also must remain in continuity and discussion with the church and its theology of the *past.*"[60] On the other hand, Zizioulas's memory of the future will help us in imagining the eschatological community that we are becoming, and we should become. In the Eucharist transpires the intersection and celebration of our common past and our teleological future. We remember our common roots (not only to the Wesleys but to Jesus Christ) and our common destiny as the eschatological *koinonia* and *familia.*

Ways Forward

Eucharistic Wesleyanism is a prophetic critique to the homogenizing and divisive forces in our tradition, and a prophetic vision heralding a better state of affairs. The *Zeitgeist* may pull us to remain on one side of the pendulum's swing, radicalize such a position and uncritically succumb to domineering and divisive alternatives. It is during these times that we are once again called to aim for a *via media.* This can be achieved by considering several factors, starting with the following:

1) Leveling the Field

A. Wati Longchar explains that globalization can help countries cooperate in the pursuit of peace, prosperity and multilateral community building, but powerful players can "look at the global village as an order or mechanism for greater economic exploitation and political oppression."[61] However, one is mistaken to deduce that such a tendency is inherent only to Westerners. The same dominating ethos can be found in many nationalist-, pragmatist-, and context-driven theologies from the non-Western worlds. Nevertheless, it remains true, considering that published studies on Wesleyanism outside the West are a tiny fraction, that the West may still be dominating the scene. This might endure as a problem because the increase of academic publications coming out of Africa, Asia, and Latin America is crippled by a lack of resources. Unless a radical leveling of the playing fields—financial field, linguistic field, access to the field—global Wesleyanism will remain

60. Ott, "Globalizing Theology," 312.

61. Longchar, "Globalization," 67.

prescriptive, with the West speaking and the rest listening.[62] Related to this is the necessary abolition of the "hegemony postulate," in which everyone is required to play by the dictates of Western logic and rules.[63] The dominant voice in this field, in need of the most leveling, is the academia, or "the monstrous regiment of systematic theologians."[64] What might be needed is the closing down of what Peter Berger refers to as "faculty club culture,"[65] where theology is "done by experts and then 'trickled down' to the people for their consumption."[66] Theological pluralism and the accursed Enlightenment propaganda for intellectual freedom have made the academia as much a quagmire of hullabaloo as a sanctuary for answers. As such the plurality of views is nothing more than "educated opinions" competing for allegiance, which results in confusion rather than unity.[67]

2) Understanding Dialogue

Following Berger, a dialogue involves a sort of *aggiornamento,* a bargaining process where "one subjects oneself to mutual cognitive contamination."[68] If dialogue (of any kind) is to ensue, parties must be open to a process of rethinking which might involve giving up some elements in order to gain others. Dismissive and indifferent fortification of our denominational and cultural castles will only harden us from being self-critical and other-incorporating. The goal of our dialogue with other fellow Wesleyans is that of mutual enrichment.[69] We must realize that dialogues are a process of giving and receiving, especially if the conversation partners are outsiders. In our increasingly eclectic world, where tolerance, indigenization, and culture are emphasized, there will be a continuous bargaining process.

---

62. Ott, "Globalizing Theology," 332.

63. Frostin, "The Hermeneutics of the Poor," 131.

64. Vanhoozer, "'One Rule to Rule Them All?,'" 91.

65. Berger, "Four Faces of Global Culture," 24–25.

66. Bevans, *Models of Contextual Theology*, 18.

67. A quick review of the articles in the *Wesleyan Theological Journal* reveals a plethora of competing interpretative voices, each with a claim for legitimacy to oppose one another's views and offer an alternative. For instance, see Collins, "The State of Wesley Studies in North America," 7–38; and Laurence's W. Wood's response "The Need for a Contextual Interpretation of John Wesley's Sermons," 259–67.

68. Berger, *A Rumor of Angels*, 26–27.

69. Beck, "Prospects for Methodist Teaching," 18.

This means engaging diverse cultures and other denominations, which will likely result in a transformation of Wesleyanism. Such dialogue requires a great deal of vulnerability and humility, making it a risky, yet necessary, endeavor.

3) Recontextualizating the Local

Theology must be particular, or else it is bogus: bogus because it relates to no recognizable community of faith. This is the significance of the local community, gathering in its self-identification and self-actualization as a Wesleyan body in such a particular spatio-temporal coordinate. But the local church is not only encompassed within its immediate context, it is also part of a global village. What is necessary, therefore, is a comprehensive and all-inclusive understanding of situatedness: a glocal self-identification. This is important, because as Jonathan Sachs claims, "The scope of our interconnectedness defines the radius of responsibility and concern."[70] The world is our parish: to serve, to establish networks, to share resources, and never to dominate. The local church must be the decentered center. If Wesleyanism is a global village, then talks about "shifts to the South," must not entail the creation of a new Constantinople from Rome, or the shifting of ecclesio-political powers from one to another, but a movement towards deterritorialization and decentralization.

Conclusions

Wesleyanism enjoys a global presence. This reality is accompanied by challenges regarding identity, government, authority, and catholicity. This essay responds to two polar approaches to Wesleyan unity: (1) the oppressive homogenizing tendencies inherent in centralized government, which achieves unity by imposing criteria that all parties should adhere to, and (2) the isolationist agenda, which achieves unity by promoting an uncritical toleration of each other's differences. Isolationism and centralization are twin ogres. The way forward is what I called Eucharistic Wesleyanism, where unity and diversity are both celebrated. We gather not for competition or for furthering our own agenda, but for present fellowship, in celebration of our common past and future. The Eucharist does not impose

70. Sachs, *The Dignity of Difference*, 121.

but invites. As the decentered center, it does not dominate but incorporates the plurality of selves into a *koinonia* of unity.

Bibliography

Abraham, William J. "The End of Wesleyan Theology." *Wesleyan Theological Journal* 40 (2005) 7–25.

Beck, Brian E. "Prospects for Methodist Teaching and Consensus." In *What Should Methodists Teach? Wesleyan Tradition and Modern Diversity*, edited by M. Douglas Meeks, 13–22. Nashville: Abingdon, 1990.

Bello, Walden. *The Future in the Balance: Essays on Globalization and Resistance.* Quezon City, Philippines: University of the Philippine Press, 2001.

Bevans, Stephen B. *Models of Contextual Theology.* Maryknoll, NY: Orbis, 1992.

Blumhofer, Edith L. *Restoring the Faith: The Assemblies of God, Pentecostalism, and American Culture.* Urbana: University of Illinois Press, 1993.

Bonino, Jose Miguez. "Reflections on the Church's Authoritative Teachings on Social Questions." In *What Should Methodists Teach? Wesleyan Tradition and Modern Diversity*, edited by M. Douglas Meeks, 58–68. Nashville: Kingswood, 1990.

Bundy, David. "The Historiography of the Wesleyan-Holiness Tradition." *Wesleyan Theological Journal* 30 (1995) 55-77.

————. "The Holiness Movements in World Christianity: Historiographical Questions." *Wesleyan Theological Journal* 38 (2003) 21-53.

Cavanaugh, William T. *Theopolitical Imagination.* London: T. & T. Clark, 2002.

Cho, Chongnahm. "The Impact of John Wesley's Ministry and Theology on the Korean Church." In *The Global Impact of the Wesleyan Traditions and Their Related Movements*, edited by Charles Yrigoyen Jr., 157–69. Lanham, MD: Scarecrow, 2002.

Cubie, David L. "A Wesleyan Perspective on Christian Unity." *Wesleyan Theological Journal* 33 (1998) 198-229.

Dayton, Donald W. "The Global Impact of the Wesleyan Traditions and Their Related Movements." In *The Global Impact of the Wesleyan Traditions and Their Related Movements*, edited by Charles Yrigoyen Jr., 3-11. Lanham, MD: Scarecrow, 2002.

————. *Theological Roots of Pentecostalism.* Peabody, MA: Hendrickson, 1987.

Dieter, Melvin E. "Wesleyan-Holiness Aspects of Pentecostal Origins." In *Aspects of Pentecostal Charismatic Origin*, edited by Vinson Synan, 55–80. Plainfield, NJ: Logos International, 1975.

Drury, Keith. "The Death of the Holiness Movement." *Holiness Digest* 8 (1994) 13-15.

Friedman, Thomas L. *The World Is Flat: A Brief History of the Twenty-first Century.* New York: Picador, 2007.

Frostin, Per. "The Hermeneutics of the Poor: The Epistemological 'Break' in Third World Theologies." *Studia Theologica* 39 (1985) 127–50.

Gonzalez, Juan. *Wesley: Herencia y Promesa.* San Juan: Publicaciones Puertorequenas, 1998.

Hiebert, Paul. "Beyond Anticolonialism to Globalism." *Missiology* 9 (1991) 263-82.

Jenkins, Philip. *The New Faces of Christianity: Believing the Bible in the Global South.* Oxford: Oxford University Press, 2006.

————. *The Next Christendom: The Coming of Global Christianity*. Oxford: Oxford University Press, 2002.

Khiok-khng, Yeo "Salvation by Grace through Faith." In *The Wesleyan Tradition: A Paradigm for Renewal*, edited by Paul W. Chilcote, 66–77. Nashville: Abingdon, 2002.

Kunishige, Kiyoshi Nathanael. "Alternate Wesleyan Influence: The Impact of 18th Century British Methodism and 19th Century American Revivalism on a Japanese Indigenous Holiness Church." In *The Global Impact of the Wesleyan Traditions and Their Related Movements*, edited by Charles Yrigoyen Jr., 143–56. Lanham, MD: Scarecrow, 2002.

Longchar, A. Wati. "Globalization: A Challenge to Theological Education." In *Glocal in the Market Place: Theological Perspectives on Globalization*. Assam, India: South Asia Regional Solidarity Committee, 2006.

McCormack, Bruce. *Karl Barth's Critical Dialectical Theology: Its Genesis and Development, 1909-1936*. Oxford: Clarendon, 1997.

Menzies, William W. "The Non-Wesleyan Origins of the Pentecostal Movement." In *Aspects of Pentecostal Charismatic Origins*, edited by Vinson Synan, 81–98. Plainfield, NJ: Logos International, 1975.

Millard, Joan A. "Are They Not Methodists Too? Case Studies of Some African Independent Churches That Call Themselves Methodists." In *The Global Impact of the Wesleyan Traditions and Their Related Movements*, edited by Charles Yrigoyen Jr., 105–17. Lanham, MD: Scarecrow, 2002.

Oden, Thomas C. *Doctrinal Standards in the Wesleyan Tradition*. Nashville: Abingdon, 2008.

Ott, Craig. "Globalizing Theology." In *Globalizing Theology: Belief and Practice in an Era of World Christianity*, edited by Craig Ott and Harold A. Netland, 309–36. Grand Rapids: Baker Academic, 2006.

Outler, Albert "Methodists in Search of Consensus." In *What Should Methodists Teach? Wesleyan Tradition and Modern Diversity*, edited by M. Douglas Meeks, 23–38. Nashville: Kingswood, 1990.

————. *Theology in the Wesleyan Spirit*. Nashville: Tidings, 1975.

Sachs, Jonathan. *The Dignity of Difference: How to Avoid the Clash of Civilizations*. London: Continuum, 2002.

Schreiter, Robert J. *Constructing Local Theologies*. Maryknoll, NY: Orbis, 1993.

Shenk, Wilbert R. "Recasting Theology of Mission: Impulses from the Non-Western World." *International Bulletin of Missionary Research* 25 (2001) 98-107.

Shepherd, Victor A. *Mercy Immense and Free: Essays on Wesley and Wesleyan Theology*. Toronto: Clements Academic, 2010.

Stackhouse, Max L. *Apologia: Contextualization, Globalization, and Mission in Theological Education*. Grand Rapids: Eerdmans, 1988.

Synan, Vinson. *The Century of the Holy Spirit: 100 Years of Pentecostal and Charismatic Renewal*. Nashville: Thomas Nelson, 2001.

————. *The Holiness-Pentecostal Movement in the United States*. Grand Rapids: Eerdmans, 1971.

Tanner, Kathryn. *Theories of Culture: A New Agenda for Theology*. Minneapolis: Augsburg Fortress, 1997.

Vanhoozer, Kevin J. "'One Rule to Rule Them All?' Theological Method in an Era of World Christianity." In *Globalizing Theology: Belief and Practice in an Era of World*

Christianity, edited by Craig Ott and Harold A. Netland, 85–126. Grand Rapids: Baker Academic, 2006.

Wesley, John. "11 June 1739." In *The Works of John Wesley*, edited by Albert C. Outler, 19:65-68. Nashville: Abingdon, 1990.

———. "Farther Thoughts on Separation from the Church." In *The Works of John Wesley*, edited by Albert C. Outler, 9:538–40. Nashville: Abingdon, 1990.

———. *The Letters of John Wesley*. Edited by John Telford. London: Epworth, 1931.

———. "Of the Church." In *The Works of John Wesley*, edited by Albert C. Outler, 3:52. Nashville: Abingdon, 1990.

———. "On Schism." In *The Works of John Wesley*, edited by Albert C. Outler, 3:59–69. Nashville: Abingdon, 1990.

———. "Ought We to Separate from the Church of England?" In *The Works of John Wesley*, edited by Albert C. Outler, 9:567–80. Nashville: Abingdon, 1990.

———. *A Plain Account of Christian Perfection*. Kansas City: Beacon Hill, 1971.

———. "Reasons Against a Separation from the Church of England." In *The Works of John Wesley*, edited by Albert C. Outler, 9:332–49. Nashville: Abingdon, 1990.

Weyer, Michael. "The Early Impact of Wesleyanism on Continental Europe." In *The Global Impact of the Wesleyan Traditions and Their Related Movements*, edited by Charles Yrigoyen Jr., 231–43. Lanham, MD: Scarecrow, 2002.

Wondra, Ellen K. "Participating Persons: Reciprocity and Asymmetry." *Anglican Theological Review* 86 (2004) 57–73.

Wright, John W., and Harrison, J. Douglas. "The Ecclesial Practice of Reconciliation and the End of the Wesleyan." *Wesleyan Theological Journal* 37 (2002) 194-214.

Yrigoyen, Charles, Jr. "Introduction." In *The Global Impact of the Wesleyan Traditions and Their Related Movements*, edited by Charles Yrigoyen Jr., xvii–xxiv. Lanham, MD: Scarecrow, 2002.

Zizioulas, John. *Being as Communion: Studies in Personhood and the Church*. Crestwood, NY: St. Vladimir's Seminary Press, 1985.

6

The Hermeneutics of Wesley and "Wesleyan Hermeneutics"

———— Ben Boeckel ————

The Hermeneutics of Wesley and "Wesleyan Hermeneutics"

It is a truism to say the last fifty years have witnessed a proliferation of ways to interpret the Bible. Among the most significant contributions made to biblical studies in recent years is the recognition that interpreters approach the Bible with their own experiences and biases in tow and, consequently, arrive at various methods for understanding scripture. Given this, it is quite appropriate to ask how Wesleyans approach the biblical text. However, answering this question is complicated by the fact that Wesleyans come in many different shapes and sizes; we are women and men from many different cultural contexts and social demographics. Wesleyans include rich and poor, clergy and laity, scholars with doctorates in biblical interpretation and Christians who have only recently been introduced to the Bible. All of these sub-groups have legitimate claims on what is a Wesleyan interpretation. As such, outlining a hermeneutic for these various people groups is a daunting task; indeed, it is impossible to find one mode of interpretation that describes how every Wesleyan can and should interpret the Bible.

Therefore, the primary thesis of this chapter is that there is not *a* Wesleyan hermeneutic. Thus, if the reader is seeking *the* Wesleyan way to interpret scripture or some seven-step methodological apparatus for arriving at *the* Wesleyan way to read the Bible, I suggest looking elsewhere. Wesleyans are too diverse to limit to one all-encompassing hermeneutic. That said, although there is not a single, unified, Wesleyan hermeneutic, there do exist Wesleyan hermeneutics (plural). When Wesleyans interpret, there are certain themes that hint at an underlying continuity among Wesleyans. In other words, Wesleyan interpreters tend to display certain family resemblances. The task of this chapter is to outline some of these common features and to understand the hermeneutical commitments typical of Wesleyan interpreters. As such, the goal of this chapter is descriptive rather than prescriptive. In other words, I intend primarily to *describe* how Wesleyans tend to interpret; I generally refrain from prescribing how they should interpret. Such prescriptive arguments must be the focus of their own project and are therefore (mostly, not entirely) bracketed here.

As we embark on this investigation, it should be noted that not all Wesleyans will agree to what is said in this chapter. Whether it is the way in which I frame the discussion, or the particulars of my argument, there will be Wesleyans who disagree. Even so, it is my hope that at the end of the chapter we will have a better grasp of the general contours of Wesleyan hermeneutics, and a start at articulating certain features that are foundational to most Wesleyan interpretations. To begin, we should first understand the term "hermeneutics."

Defining Hermeneutics

Hermeneutics' is defined in many ways. Some use it synonymously with exegesis, the act of determining the meaning behind the text. Others believe "hermeneutics" refers to the act of making a text applicable to a modern context. For this chapter, I understand "hermeneutics" to refer to the entire process by which one encounters meaning in a text; hermeneutics is the process of interpretation.

A metaphor for how this process works may aid our understanding. Thankfully, various illustrations are available. Some refer to a hermeneutical circle, or spiral, in which the presuppositions that interpreters bring to the Bible both influence the meaning found in the text and are influenced by the new understanding gained from the text.[1] This metaphor has certain merits, but there is another one that will be helpful for our study.

I prefer comparing the process of hermeneutics to the process by which water flows from its springs in an ecosystem to the tap that comes out of one's kitchen sink. In this process the water is influenced (intentionally and unintentionally) by various forces. Working with this analogy, I surmise that there are (at least) three springs that feed one's hermeneutic. First, one operates with presuppositions regarding where meaning is to be located with reference to the text. For some interpreters, the Bible's meaning is found in authorial intent (author-centered). Others believe the biblical text itself generates meaning (text-centered). And still others argue that meaning is a creation of the reader (reader-centered).[2] The locus in which one finds meaning necessarily influences one's interpretation. The second spring feeding the hermeneutical process is the interpretive community in and for which one interprets. Oftentimes, this community influences (or dictates) which interpretations are permissible.[3] Finally, the third spring feeding the hermeneutical process is the interpreter's epistemology, which governs how one justifies an interpretation and the kind of evidence one allows to warrant such justification.

These three springs coalesce as tributaries into a river and combine to form a hermeneutical purpose or agenda for interpreting the text. There are many reasons one may have for interpreting the Bible. For example, some feminists deconstruct or resist so-called literal interpretations by interpreting the Bible in order to identify the ways in which it suppresses women's voices. Often times, though certainly not always, this leads to a repudiation of the Bible's theological authority since it becomes perceived as a tool for perpetuating patriarchy and female oppression.

Others interpret in more explicitly confessional ways for the purpose of nourishing a body of believers. We find examples of this hermeneutical

1. Bernard Lategan provides a good synopsis of the hermeneutical circle in his article in the *Anchor Bible Dictionary*. See Lategan, "Hermeneutics," 149–50.

2. It is important to realize that these positions are not mutually exclusive. For instance, many scholars advocate a two or three step approach to interpretation with step one focusing on the text's historical context and considerations about its original (and/or authorial) meaning. Step two, for such interpreters, uses step one as a foundation for further applications in theology for modern readers. For good examples of this, see the chapters by Craig Blomberg and Merold Westphal in Porter and Stovell, *Biblical Hermeneutics*.

3. E.g., interpretations that deny the virgin birth will not be permitted in many Christian congregations since this is axiomatic for traditional Christian communities.

purpose in many Sunday sermons preached from mainline Evangelical pulpits.[4] There are many reasons for interpreting the Bible and the development of these reasons is impacted by the ways in which the three hermeneutical springs influence both each other and one's understanding of the Bible.

After acquiring one or more reasons for interpreting the text, we necessarily use some kind of methodology to make sense of the words in the Bible. Returning to our aquatic metaphor, we can understand this step as analogous to the point where water is shunted into a water treatment facility. Here, things are done to the water to make it potable. Similarly, one's hermeneutic requires methods for finding meaning. Sometimes one simply reads the words of scripture and interprets their *prima facie* meaning. Other times one pulls the text apart to analyze its composition-history. Still other times one focuses on particular aspects of a text, such as the characterization of somebody in a biblical story. There are many methodologies that one may use depending on the purpose of one's interpretation. Both literary-critical methods and diachronic methods remain useful in (post)modern biblical interpretation.[5] As Wesleyans, we have a variety of methods at our disposal in the process of interpretation.

The last step in the process is applying one's method to a particular text and discovering (or creating, depending on one's presuppositions) its meaning. Each text is unique and the application of one's hermeneutic to one text will look different than it does for another text. Using my metaphor, we can understand the text as a final filter through which one's interpretive river flows before coming out of one's tap. Regardless of what has happened earlier in the interpretive process, the text allows for and precludes certain interpretations. Of course, some interpreters bypass the filter and so create readings that do not follow from the text, but in my experience, most

---

4. This is, certainly, *not* to say that feminist and confessional/Evangelical interpretations are mutually exclusive. That said, there is a marked hermeneutical difference between third-wave feminist exegesis, which typically resists the ideology of the biblical text, and that of most Evangelicals who are generally prone to accept a biblical worldview.

5. In biblical studies, "diachronic methods" typically describes methodologies that go "behind" the text to study its various stages of development. The most commonly recognized diachronic approaches would be source criticism, redaction criticism and textual criticism. By contrast, "synchronic methods" deal with the final form of the text as a literary whole; these methods typically bracket questions about the text's development through time. Examples of synchronic approaches would be narrative criticism, rhetorical criticism, and reader-response criticism.

interpreters are content to interpret the text on its own terms rather than intentionally imposing their own agenda onto the text.[6]

This aquatic metaphor for hermeneutics is not the only way to understand the process of interpretation and does have limitations.[7] However, there are merits to this analogy. Specifically, this metaphor illustrates the various sources (springs) upon which one draws while interpreting a text. Additionally, it accounts for the existence of various types of interpreters within a given school. For instance, there may be different kinds of Wesleyan interpreters because the mixture of the springs feeding, and the methods used, in interpretation will differ among Wesleyans.

I propose that Wesleyan approaches to the Bible constitute a hermeneutical agenda or purpose. This does not mean that a Wesleyan hermeneutic is uncritical (or post-critical). Rather, it means that when one interprets as a Wesleyan, even if one seeks to understand the authorial intent of the Bible, the reason that one engages in this study is in service to a Wesleyan theology. Obviously, there will be different kinds of Wesleyan interpretations because there are different articulations of Wesleyan theology. For instance, pastors of more "traditional," often more theologically conservative, Wesleyan churches tend to (though certainly not always) render interpretations of the Bible that look different from postmodern Wesleyan interpretations found elsewhere.[8] The differences between these

6. By contrast, many interpreters utilizing forms of postmodern and recent literary-critical approaches (e.g., poststructuralism, deconstructionism, and sometimes reader-response interpretations) tend to interpret the text in ways that reject the notion that the text has its own meaning (as is exemplified in Esther Fuchs' statement, "all interpretations are anchored in the reader, rather than the text." Cf., Esther Fuchs, *Sexual Politics in the Biblical Narrative*, 17. These interpreters generally reject earlier literary-critical methods and theoretical frameworks such as formalism, structuralism, and new criticism, which construe the text as autonomous and containing meaning in and of itself. Wesleyan interpreters have typically sided with those who argue the text has meaning, but there are those who utilize postmodern forms of interpretation; whether such approaches are consistent with a Wesleyan theology—particularly as it relates to scripture—is a discussion for another time.

7. E.g., it does not adequately account for the ways in which one's final interpretation of the text can then challenge and reorient earlier stages in the process. This is captured better by the hermeneutical circle analogy mentioned earlier.

8. Granted, terms like "traditional" can be problematic if this is taken to mean that the Church was ever completely uniform in its doctrine and praxis. Recognizing this, we must also recognize that throughout the past two millennia certain tendencies have been dominant among Christians who are creedally orthodox. Those who typically adhere to the creeds and historic teachings of the Church on Christian belief and practice and who bolster such positions by appeal to scripture exemplify the sort of interpreters I have in

interpretations often derives from differences regarding where one expects to find meaning with reference to the text, the interpreters' epistemologies, what is acceptable to their respective interpretive communities, etc.[9]

Given these differences, is it *really* legitimate to call both of these interpretations "Wesleyan?" Yes, because each of these participates in the Wesleyan tradition. Whereas postmodern interpretations produced by, say, someone in the academy might be "Wesleyan" by exhibiting intentional coherence either with what John Wesley said or would say, the interpretation offered by pastors and Sunday School teachers outside the academy is also Wesleyan inasmuch as it is offered to God's people in order to foster holiness. This, however, should make us inquire, what holds these interpretations together?

John Wesley and Scripture

Whatever holds the various Wesleyan interpretations together will likely demonstrate some coherence with the namesakes of the Wesleyan tradition. Recognizing this, most realize the difficulties of using John Wesley's hermeneutic today since there are many differences between Wesley's eighteenth century context and ours.[10] Consequently, a (post)modern Wesleyan hermeneutic is not Wesley's hermeneutic, per se. Two reasons for this present themselves immediately. First, as the aquatic metaphor above shows, one's audience, and one's historical context, impact how one interprets. Thus, Wesley preaching to the first Methodists will look different from the pastor in the Church of the Nazarene whose congregation is influenced by an admixture of Wesleyanism and the American Holiness Movement. Secondly, (post)modern Wesleyans have different epistemological presuppositions than Wesley, which results in differing hermeneutics. For

Key

---

mind with the term "traditional" interpretation or hermeneutic.

9. Unfortunately, these differences often create factions within the Church. Wesleyans from so-called "conservative" contexts have a knack for caricaturizing all postmodern interpreters as liberals and/or heretics who forsake sound doctrine while postmodern interpreters often describe their more conservative counterparts as "fundamentalists." Neither caricature is true; both wound Christ's body.

10. For one thing, we know a lot more about the way in which the Bible came into existence today than Wesley did. Second, we know much more about biblical authors' historical contexts, which should inform our interpretations. The fact that Wesley did not consider this information is not a black mark on his record; rather, he did not have access to this information and cannot be expected to have accounted for it.

instance, Wesley's doctrine of inspiration included a notion of biblical inerrancy, in some sense.[11] This position, however, is not universally shared by Wesleyans today. These philosophical differences mean that contemporary Wesleyans will undoubtedly differ from Wesley in their interpretations of the Bible.

Although there will be differences between Wesley's hermeneutic and contemporary Wesleyan hermeneutics, there are also certain continuities. Among these similarities we might include the way in which Wesley and Wesleyans typically understand scripture's theological purpose (or at least one of its purposes) as well as a predilection for certain methods of biblical interpretation. Three points warrant discussion here.

First, for Wesley, scripture's purpose was soteriological; it made known the way of salvation.[12] Wesley's often quoted preface to his sermons warrants reproduction:

key emphasis

> I want to know one thing,—the way to heaven; how to land safe on that happy shore. God himself has condescended to teach the way: For this very end he came from heaven. He hath written it down in a book. O give me that book! At any price, give me the book of God! I have it: Here is knowledge enough for me. Let me be *homo unius libri.* . . . In [God's] presence I open, I read his book; for this end, to find the way to heaven.[13]

Wesley did not read the Bible primarily to articulate propositions for inclusion in a systematic theology (as evidenced by the fact that Wesley never authored such a work). Rather, scripture was read to make believers "wise unto salvation" (2 Tim 3:15).[14] It is difficult to overstate the importance of salvation to Wesley's use of scripture. For Wesley, biblical interpretation was about salvation and learning how one can be saved.[15] Consequently, in the act of interpreting the Bible, the questions Wesley asked and the answers

non-systematic emphasis

11. Although, Richard Thompson correctly observes that we should not understand this in terms of "contemporary inerrancy debates within fundamentalist circles" (see, Thompson, "Inspired Imagination," 61). Thompson also notes that inerrancy is just one of several components of Wesley's conception of inspiration.

12. See, Shelton, "John Wesley's Approach to Scripture in Historical Perspective," 38–40; Wall, "Toward a Wesleyan Hermeneutic of Scripture," 51–52; and Green, "Is There a Contemporary Wesleyan Hermeneutic?," 130–32.

13. Wesley, *Sermons on Several Occasions,*105–6.

14. Wesley, *OT Notes,* §18.

15. Jones, *John Wesley's Conception and Use of Scripture,* 104. Cf., Shelton, "John Wesley's Approach to Scripture in Historical Perspective," 38–39.

he found connected to his understanding of salvation and sanctification: scripture revealed the way to heaven; its central message disclosed God's plan of salvation.

William Abraham makes the astute observation that what we have in Wesley is the beginning of a theology of scripture.[16] When fully articulated, this conception of scripture can relocate scripture within the doctrine of the Church as a means of grace.[17] This speaks to a second important component of Wesley's hermeneutic: he believed Bible reading was an ordained "means of grace," which he defined as "outward signs, words, or actions, ordained by God . . . to be the ordinary channels whereby he might convey to men, preventing, justifying, or sanctifying grace."[18] Reading scripture does not generate grace in itself but is a conduit through which God's grace flows to us.[19]

Scripture reading, then, was sacrament-like for Wesley; it facilitated "the renewal of your soul in righteousness and true holiness" through the power of the Holy Spirit and the work of Jesus.[20] If the means of grace failed to accomplish this, Wesley said, "they are dung and dross."[21] Scripture reading is viewed as a spiritual practice; it is done under the aegis of the Holy Spirit and is saturated with prayer.[22]

We have now seen that, in Wesley's view, scripture has a soteriological purpose and functions as means of grace. To this we must add a third feature, the "simultaneity of scripture."[23] This refers to Wesley's belief that the Bible must be read as a whole.[24] Scripture's wholeness consists

---

16. Abraham, "Scripture and Divine Revelation," 122.

17. Ibid., 122. Abraham also notes that it could relocate scripture within the doctrine of sanctification.

18. Wesley, Sermon 16, 381. It should be noted that although these means are ordained by God, Wesley clearly states that God's grace can be conveyed in other ways as well. See, Ibid., 395 and "Sermon 98," 385. See also, Maddox, *Responsible Grace*, 192–229.

19. Wesley, "Sermon 16," 381–83.

20. Ibid., 396–97. Cf., Wall, "Toward a Wesleyan Hermeneutic of Scripture," 46–48.

21. Wesley, "Sermon 16," 397.

22. In Wesley's preface to his *OT Notes*, he outlines a process for reading the Bible in which prayer plays an integral role. Cf., *OT Notes*, Preface, §18.

23. Wall, "Toward a Wesleyan Hermeneutic of Scripture," 48–51.

24. Ibid., 49. Reading scripture holistically attempts to prevent one from adopting a canon within the canon. This is consistent with Wesley's belief that scripture as a whole "is a most solid and precious system of divine truth. Every part is worthy of God and all together are one entire body, wherein is no defect, no excess" (*NT Notes,* Preface, §10).

in the doctrines that run throughout the Bible, what Wesley designated the "general tenor of scripture."[25] This is where Wesley's use of the analogy of faith becomes important.

An explicit definition of Wesley's view of the analogy of faith is difficult since Wesley does not define exactly what he means by the term. Scott Jones offers a helpful explanation by observing that Wesley's analogy of faith is the "system of doctrine whose content is the order of salvation and whose function is to serve as a normative guide and limit for theology and as a rule for interpretation."[26] For Wesley, the analogy of faith was the "connection and harmony there is between those grand, fundamental doctrines of original sin, justification by faith, the new birth, inward and outward holiness."[27] Put differently, the analogy of faith connects the doctrines found in scripture and gives coherence to its overarching message when read as a whole.[28] Given Wesley's emphasis on soteriology, it is unsurprising that his conception of the analogy of faith includes doctrines pertaining to salvation (e.g., sin and justification).

On a practical level, the analogy of faith establishes for Wesley a theological rubric by which he can allow scripture to interpret itself.[29] In other words, a difficult text can be interpreted by another text. The danger here, however, is determining the validity of the intertextual comparison. The Church Father Irenaeus recognized that heretics also employed intertextual exegesis, but connected texts in such a way as to distort the original or intended picture of the Bible.[30] One way to prevent such distortion is to use the analogy of faith, which for Wesley consisted in the way in which he connected the several doctrines mentioned in the previous paragraph.[31]

25. Jones, *John Wesley's Conception and Use of Scripture*, 47–48.

26. Ibid., 49.

27. Wesley, *OT Notes*, §18. Cf., *NT Notes*, Rom.12:6.

28. Wesley, *OT Notes*, §18; *NT Notes*, Rom 12:6. Cf., Jones, *John Wesley's Conception and Use of Scripture*, 43–53.

29. See, Wesley, "Sermon 64," 501.

30. Irenaeus, *Against Heresies*, 326.

31. Unfortunately, space does not allow for an in depth example of Wesley's use of the analogy of faith. It is difficult to know when he understands himself to be using this because he never gives an explicit example of how it would work. Perhaps one place we see the analogy at work is in Wesley's sermon, "Working Out Our Own Salvation," where he explains the Christian's working out of salvation (Philip. 2:12) in terms of prevenient grace, convincing grace/repentance, justification, and sanctification. In this sermon, Wesley explains a potentially confusing passage by using his understanding of soteriology to appeal to other biblical texts. See, Wesley, "Sermon 85," 203–4.

To summarize, I have outlined three important features of Wesley's understanding and interpretation of scripture: it is soteriological, it is a means of grace, and it is interpreted as a whole using the analogy of faith. Admittedly there is much more to be said about Wesley's hermeneutic, but what I have offered here lays the essential groundwork for a discussion of what constitutes Wesleyan hermeneutics today.[32] It is to this topic that we now turn.

Wesleyans Practicing Hermeneutics

At the outset of our discussion, it should be reiterated that Wesley's hermeneutic is not synonymous with Wesleyan hermeneutics. Because of the advancements in biblical studies, the modern interpreter can access many tools (e.g., literary criticism, redaction criticism, form criticism, etc.) that were unavailable to Wesley because Wesley was limited by his eighteenth century context (as we are limited by ours). Consequently, it is unsurprising that the interpretations of Wesley's followers exhibit differences from Wesley's hermeneutic.

However, before addressing the attributes of Wesleyan hermeneutics, one further observation should be made: the reason we are unable to use Wesley's hermeneutic today is the same reason we cannot speak of a singular Wesleyan hermeneutic. Just as Wesley lived in a particular context, so also Wesleyans live in many different contexts that influence our hermeneutics. Admitting that there are various kinds of Wesleyan interpreters is hardly a new recognition; in 1983, George Lyons remarked that referring to "'the Wesleyan interpreter' suggests a non-existent uniformity among those who choose so to identify themselves."[33]

This diversity among Wesleyans runs deeper than superficial matters such as interpreter A's metaphorical understanding of Genesis 1 and interpreter B's advocacy of 7-day creationism. Rather, Wesleyan interpretations often attest fundamentally different understandings of scripture's function

32. Especially insufficient in this section has been my examination of Wesley's methodological moves in biblical interpretation, particularly pertaining to prayer and the work of the Holy Spirit. Other important topics that remain unaddressed relate to Wesley's conceptions of the authority of scripture and scriptural infallibility. For further study, see Jones, *John Wesley's Conception and Use of Scripture*; Wall, "Toward a Wesleyan Hermeneutic of Scripture"; and Green, "Wesley as Interpreter of Scripture and the Emergence of 'History' in Biblical Interpretation," 47–62.

33. Lyons, "Hermeneutical Bases for Theology," 63.

within theology: some Wesleyans use the Bible primarily to secure propositions for Christian theology while others emphasize different functions like scripture's role as a means of grace. We can find examples of the first of these models in local church contexts in many Wesleyan Sunday school classes. Somewhat differently, in other contexts such as the university setting or meetings of the Wesleyan Theological Society, (vocational) Wesleyan theologians are more likely to understand scripture primarily as a means of grace, but without believing that its primary purpose is to offer propositions of the kind used in our the Sunday school class above.[34]

Both models represent essential components of the Wesleyan tradition. One group emphasizes (with Wesley) the Protestant concern that the Bible serve as the primary source for theology; the other makes the necessary observation (again, with Wesley) that in the Bible we find more than statements about correct belief—we also meet the Word and are nourished by God's Spirit. Granted, both of these approaches have times when they are more or less difficult to apply and perhaps times when they cannot or should not be applied. For instance, interpreters using scripture to find propositions for theology might have difficulty with books like Psalms and Lamentations (though they might argue that propositions can be derived from such texts). Similarly, those preferring more theological/soteriological uses of scripture are often wont to defer to scriptural propositions they deem helpful (e.g., "God is love").

In any case, the differences between these two models run deeper than the observation that Wesleyans appropriate Wesley in different ways. Indeed, different hermeneutics are at work here. Returning to the categories in our aquatic metaphor, many Sunday school teachers might operate with a certain epistemology (i.e., the Bible as the sole source for theology), and use some sort of an intertextual method to reach their conclusions. On the other hand, a Church historian in a Wesleyan university, addressing students or peers in scholarly settings, may employ a somewhat different epistemology (one that, among other things, more readily draws upon tradition) and may use any number of exegetical methods (e.g., perhaps the fourfold method of Medieval exegesis).

Of course, these two approaches are not mutually exclusive. For instance, if our Church historian happens to teach a Sunday school class, she

---

34. Admittedly, these examples utilize stereotypes of Sunday school and the academy and therefore fail at certain points. That said, as one who has occupied both positions (Sunday school teacher and academic), I can testify that that there is a ring of truth to these generalizations.

could use the same method she employs in more scholarly settings. That said, this hypothetical scenario is an exception that proves the rule; the average Sunday school teacher is often unaware of the exegetical methods to which a historian may have been exposed. Consequently, we might say that one's hermeneutic is affected by formal education, which makes certain interpretive tools more accessible to one interpreter than another with less formal education (e.g., in my own experience, my interpretation of the Bible today is very different than it was when I received by Bachelor of Arts degree).[35]

Given these differences within Wesleyanism, which lead to different interpretive approaches, we must ask, "Is talking about Wesleyan hermeneutics a lost cause?" I do not think so. Though Wesleyans interpret in many ways and in various contexts, there are certain themes that seem fundamental to Wesleyan hermeneutics. We might view these as the hermeneutical bedrock on which the edifices of Wesleyan interpretations are built. I will now attempt to summarize what I believe to be minerals that make up this bedrock.

Soteriological Emphasis

Soteriology was so essential to Wesley's teaching on the Bible that Wesleyan hermeneutics would be unrecognizable without this emphasis. However, not just any soteriology will do; Wesleyans read with a Wesleyan understanding of salvation.[36] Scripture illuminates the way in which Christ restores the image of God that was lost in Genesis 3. Through faith in Jesus, the Wesleyan understands that we are forgiven for sins (justification).

---

35. It is for this reason that quality Wesleyan curricula are an essential resource for the Church. We cannot, nor should we, expect every Sunday school teacher to have an advanced degree in biblical studies before teaching a class on scripture. A Church curriculum can go a long way towards placing the fruits of formal education in biblical studies and theology into the hands of our Wesleyan laity.

36. Of course, this is not a clear cut endeavor since Wesley's understanding of salvation also requires an interpretation of Wesley and his works. This introduces an important hermeneutical conundrum: our understanding of our Wesleyan heritage is as much an interpretive issue as our understanding of scripture. Thus, we come to the question of which interpretation receives priority in theology: what ought Wesleyans to do if a biblical text is at odds with their understanding of Wesleyan theology? Do they perform exegetical gymnastics to make scripture consistent with the interpretation of Wesley, or do they tweak the understanding of Wesley to conform to scripture? For now, I will leave this investigation to the theologians.

After this, there is growth in grace and filling with the Holy Spirit (entire sanctification).

Biblical passages that cohere with this framework will be used *via* the analogy of faith to interpret other passages. This does not mean we read salvation into every text, however. Rather, the analogy of faith silhouettes those texts that do not address salvation; it becomes a backdrop against which we understand the whole of scripture. For instance, it would be difficult to find salvation in the Ark Narrative of 1 Samuel 4:1–7:2, which describes the ark's excursion into Philistia and its eventual return to Israel. Clearly, this story is not about salvation.

However, in making sense of this text, Wesleyan interpreters can use the analogy of faith to situate the text within the framework of biblical history. For instance, the death of those who inappropriately handled the ark (1 Sam. 6:19) can be explained by examining other texts that address this topic. Similarly, the analogy of faith helps us understand how the Ark Narrative fits into Israel's salvation-history: by explaining what happened to the ark in the pre-monarchic period, the story anticipates David, who brought the ark to Jerusalem in 2 Samuel 6. In the following chapter, David wanted to build a temple in which the ark could be placed; this occasioned the Davidic promise of an eternal dynasty of which Jesus is a part.

We see from this brief example that, though salvation is not part of the Ark Narrative itself, the use of the analogy of faith allows us to situate the story within the history of God's salvific activity. Of course, there are other ways in which Wesleyans can interpret the Ark Narrative; this has been only one example.[37] Conveniently, it has also provided a helpful transition to the next essential feature of Wesleyan hermeneutics.

Analogy of Faith

As was noted above, Wesley used the analogy of faith to allow scripture to interpret itself.[38] This principle would be considered a hermeneutical methodology that is applied to the text. In this endeavor, one's background (e.g., one's theological presuppositions) influences one's deployment of the analogy of faith. Rob Wall notes that different theological traditions "find different analogical meanings apropos to their particular theological and

---

37. For another, see, Mellish, *1 & 2 Samuel*, 74–75.

38. See Jones, *John Wesley's Conception and Use of Scripture*, 122. Cf., Wesley, "Sermon 64," 501.

✳ ⎰ecclesial locations."[39] Consequently, different people may interpret ambiguous scriptures by appealing to different sets of texts depending on their theological contexts.[40] For Wesleyans, as for Wesley, the analogy of faith is a tool whereby one can say that scripture offers a soteriological message.[41]

The example above of the Ark Narrative has already shown that the analogy of faith is important to a Wesleyan interpreter's methodology. Although it is possible to deploy a Wesleyan hermeneutic without the analogy of faith, most Wesleyans will find the analogy of faith helpful since it allows us to understand difficult texts by appealing to ones that are less ambiguous. By using scripture to explain itself, Wesleyans continue the tradition of their theological father. That said, the analogy of faith is not the only methodology to be employed by Wesleyans (e.g., critical methodologies have their appropriate time and place). The analogy of faith is only emphasized here due to its prevalence among Wesleyan interpreters.

Joel Green and Contemporary Wesleyan Hermeneutics

Joel Green's work on contemporary Wesleyan hermeneutics warrants sustained discussion here since he provides important methodological insights. Green offers four observations for the contemporary Wesleyan interpreter: first, Wesleyans "find ways of being critical [with respect to the nature and interpretation of scripture] that cohere with the Bible's character as Scripture."[42] In this, we follow Wesley, who was a critical interpreter of scripture. "Critical" here refers to the quality of being concerned with the validity of one's interpretation, which is certainly true of Wesley who

39. Wall, "Toward a Wesleyan Hermeneutic of Scripture," 49–50.

40. Two points must be made here. First, two interpretations using the analogy of faith differently can both offer legitimate interpretations. That said, determining which one is more justifiable, appropriate, literal, etc., is a separate discussion that space prohibits here. Secondly, it should be noted that postmodernists have an important insight about the analogy of faith: though it arises out of one's reading of scripture, the themes to which one gravitates and the passages that one believes disclose "the general tenor" of scripture (to use Wesley's term) involve subjective and interpretive decisions. This returns us to my first point: determining which conception of the analogy of faith is most appropriate is a separate discussion that we cannot enter here (neither can we discuss any connections between the Christian's use of the analogy of faith and the Holy Spirit's guiding).

41. Koskie, "Can We Speak of a Wesleyan Theological Hermeneutic of Scripture Today?," 203.

42. Green, "Is There a Contemporary Wesleyan Hermeneutic?," 125.

adjudicated between competing interpretations of biblical texts (using tools like textual criticism). Likewise, Wesleyans endeavor to offer "critical" interpretations of scripture and use critical methodologies.

Green's second observation is that Wesleyan hermeneutics operate with a "properly chastised concern with the 'literal meaning' of Scripture."[43] This literal meaning, however, is not necessarily scripture's "historical meaning."[44] Rather, Green argues that Wesleyans should prioritize the meaning of scripture in its canonical form over the meaning behind the text (e.g., authorial intent).[45]

Green is correct that the final (i.e., canonical) form of the Bible is important for Christian interpreters. However, I am reluctant to relegate historical criticism to a secondary status in Wesleyan hermeneutics. First, not all Wesleyans grant Green's assumption that the text itself is the primary locus in which the interpreter finds meaning. Along with this, a related problem with overemphasizing the canonical form of the text is that it makes a theological interpretation far too easy to vitiate if the text is corrupt.[46] It is better for interpreters to be equipped to address the historical problems behind the text and to give an account for why the interpretation on offer remains valid in light of those issues. Second, historical approaches to the text are important for Wesleyans inasmuch as the Bible makes historical assertions (something Green recognizes). If Christianity is to be credible, the text on which its theology (and theological interpretations) rests must be subject to the kind of historical study that Green subordinates to the final form of scripture; Wesleyans need to know both the content of the Bible and the veracity of its historical claims.[47]

43. Ibid., 127. Cf. ibid. 127–28 for Green's response to postmodernity's concern that literal readings are the product of the reader. See also, Abraham, "Scripture and Divine Revelation," 120–21.

44. Green, "Is There a Contemporary Wesleyan Hermeneutic?," 128.

45. Ibid.

46. A case in point is 1–2 Samuel. Textual criticism reveals various manuscript traditions of this book and the Masoretic Text (which underlies most English Bibles) does not appear to be the original; neither is the Masoretic Text the canonical version of the early Church (that version is reflected by the Septuagint—the Greek translation of Samuel—which is substantially different from the Masoretic Text). In this situation, prioritizing the canonical form of the text is problematic because we must ask, "Which text is canonical?"

47. In fairness, Green does offer legitimate critiques of historical criticism (as it is typically conceived), especially in his 2011 article, which outlines historical criticism's presuppositions as well as different meanings of "historical criticism" (Green,

Green's third point is that a Wesleyan hermeneutic "will be characterized by soteriological aims."[48] This is certainly true, but Green unfortunately pits this against historical criticism. He justifiably rejects historical critical attempts to interpret scripture like a functional atheist, unwilling to accept God's activity in the text. That said, we should avoid throwing out the baby with the bathwater; making soteriological assertions about scripture does not exclude an ability to talk about what happened in the past (though it does necessarily challenge certain assumptions regarding how history is to be written).[49]

Green's fourth point calls for the demolition of barricades that isolate biblical studies from other disciplines (e.g., theology and ethics).[50] This demolition can happen by allowing biblical studies and other disciplines to interpenetrate. Taking theology as an example, as biblical scholars, Wesleyans should—and I admit that I am prescribing more than describing here—mine the depths of the Bible using both diachronic/historical-critical and synchronic/literary exegetical methods to ascertain what the text says. Similarly, as theologians, we should engage in thoughtful and systematic reflection about how the text informs and influences a Wesleyan understanding of God and our identity as God's holy people.

This connects with what is perhaps Green's most important observation: an essential ingredient of Wesleyan hermeneutics is a Wesleyan interpreter.[51] There is no singular methodology that can be applied to a text that will ensure a Wesleyan interpretation at the end of the process.

"Rethinking 'History' for Theological Interpretation," 160–61). In that article, he concludes that study of the "historical situation within which the biblical materials were generated" is important for theological interpretation, but it remains unclear how this study can be accomplished without adopting the framework Green proscribes (i.e., the task of reconstructing past events to narrate a story, an activity that he deems "inimical" to theological interpretation). My worry is that historical criticism is more important for Wesleyan hermeneutics than Green allows. Granted, not all Wesleyans agree on this matter, but many of them place a premium on the meaning *behind* the text. What we need is a framework by which theologians can agree with Green on what are historical criticism's problems while affirming the need to conduct robust historical investigation in order that Christian belief may be sufficiently warranted (which presupposes knowing whether certain events did or did not happen).

48. Green, "Is There a Contemporary Wesleyan Hermeneutic?," 130.

49. Green, "Rethinking 'History' for Theological Interpretation," 160–62. See also, Abraham, *Divine Revelation and the Limits of Historical Criticism*.

50 Green, "Rethinking," 132–33.

51. Green, "Is There a Contemporary Wesleyan Hermeneutic?," 124.

What is needed is a Wesleyan exegete who will find Wesleyan insights in the text and communicate these to the Church. In saying this, Green is not contradicting everything else that he offers as characteristic of Wesleyan hermeneutics (e.g., being critical, literal, soteriological, etc.). Rather, these characteristics are simply accidental—in the philosophical sense of the term—to Wesleyan interpretation whereas a Wesleyan interpreter is essential.

Knowledge and Vital Piety

The final attribute that I would observe is fundamental to Wesleyan hermeneutics is the recognition that reading the Bible is both a spiritual and academic enterprise. Studying scripture involves both learning about salvation and meeting the Savior. It is a chance to receive God's grace and to deepen our knowledge of God. Consequently, Wesleyan interpreters heed the words of Charles Wesley, "Unite the pair so long disjoined: knowledge and vital piety."[52] For Wesleyans, biblical interpretation is both a spiritual discipline and an academic endeavor; it involves pietism and criticism working in concert.

This, however, does not mean that all Wesleyan interpretations will marry piety and criticism in the same way. For instance, I have heard quite a few Wesleyans interpret scripture at the annual meetings of the Wesleyan Theological Society, but very few of these would make good sermons (they presume a different audience). Conversely, I have heard many Wesleyan sermons, but even fewer of these would be well received at an academic gathering of Wesleyans. The important point here is not that one interpretation is more authentically Wesleyan than the other, but that the different groups of Wesleyans use different hermeneutics for different purposes while retaining a concern for deepening both spiritual knowledge and spiritual discipline.

Conclusion

Having surveyed some of the overarching characteristics of Wesleyan hermeneutics, we must remember that these do not constitute *the* Wesleyan way of reading the Bible. There is no "Wesleyan hermeneutic" because

---

52. Wesley, "At the Opening of the School in Kingwood," 36.

hermeneutics are integrally connected with a number of factors on which there is little agreement in the Wesleyan tradition. Another reason there is not *a singular* Wesleyan hermeneutic relates to the social-location of the interpreters. Hermeneutics are affected by (though I do not think they are constrained by) one's social context. Thus, different traditions of Wesleyanism (United Methodist, Church of the Nazarene, etc.) will occasionally accentuate different nuances within the biblical text. These different accents derive from hermeneutical approaches that, while being very similar, also differ in certain ways (e.g., different interpretations of Wesley). Nevertheless, what unites Wesleyan interpreters is a family resemblance; they will generally (though not unanimously) agree to what has been outlined in section three of this chapter.

However, the question should be asked, what distinguishes these Wesleyan hermeneutics from any other Christian hermeneutic? On one level, not much. If the goal is to obtain a "literal" translation of the Bible, just about everyone will translate the first words of John 1:1 something like "in the beginning was the Word . . . " and this will be the case regardless of one's theological identity (whether Wesleyan, Roman Catholic, Reformed, Orthodox, etc.).

On the other hand, differences begin to emerge when we step beyond the so-called literal interpretation to ask what this text means. This task requires locating a given text within one's theological framework and one's interpretation of other biblical passages. It is here that the Wesleyan interpreter's theological identify is most visible, particularly in our use of soteriology to interpret.[53] In this emphasis we reflect the sentiment of our forbearer who wanted to know one thing: "the way to Heaven."[54] Now, it may correctly be argued that many Christian hermeneutics could focus on this theological concept. However, the distinctly Wesleyan component in this case is not the fact that soteriology influences the hermeneutic but the fact that the soteriology will be articulated in Wesleyan ways. Put differently, the Wesleyan flavor will be identified by the Wesleyan soteriology.

To conclude, the recognition that there is no single Wesleyan hermeneutic should not cause despair. If there was only one or a few ways to interpret as Wesleyans, there would be only one or a few ways for Wesleyans

---

53. Robert Wall makes an important observation in relation to this point: "my hunch is that the differences between Christian interpreters are often less a matter of methodological or epistemological disagreements and more a matter of confessional differences." See, Wall, "The Canonical Response," 195.

54. Wesley, *Sermons on Several Occasions*, 105–6.

to make the Bible speak to the (post)modern Church. Thus, it is providential that the Holy Spirit works in various ways to meet us in the Bible. Through the service of various Wesleyans using various hermeneutical approaches, the Holy Spirit nourishes Christ's Church. Therefore, let us thank God that Wesleyan biblical interpretation is not bound to one method of interpretation!

Bibliography

Abraham, William. *Divine Revelation and the Limits of Historical Criticism.* Oxford: Oxford University Press, 2000.

———. "Scripture and Divine Revelation." In *Wesley, Wesleyans, and Reading Bible as Scripture,* edited by Joel B. Green and David F. Watson, 117–32. Waco: Baylor University Press, 2012.

Fuchs, Esther. *Sexual Politics in the Biblical Narrative: Reading the Hebrew Bible as a Woman.* Journal for the Study of the Old Testament Supplement 310. Sheffield: Sheffield Academic Press, 2000.

Green, Joel. "Is There a Contemporary Wesleyan Hermeneutic?" In *Reading the Bible in Wesleyan Ways,* edited by Barry Callen and Richard Thompson, 123–36. Kansas City: Beacon Hill, 2004.

———. "Rethinking 'History' for Theological Interpretation." *Journal of Theological Interpretation* 5 (2011) 159–73.

———. "Wesley as Interpreter of Scripture and the Emergence of 'History' in Biblical Interpretation." In *Wesley, Wesleyans, and Reading Bible as Scripture,* edited by Joel B. Green and David Watson, 47–62. Waco: Baylor University Press, 2012.

Irenaeus. *Against Heresies.* In vol. 1 of *The Ante-Nicene Fathers.* Edited by Alexander Roberts and James Donaldson. 1885–87. 10 vols. Reprint, New York: Scribner's, 1913.

Jones, Scott J. *John Wesley's Conception and Use of Scripture.* Nashville: Kingswood, 1995.

Koskie, Steven. "Can We Speak of a Wesleyan Theological Hermeneutic of Scripture Today?" In *Wesley, Wesleyans, and Reading Bible as Scripture,* edited by Joel B. Green and David Watson, 195–209. Waco: Baylor University Press, 2012.

Lategan, Bernard. "Hermeneutics." In *Anchor Bible Dictionary,* edited by David Noel Freedman et al., 3:149–54. New York: Doubleday, 1992.

Lyons, George. "Hermeneutical Bases for Theology: Higher Criticism and the Wesley Interpreter." *Wesleyan Theological Journal* 18 (1983) 63–78.

Maddox, Randy L. *Responsible Grace: John Wesley's Practical Theology.* Nashville: Kingswood, 1994.

Mellish, Kevin. *1 & 2 Samuel: A Commentary in the Wesleyan Tradition.* New Beacon Bible Commentary. Kansas City: Beacon Hill, 2012.

Outler, Albert, ed. *The Works of John Wesley.* Vols. 1–4, *The Sermons.* Bicentennial ed. Nashville: Abingdon, 1984.

Porter, Stanley, and Beth Stovell, eds. *Biblical Hermeneutics: Five Views.* Downers Grove: IVP Academic, 2012.

Shelton, R. Larry. "John Wesley's Approach to Scripture in Historical Perspective." *Wesleyan Theological Journal* 16 (1981) 23–50.

Thompson, Richard. "Inspired Imagination: John Wesley's Concept of Biblical Inspiration and Literary-Critical Studies." In *Reading the Bible in Wesleyan Ways*, edited by Barry Callen and Richard Thompson, 57–79. Kansas City: Beacon Hill, 2004.

Wall, Robert. "The Canonical Response." In *Biblical Hermeneutics: Five Views*, edited by Stanley Porter and Beth Stovell, 188–200. Downers Grove: IVP Academic, 2012.

———. "Toward a Wesleyan Hermeneutic of Scripture." In *Reading the Bible in Wesleyan Ways*, edited by Barry Callen and Richard Thompson, 39–55. Kansas City: Beacon Hill, 2004.

Wesley, Charles. *Hymns for Children and Persons of Riper Years*. 4th ed. London: Paramore, 1784.

Wesley, John. *Explanatory Notes Upon the New Testament*. London: Epworth, 1958.

———. *Explanatory Notes Upon the Old Testament*. 1765. Reprint, Salem, OH: Schmul, 1975.

Part 3

Renewing Classical Wesleyanism

Back to a Wesleyan Future via a Usable Past

———— Susie C. Stanley ————

M y experience as an activist working for passage of the Equal Rights
Amendment (ERA) in the early 1970s illustrates the need for a usable past. I encountered opposition not only in the public arena but also in
the church. Growing up in the Wesleyan/Holiness branch of Wesleyanism
had led me to believe that my heritage supported my feminism. It became
obvious that I needed to find evidence beyond my personal experience to
augment my theology and my activism. Opponents of feminism sent me
in search of a usable past even though I was unfamiliar with this phrase at
the time. Because Wesleyan scholarship has flourished over the past several decades, the new generation of Wesleyan scholars has an abundance
of material to mine for a usable past. The challenge for new scholars is to
appropriate the past supplied by Wesleyan scholarship and practice as a
tool for informing the present and shaping a vision of the future. The past
becomes usable as it is appropriated for this task.

Literary critic Van Wyck Brooks coined "usable past" in 1918. In the
context of American literature, he advocated adopting a "shared cultural
history" because "the past is an inexhaustible storehouse of apt attitudes
and adaptable ideas. . ."[1] For Brooks, a usable past was "an invention or at
least a retrospective reconstruction to serve the needs of the present."[2] Now

1. Brooks, "On Creating a Usable Past," 341, 339.
2. Olick, "From Usable Pasts to the Return of the Repressed."

widely utilized in several academic disciplines, it is particularly apropos for theology and Christian ethics.

I first encountered the phrase "usable past" in Letty Russell's *Human Liberation in a Feminist Perspective—A Theology* (1974).[3] She described the methodology underlying my historical efforts and provided a theological framework utilizing liberation theology: "Human beings need to find identity and strength from the images of past history which can help to guide them in shaping their present and future. . . . it becomes a *usable* past through reflection on its meaning and mistakes in such a way that human beings build a common sense of direction toward the future."[4]

Russell described my quest to resolve the disconnect between my views and those of Christians and others who opposed the ERA. I hoped to counteract those who denied there was any Christian precedent for supporting the ERA but I was not sure of the outcome. I had read Mary Daly's *Beyond God the Father* [5]where she presented a convincing case for the complicity of the church in women's oppression, not only in the church but also in society. Daly's arguments tempted me to leave my Christian tradition and perhaps even Christianity.

George Pickering, an ethicist at University of Detroit, helped facilitate my initial search for a usable past. My reading focused on women abolitionists and suffragists of the nineteenth century. Some scholars researching this era dismissed Christianity as a hindrance to women's equality in society and in the home. They either minimized or ignored the positive role of Christianity in the movements themselves or in the lives of individual women. So, the first goal was to examine primary documents to ascertain if the interpretation of history advanced by these scholars accurately reflected information from these sources. *History of Woman Suffrage*[6] was an important resource. With first-hand accounts of meetings and other activities, its 5,555 pages were a gold mine. Not only was there support from Christian women and men for suffrage and other women's rights but this history chronicled the existence and involvement of at least forty-five women clergy. Of course, there were Christian opponents, too. My task was not to ignore this information. One of my first academic papers was "The

---

3. Russell, *Human Liberation in a Feminist Perspective*, 72–103.

4. Ibid., 72.

5. Daly, *Beyond God the Father*.

6. Stanton, Anthony, and Gage, *History of Woman Suffrage*, vols. I–III; Anthony and Harper, vols. V–VI.

Chief Bone of Contention: The Suffragists and Their Opponents Wrestle with the Bible."[7] Not surprisingly, it included an ethical component, urging support of the ERA.

My search for a usable past led me to the Bible as well as historical sources. This reflected the Wesleyan emphasis on the Bible as an important source of theology. This was not a quick perusal—I read every word from Genesis to Revelation. I created a chart with places in the gospels where Jesus interacted with women. This served as the basis for workshops at various churches and ultimately became a handout for my seminary and college classes.

A study of Wesleyan historical resources also uncovered a usable past in the Bible that affirmed women, especially as preachers. For instance, Phoebe Palmer's *The Promise of the Father* and B. T. Roberts' *Ordaining Women* were book-length treatises while numerous pamphlets and book chapters supplemented this positive affirmation of women's gifts and usage of those gifts in the church.[8]

Non-Wesleyans contributed to the usable past I constructed. Letty Russell documented Jesus' encounters with several women.[9] Rosemary Radford Ruether also consulted the Bible and employed its prophetic tradition to develop her liberation theology that challenged a broad range of injustices. Gary Dorrien observed: "Ruether stressed that feminist theology rested on the central tradition of the scriptural witness, the one by which biblical faith 'constantly criticizes and renews itself and its own vision.' By claiming the Bible's prophetic-liberating stream as a norm for criticizing Christianity and patriarchy, feminist theology operated in the same fashion as other liberationisms, stripping away layers of ideology and misunderstanding that concealed Christianity's emancipatory content."[10]

Both Russell and especially Ruether have been scholar-activists with whom I share a mutual ethical concern to achieve justice in society. Drawn to the work of Ruether and Russell because of their activism, I was searching for a usable past that supported Christian ethics.

---

7. Stanley, "The Chief Bone of Contention.

8. Palmer, *The Promise of the Father*; Roberts, *Ordaining Women*; Stanley, "Wesleyan Holiness Women Clergy." This resource contains texts of over seventy articles by Wesleyan/Holiness authors supporting women in ministry.

9. Russell, *Human Liberation in a Feminist Perspective*, 87.

10. Dorrien, *Economy, Difference, Empire*, 298. Dorrien's own emphasis on a usable past has anchored an activist agenda.

Two concerns need to be kept in mind when appropriating a usable past. First, there is no such thing as a golden age which can be tapped as the basis for a usable past. I have discovered, though, that referencing a usable past sometimes leads to being accused of advocating a golden age. Believe me; there is no evidence of a golden age in the ancient past of the church, much less in the early decades of Wesleyanism either in England or the United States. For example, the stories recounted by our foremothers preclude this mistaken depiction of the past. Sexism was as alive and well then as now.

"Until lions have their own historians, tales of hunting will always glorify the hunter" is an African proverb illustrating a second concern when consulting the past. Sometimes, we only have a partial history told by those in power. Groups that have been marginalized or overlooked in historical accounts have pointed this out and historians have begun including the "lions" in the historical canon.

The history of women illustrates the fact that those in power control what gets recorded as history. In 1974, Letty Russell called for an expansion of the historical canon: ". . . to create a usable past as *her-story* and not just *his-story*."[11] Early histories of the civil rights movement illustrate the omission of women. A reader of these accounts could not be faulted for assuming that few women played leadership roles in the movement. Subsequent historians have pointed out the importance of women in the movement, from Ella Baker to Fanny Lou Hamer. For instance, a recent biography of Rosa Parks by Jeanne Theoharis documented that she was an activist long before she inspired the Montgomery Bus Boycott by refusing to give up her seat on a bus. Her support of the Black Panther movement exemplifies her ongoing pursuit of justice for African/Americans. Theoharis credited Parks' Christian "faith in God's vision of justice on earth" for sustaining her through the years.[12] An active member of the African Methodist Episcopal Church, Parks claimed that she relied on prayer which resulted in inner peace as she dealt with the trauma and terror related to the boycott.[13]

Just as women such as Parks were often invisible from the historical canon until recently, the same was true for John Wesley and Wesleyan

11. Russell, *Human Liberation in a Feminist Perspective*, 81.

12. Theoharis, *The Rebellious Life of Mrs. Rosa Parks*, 30. This is the first biography of Parks written for adults. It puts to rest the mistaken notion that Parks was a meek and mild woman who simply was too tired to move when the bus driver ordered her to give up her seat.

13. Ibid., 102, 124.

theology. A prominent Wesleyan theologian once reflected that he never encountered John Wesley's theology in his graduate curriculum. One hopes the days are past when Wesley was absent from the pantheon of theologians studied in graduate school. The historian Douglas John Hall employed a usable past, contending that "by its nature Christian theology requires dialogue with and help from a 'usable past' .... It requires a tradition, a past, with which to struggle and from which to learn." However, he limited the parameters of a usable past when he continued: "And it is beyond question that the 'past' of this particular mode of theological reflection in the Protestant mode is to be located in the history and literature of Germanic Protestantism."[14] Hall's emphasis reflects the use of a Reformed lens that still overlooks John Wesley. Even with an abundance of research and writing about Wesley and Wesleyan theology, unfortunately, in some cases, the case still needs to be made for incorporation into the canon. Sometimes the role of a historical theologian involves doing more than mining the past for what is usable. It may require uncovering and promoting portions of history that previously had been invisible.

My search for a usable past supported my decision to stay in the church. Employing the methodology of a usable past has guided both my activism and my career as an academic. "Empowered Foremothers: Wesleyan/Holiness Women Speak to Today's Christian Feminists" is one example which demonstrates this by uniting material from a usable past with an emerging feminist ethic.[15]

Possessing a historical consciousness is not enough for Wesleyans. Exploring history for a usable past is an obligation for new scholars who must avoid the pitfall of falsely identifying a golden age that we need to emulate. Likewise, a usable past must not be constructed solely from a history told by those in power. Stories of the marginalized need to be included. With these caveats in mind, appropriating a usable past derived from Wesleyan theology and behavior becomes a means of positively influencing the present and envisioning the future.

Bibliography

Anthony, Susan B., and Ida Husted Harper, eds. *History of Woman Suffrage.* Vol. 4. Indianapolis: Hollenback, 1902.

14. Hall, *Bound and Free*, 73.
15. Stanley, "Empowered Foremothers," 103–116.

Brooks, Van Wyck. "On Creating a Usable Past." *The Dial*, April 11, 1918. http://archive. org/stream/dialjournallitcrit64chicrich#page/336/mode/2up.

Daly, Mary. *Beyond God the Father: Toward a Philosophy of Women's Liberation*. Boston: Beacon, 1973.

Dorrien, Gary. *Economy, Difference, Empire: Social Ethics for Social Justice*. New York: Columbia University Press, 2010.

Hall, Douglas John. *Bound and Free: A Theologian's Journey*. Minneapolis: Fortress, 2005.

Harper, Ida Husted, ed. *History of Woman Suffrage*. Vols. 5–6. New York: J. J. Little & Ives, 1922.

Olick, Jeffrey K. "From Usable Pasts to the Return of the Repressed." *The Hedgehog Review* 9 (2007) 19–31. http://www.iasc-culture.org/THR/archives/UsesPast/Olick.pdf.

Palmer, Phoebe. *The Promise of the Father; or, A Neglected Specialty of the Last Days*. 1859. Reprint, Salem, Ohio: Schmul, 1981.

Roberts, B. T. *Ordaining Women*. 1891. Reprint, Indianapolis: Light and Life, 1992.

Russell, Letty M. *Human Liberation in a Feminist Perspective—a Theology*. Philadelphia: Westminster, 1974.

Stanley, Susie C. "The Chief Bone of Contention: The Suffragists and Their Opponents Wrestle with the Bible." Paper presented at the annual meeting of the American Academy of Religion, New York, 1982.

———. "Empowered Foremothers: Wesleyan/Holiness Women Speak to Today's Christian Feminists." *Wesleyan Theological Journal* 24 (1989) 103–16.

Stanton, Elizabeth Cady, et al., eds. *History of Woman Suffrage*. Vols. 1–3. Rochester: Charles Mann, 1881–86.

Theoharis, Jeanne. *The Rebellious Life of Mrs. Rosa Parks*. Boston: Beacon, 2013.

Intra-Methodist Ecumenism?

The (Pan)Denominational Search for Methodistic Methodism

———————— Andrew J. Wood ————————

This chapter is a call for a renewal of "Intra-Methodist Ecumenism." Or, if one prefers, this ecumenism could be labeled "Pan-Methodist," "Pan-Wesleyan," or simply "Wesleyan." But, "Intra-Methodist" may be as good as any other label. There is a shared Wesleyan-Methodist tradition, comparable in its complexity and importance for Christian history with the Reformed tradition, for example.[1] But when specific denominational adherents to this shared Wesleyan-Methodist tradition speak of ecumenism, they most often have in mind conversations between Wesleyans and other religious groups. However appropriate these *extra*-Methodist conversations may be, they are seriously weakened by the sad state of ecumenical conversations *within* the Wesleyan-Methodist tradition. The state of Intra-Methodist ecumenism is tragically weak. But it is not only our extra-Methodist ecumenism that is weakened by our lack of Intra-Methodist ecumenism. So too, is our

———————————————————————

1. When we speak of the shared tradition in broad terms, we need not include "theological" as a modifier i.e., "Wesleyan theological tradition." In the same way we can speak of a "Reformed tradition," we can speak of a Wesleyan tradition or Methodist tradition. The addition of the modifier "theological" to refer to the shared tradition implies that we have nothing in common but theology. *Methodism is not a theological school of thought. It is a major Christian tradition.*

own understanding of what it means to be Wesleyan, what it means to be Methodist.

The search for a truly "Methodistic" Methodism is ongoing in the various denominations that make up this shared tradition. Calls for reform, revival and renewal abound.[2] It is, of course, a conversation that began early and can be found in every era and corner of Methodist history. But we are failing to benefit from one another because we are not having a shared conversation about what a "Methodistic" Methodism looks like as opposed to an "Unmethodistic" Methodism.

Before turning to specific examples of shared history and its potential to aid us in the present, a word about descriptive language is in order. "Methodist" or "Methodistic" are more accurate descriptors of this shared tradition in many cases than is the word "Wesleyan." The reason is simple: we have a general habit of using Wesleyan to refer to the life, thought and actions of John and/or Charles Wesley. Too often this results in obscuring the rich and expansive history of this tradition after 1791. The churches that owe their origin to Martin Luther are called Lutheran. The primary descriptor of those looking to Wesley has been Methodist (similarly, Calvin's followers belong to the Reformed tradition).[3] If we were to use the word Wesleyan in its more general sense to refer to the wider tradition—as many do—its use might be adequate for this task. But since so often it is used to mean "of John Wesley," whereas the use of "Methodist" does not normally denote a similar narrowing of geography or biography or chronology, "Intra-Methodist" seems the better terminology. "Wesleyan-Methodist" may be the most inclusive usage of all, since all the churches belonging to this tradition will readily claim at least one of these terms if not both.

Doctrine is one area where common identity is generally recognized among these churches. Many would also be open to the notion that there might be a shared ethical tradition, though the political aspects of that tradition (those having to do with the state) have, as yet, been grossly understudied. But it is in the area of polity that a shared tradition has been

---

2. Recent examples include Hunter, *The Recovery of a Contagious Methodist Movement*; Vickers, *Minding the Good Ground*; Kisker, *Mainline or Methodist?*; Matthews, *The Renewal of United Methodism*; Scott and Scott, *Restoring Methodism*; and Heath and Kisker, *Longing for Spring*.

3. Denominational titles alone suggest as much, as does the membership of the respective denominations since 1784. "Wesleyan" has been an important, though secondary, label for the tradition. In fact, more of these denominations carry the word "Episcopal" in their title than carry the word "Wesleyan."

tragically unacknowledged. For the purposes of this essay, we will include the seven churches based in the USA that have Methodist forms of polity and whose membership in the World Methodist Council indicates both Methodist identity and openness to intra-Methodist dialogue.[4]

Intra-Methodist Polity

The first task in this area is, quite simply, to recognize that there is a *shared Methodist tradition in polity*. The second task, having recognized that there is a Methodist tradition in polity, is to engage our fellow Wesleyans, our fellow Methodists, in two areas:

1. Intra-Methodist ecumenical conversations that entail discussions about this shared polity tradition. The aim here is a clearly ecumenical aim—to recognize, affirm, and appreciate our common heritage and mission.

2. Intra-Methodist ecumenical conversations that specifically enable us to hear one another's internal conversations about polity changes and denominational identity. The aim here is to aid each of our respective denominations in their task of pursuing faithfulness to Christ in the Wesleyan-Methodist tradition, i.e., to share information and perspectives that we all might be truer to "Methodistic" Methodism.

Polity and political debates are often claimed as key denominational markers *inside* denominations but rarely discussed in connection with other denominations, hence the need for "Intra-Methodist" ecumenism. If one were to attend Nazarene General Assemblies and United Methodist and AME General Conferences, many of the family resemblances and relationships

---

4. These seven churches are the United Methodist Church—representing mainline Methodism, the African Methodist Episcopal Church, African Methodist Episcopal Church, Zion, and the Christian Methodist Episcopal Church—each representing African American Methodism, and the Church of the Nazarene, Wesleyan Church, and Free Methodist Church—each representing holiness Methodism. Many other churches might have been included that have claims to membership in the wider tradition (e.g., The Salvation Army, The Church of God, Anderson, the Congregational Methodist Church), but these churches are not in scope here because while they are Wesleyan in their theology they do not have polities that fit the wider mold, nor are they members of the World Methodist Council. For those two reasons, they made less sense in a chapter that is not about *pan-holiness theological* ecumenism (with the Wesleyan Theological Society as an institutional example) but about *pan-Methodist polity* ecumenism (with the World Methodist Council as an institutional example).

would be readily apparent. Some of them have to do with doctrine. Many of them have to do with polity (or if preferred, decision-making and mission) and politics (or if preferred, social ethics). We have far more in common than John's sermons and Charles' hymns, largely because we share a history that extends far beyond the year 1791. Much of this common ground was forged in the American context in the great mass of Methodist history that happened between John's death in 1791 and Albert Outler's kick-starting of "Wesley Studies" in 1964.[5]

If we include polity, we might more readily see what is Wesleyan or "Methodistic" about Nazarenes, the United Methodist Church, the AME Church, etc. Without discussing polity, we will continue to struggle separately to come to terms with what we should do with the various organizational and missional proposals that come to our churches every four years.

There are common core themes of Methodist identity among the seven major Methodist denominations in the USA: United Methodist, AME, Nazarene, AMEZ, Wesleyan, CME and Free Methodist. Each is self-consciously Wesleyan and each makes frequent claims internally about what it means to be truly Wesleyan or Methodist, but rarely have those internal discussions been shared with others inside the wider tradition. The argument here is for a greater recognition of shared identity and history with the additional call to students of each of these traditions and theologians working out of them to take this shared identity and history more seriously. The aim is to bring these intra-denominational conversations to an Intra-Methodist ecumenical table.

The great weakness in Intra-Methodist discussions has been the lack of recognition of common ground in polity, and this has weakened each denomination's attempts at the renewal and refreshing of their mission and ministry. This also inhibits the ability of these bodies to understand and appropriate their shared pasts. Our understanding of past polity discussions, including those with strong ethical implications, are undermined because we interpret them through the lenses of Wesleyan doctrine alone. Polity has

---

5. Of the seven denominations most commonly included in lists of American churches with ties to the Wesleyan-Methodist tradition, only the United Methodist Church claims a starting date before 1791 (1784). The dates of origin for the AME, AMEZ, Wesleyans and Free Methodists are before the American Civil War. The dates for the CME and Church of the Nazarene are after that war, but the latest is 1908 (Nazarenes). All seven of these denominations are members of the World Methodist Council. The largest three—UMC, AME and Nazarene, in that order—are representative of the three broad wings of this tradition in the USA (Mainline, African American, and Holiness).

its own theological implications that are not easily understood by appeals to a Wesleyan quadrilateral, "social/personal holiness," or prevenient grace.

When asked what it meant to be a Methodist, our forebears consistently included polity in their answer.[6] If you asked that question of budding Wesleyan clergy today, far too few would be able to provide any affirmative, much less distinctive, notions about Methodist polity in their answer. Few would argue that John Wesley was disinterested in the question of how we should organize ourselves for mission and ministry in the world. But his descendants of late have largely divorced those questions from any notion of what it means to be a Wesleyan. Thus, polity questions are treated as merely practical, pragmatic, or fiscal issues entirely without reference to what is a rich historic tradition of pan-Methodist or pan-Wesleyan polity.

Polity is not just how we are organized however. It is also about how we will make decisions and solve problems, and perhaps more pointedly, how we will go about arguing and debating with each other. Taken in this way, its practical theological implications are readily apparent. So too is the large scale failure of the denominations in this tradition to think together in meaningful ways about these issues. Each denomination handles its own polity debates without reference to shared tradition, even while the term "Wesleyan" is taken only as a descriptor of doctrine or social ethics. It has been difficult for us to apply the lessons of polity histories that we do not know. We are leaving wisdom unapplied.

Who We Are

Methodists are heirs to a rich tradition. The tradition has many elements and influences. It has been shaped by so many interrelated streams that it can fairly be called evangelical, Protestant, pietistic, Anglican, and revivalistic.

Methodism is also a deeply idealistic tradition. Methodists inherited the "tripartite division of history" from the Protestant Reformation, which was itself influenced by the Renaissance. This idea of history divides the past—or a particular past—into three parts. The first is an ancient or older "golden age," when someone "had it right," when in the judgment of those

---

6. For examples of earlier primers that addressed polity distinctives in considerable depth, one representing a predecessor denomination of the United Methodist Church, the other the AME Church, see Hudson, *The Methodist Armor*; and Turner, *The Genius and Theory of Methodist Polity*. Both texts went through many revisions.

in later times, an ideal was faithfully and truly embodied in time and place. The second is a middle age of decline from the high ideals and achievements of the ancient golden age. The third era is a modern or current period of revival and reform by means of appreciating, recovering and appropriating salient features of the golden age. For Luther and most Protestants after him, including Wesley, the ancient golden age was the age of the Apostles and the Holy Bible, i.e., "primitive Christianity." The Puritans, one historian wrote, were endeavoring to "live ancient lives."[7] This division of history is evident throughout Western societies, originating first in the Old Testament prophets but now to be found in modern advertising, e.g., the marketing use of "classic" or "vintage."

But for many, there is a dual idealism at work here. Lutherans look to Luther while also looking to the scriptures. Methodists too have not just looked to the scriptures and apostolic age but to what many have called "primitive Methodism"—to include the Wesleys but also the age of Francis Asbury in the "golden age" of Methodist origins. For many, Methodist faith during the lifetimes of John and Charles Wesley, Francis Asbury and Richard Allen remains the idealistic heart of the tradition. That dual idealism between scriptural and Methodist origins has encouraged Methodists' ongoing and often aggressive reform efforts. Methodists have, on the whole, been a restless bunch. Our shared tradition of reforming, idealistic zeal places particular pressures on questions of polity. How will we decide what should be done? How will we handle disagreement and dissent among us? Once decided, how will we sustain and accomplish our mission together?

To Serve the Present Age

Why Intra-Methodist Ecumenism?

If the divisions of Christianity are scandalous, as many think they are, one might reasonably ask what proper steps can be taken to overcome them? Or, at the least, how might we move toward greater cooperation and affirmation of fellow Christians? It seems clear that the answer to these questions cannot be at the meta level of Protestant-Catholic-Orthodox discussion, but rather where most divisions exist within Christianity and where the greatest immediate potential for recovering common cause exists—within the various Christian traditions. The assumption of this essay

7. Bozeman, *To Live Ancient Lives.*

is that ecumenical conversations need to start with *near* neighbors, *within* the Methodist tradition first. Further, it seems the case that while the gulf between the AME Zion Church and the Roman Catholic Church may be greater, the history of recent tensions and hard feelings is much greater within the Methodist fold. We might have a long list of reasons why the Roman Catholics and United Methodists will not unite, but do we really have a long list of *good* reasons why the Wesleyans and Nazarenes will not?

Why Polity? Who Cares about Polity Anyway?

One classic history of Methodism in America was titled *Organizing to Beat the Devil*.[8] Polity delineates the process for how decisions are made (and who will be involved in making those decisions). Polity is how visions are enacted and furthered. Polity is how doctrine is spread, changed, and reinterpreted. Polity is the means through which renewal and revitalization will come, if not for individuals certainly for larger groups like denominations. All of these denominations in view have strong notions and practices of *connectionalism*. In many respects, connectionalism is largely a synonym for "Methodist polity." We are bound together. We are connected. We cooperate and thus do more together than we would ever do apart. We embrace a vision of organizing ourselves for ministry that attempts to embody Psalm 133: "How good and pleasant it is when God's people live together in unity . . . for there the LORD bestows his blessing." For a tradition so steeped in connectionalism, our ecumenical failure with each other is especially discouraging. Again, our common ground is *cooperation and connection*. And yet because we ignore polity in our conversations, we never arrive at the core Methodist practices of connection *with each other*. Our theological discussions do not achieve missional aims because we are ignoring missional means (polity). To state it another way, Intra-Methodist ecumenical relations are lacking in graciousness because we fail to engage one another in the means of grace.

Affirming that we Wesleyans believe in prevenient grace is well and good. But once we turn to the question, "What would it mean for us to be a connection shaped by a belief in God's prevenient grace?" we have moved squarely into the realm of polity, into the realm of decision making, prioritizing, institutional will, and missional focus. And make no mistake, if Methodists do not get to polity, they have left vital work undone. Methodists

8. Ferguson, *Organizing to Beat the Devil*.

have long understood themselves to be responsible, not just for having the right opinion of or theory about this or that religious, social, moral or political issue but also for doing something about it. For Methodists, doctrine and ethics must be translated into polity, mission, and action. We have revived "Wesley Studies." We have elevated "Wesleyan Theology." But where is Wesley's *revival*? Polity is the step between theology that deserves the name Wesleyan and the *vital piety* that deserves the name Methodist. Without practicing polity, our ugly divisions will remain unaddressed and unresolved. Let spreading scriptural holiness begin within and among the Methodist tradition. Let Methodists from the various denominations conference with one another.

How to Begin?

We need a gathering aimed at thinking through the common polity ground we share. This gathering must be broadly representative and should aim at three goals. First, we must affirm what we have in common in terms of organization, historically and presently. We must recognize common elements of mission. Second, we must affirm why we are organized as we are and what theological, ethical, and missional aims are or were in view in our organizational decisions. From this we will recognize common priorities and values. Third, we must begin to pray with each other and especially *for each other*. How often have you heard a United Methodist pray for the Church of the Nazarene or a Nazarene pray for the United Methodist Church? If confessions and reconciliations follow all will be better for it. If opportunities for organic union, greater cooperation, or simply warmer relations result, we will have achieved something worth achieving. Blessed is the peacemaker.[9]

Basic Features of Methodist Polity

There are many shared elements of Methodist polity. The following are generally held in common among most of the churches in the tradition.

---

9. This gathering should include official denominational representatives, historians, polity experts, district superintendents/presiding elders, clergy and laity from the seven denominations.

1. In broad terms, Methodist churches have three levels or layers of polity: the local (e.g., congregational), the regional (e.g., district, conference, and in many cases a layer beyond that, the region/jurisdiction/episcopal district), and the general (i.e., denomination-wide).

2. General Superintendents/Bishops

   A. Bishops are elders who are consecrated to the ministry of general superintendency. In most Methodist usage, "general superintendent" and "bishop" are synonyms.

   B. Methodists have itinerant general superintendency, not diocesan episcopacy. That is, Methodists elect persons to preside over the whole of the church/connection, i.e., "general," and expect them to travel throughout the church/connection, i.e., "itinerant." We do not elect persons from an area to serve only in that area.[10] Methodist notions of episcopacy are distinct, then, from other traditions that have episcopacy.

   C. Methodists have not usually claimed apostolic succession as a supportive theory for Methodist general superintendency. Most deny it.[11]

   D. For most of these churches and for most of Methodist history, bishops/general superintendents were elected by the General Conference/Assembly. That habit was maintained in mainline Methodism until the 1939 merger when jurisdictional episcopacy was introduced as a mechanism to achieve union. Most Methodist churches have largely stayed with the itinerant general superintendency theory of episcopacy inherited from pre-1939 mainline Methodism.

3. District Superintendents/Presiding Elders

4. General Conferences/Assemblies that meet on a quadrennial basis

5. Annual Conferences/Districts/District Assemblies meeting annually

10. The possible exception to this is the United Methodist practice since the 1939 merger of electing bishops by jurisdiction who preside within that jurisdiction, a radical departure from previous MEC and MECS practice. Still, the principle of itinerant general superintendency remains within the UMC and bishops still itinerate among conferences within a jurisdiction.

11. Hillary Hudson called apostolic succession, "The dogma on the strength of which High-Churchmen disfranchise non-episcopal Churches of their Christian birthrights." Hudson, *The Methodist Armor* (1889 ed.), 21.

6. The Methodist tradition has a ministry, not a priesthood

7. Methodists do not make the same claims about their polity that most other Christian traditions do. Unlike the Baptists, Catholics, Episcopalians, Presbyterians, etc., we do not claim that our polity is *the* scriptural or *the* apostolic way. We have claimed that this form of organizing ourselves for mission and ministry seemed wise and that God has blessed through it.[12]

8. Tensions between strong episcopal leadership and "preacher's rights." Throughout the Methodist churches that tend to exercise stronger episcopal leadership, there have been consistent tensions between bishops and the preachers. From a certain perspective, this might be seen to be a natural tension between a strong, coherent executive power and democratic and/or representative government. Perhaps, too, this is a Methodist version of "which came first, the chicken or the egg?" Did Wesley as bishop/general superintendent call together preachers to follow him (thus, episcopacy came first) or did a group of preachers select Wesley to provide leadership (thus, conference/the preachers came first)?

9. Denominational ownership of local church property.

10. The principles and practices of connectionalism. Methodists cooperate, confer, connect. Mission and ministry are not solitary and localized in our tradition.[13]

---

12. In his 1885 primer on Methodist polity, Bishop Henry McNeil Turner of the AME Church asked the question "20 Q. What form of Church Government does the Bible prescribe?" His answer: "A. None whatever. Dr. Bangs says, 'No specific form of church government is prescribed in the Scriptures, and therefore it is left to the discretion of the church to regulate these matters as the exigencies of time, place and circumstances shall dictate to be most expedient, and likely to accomplish the most good, always avoiding any and everything which God has forbidden.' Bishop Tomline and Mr. Watson say the same. The Bible is a mere Code of sacred principles and virtues, which may be fermented by prayer and faith in God, and appropriated to our eternal salvation; but the mode of their application is left to the highest and purest judgment of the Church."

13. For another overview of Methodists' common ground in polity, see Koskela, "Discipline and Polity," 156–170. See also, Woodruff Tait, "'Everything Arose Just as the Occasion Offered,'" 95–119.

Nazarenes as a Test Case/Example

Six of the seven churches that are clearly part of the tradition in the US have either Wesleyan or Methodist in their names. The sole exception is the Church of the Nazarene. Nazarenes are also the youngest of theses churches. They are least likely to utilize the word "Methodist" as an affirmative term applied to their own denominational identity. They are the church that has the largest number of non-Methodists among their founders, in part, because the Church of the Nazarene was an ecumenical merger movement among those who had already left other churches, not a direct split from mainline Methodism. Compared to the UMC, AME, AMEZ, CME, Wesleyans, and Free Methodists, Nazarenes appear to be the least "Methodist" of these churches. Some might even say Nazarenes are "related to" Methodism, but not *Methodist*. Early Nazarene leader C. W. Ruth wrote in 1903 that "The Church of the Nazarene is nothing in the world but old-fashioned Methodism, with a congregational form of government." [14] But, with respects to C. W. Ruth, this is actually quite misleading.

When it comes to Nazarene denominational identity, Nazarenes have two habits that obscure their Methodist polity lineage. First, Nazarenes have preferred to label themselves a "Holiness" or "Wesleyan-Holiness" church and have most often done this precisely to distinguish themselves from mainline Methodism that rejected the emphases of the holiness movement. Nazarenes have had a strained relationship with mainline Methodism, and much of Nazarene internal identity shaping has worked itself out specifically *in comparison to* "Methodism." Second, Nazarenes have long characterized their polity as a blend of "episcopal" and congregational elements. This is imprecise. Nazarene polity has strong congregational elements at the local level. But what Nazarenes call "episcopal" is, in fact, a Methodist polity or perhaps more specifically, the polity of what was called "Episcopal Methodism" (the polity of the Methodist Episcopal Church, 1784–1939, and Methodist Episcopal Church, South 1844–1939).

On each of the points of common Methodist polity above, Nazarenes fit the Methodist model. The Church of the Nazarene, in its doctrine and in its polity, is *a dissenting church within the Methodist tradition*. In this, it has common ground with the other Methodist denominations save the United Methodist Church. The African American Methodist churches

---

14. Ingersol, "Methodism and the Theological Identity of the Church of the Nazarene," 17–32.

and the Holiness churches are all dissenting churches within the tradition. The Holiness churches have common (and largely unexplored) dissenters' ground with the African American Methodist churches as fellow dissenting churches within the Methodist tradition/family. There is a long history of intra-Methodist dissent, marked not only by the debates within mainline Methodism but also the list of churches that have "come out" of mainline Methodism and frequently did so with the aim to be more "Methodist" than the mainline Methodists were. The claim of showing greater fealty to "primitive Methodism" than mainline Methodism showed is a common feature of each dissenting church in the tradition.

We see this clearly in leading early Nazarene General Superintendent Phineas F. Bresee and the first editor of the Nazarenes' *Herald of Holiness*, B. F. Haynes. Bresee and Haynes did not reject "Methodism." From 1857 to 1894, Bresee was a minister in the Methodist Episcopal Church (37 years). From 1873 to 1911, Haynes was a minister in the Methodist Episcopal Church, South (38 years). Rather than rejecting "Methodism," they believed that the Church of the Nazarene was to be what mainline Methodism said it was, and had been, but was no longer. Nazarene origins are best located in disagreements that were *internal* to Methodism. If Nazarenes by the 1910s could no longer affirm the main thrust of mainline Methodism in America, they could still find historical and current models of piety within it. Beyond John and Charles Wesley, few would have doubted the piety of Bishop Francis Asbury, E. M. Bounds, or E. Stanley Jones who lived and died as Methodists. And Nazarenes then, and now, have known *and have worked with*, dissenting Methodists who remained within the mainline Methodist world. It is ironic then, with early Nazarenes setting out to be *more "Methodistic"* than the mainline Methodists were, that more recent Nazarenes often decline to understand themselves as members of the broad Methodist family.

Nazarene dissent from mainline Methodism was not just about doctrine and ethical matters. There was a polity element too. Nazarenes are basically Methodistic in polity but decidedly more "free church" and democratic in sentiment and culture.[15] Far from being unique to Nazarenes, this "democratic" Methodism fits many of the dissenting groups in Methodist history that modified their polity to be more open or representative and less "autocratic" than mainline Methodism (e.g., the Methodist

15. Stan Ingersol has argued that instead of "free church," a more accurate description is that Nazarenes are a "believer's church," a model of ecclesiology that has much in common with various American denominations within and outside the Methodist tradition.

Protestant Church, Wesleyans, Free Methodists, and even the Evangelical United Brethren).[16] This difference usually centered on having a weaker episcopacy. Mainline Methodism has elected its bishops for life; Nazarene General Superintendents serve terms, face re-election, and have age limits to their service, each being a free church and democratic amendment to what is basically Methodist polity. Evidencing a common—if unacknowledged—conversation, each of these amendments were proposed as changes to *United Methodist episcopacy* at the 2012 United Methodist General Conference in Tampa, Florida.

Early Nazarenes were attempting to recreate the best features of "primitive" or early Methodism—attempting to reestablish and expand a *more "Methodistic" Methodism*. But again, this is not unique. Methodism has a long tradition of folks who feared that Methodists were declining in spiritual power, had lost their way and needed to get back to the piety of their former days. Those folks in Methodist history are called "croakers." Nazarenes are inheritors of the "croaker" tradition. Once again, Nazarenes are not unique. They are just some of many in the tradition who at various times have argued that Methodists (or particular Methodists) have lost their way and need to get back to the piety of former days. This is a family resemblance of Methodism (and, in broad terms, Protestantism generally).[17]

All the Methodist churches have "croakerism" in their blood. We are idealists. We want a holy church. We want our church to be all it should be. Further, it is not the case that Methodists start arguing with themselves only after decline has set in. United Methodists in particular have endured almost a half century of membership decline. But their Methodist forebears were arguing vigorously with themselves during the 19th century when Methodism grew rapidly and spread itself around the world! Nazarene idealism—some might say perfectionism—is not a special feature of the holiness wing of the tradition. The entire Methodist tradition has deep roots in croaker idealism influenced by a tripartite view of history. This continuous push to reform ourselves for faithful ministry in the world by reference to an inspiring past characterizes all of the churches in the Methodist tradition. It is Methodism searching to be a more "Methodistic" Methodism. Though that push has often occasioned our divisions into different denominations,

16. For polity in the E.U.B. tradition and its differences with mainline Methodism, see Kirby, "Episcopacy and Ordination," 139–49.

17. For an excellent discussion of Methodist "croakerism" and its similarities and differences with the Puritans' earlier jeremiads, see Wigger, *Taking Heaven By Storm*, especially chapter 8 "Methodism Transformed," 173–95.

and the tensions *within* our denominations, the impulse itself is *common* ground. Because of this common search for faithful solutions to the various trials our connections face, we have an opportunity to pray for each other and learn from one another's successes and mistakes. Proposals for reform and renewal of mission and identity abound in all of our churches. Could we not, should we not, confer *together*?

Bibliography

Bearden, Harold I., ed. *African Methodist Episcopal Church Polity.* Nashville: AMEC Sunday School Union, 1984.

Buckley, James M. *Constitutional and Parliamentary History of the Methodist Episcopal Church.* New York: Eaton & Mains, 1912.

Frank, Thomas J. *Polity, Practice, and the Mission of the United Methodist Church.* Nashville: Abingdon, 2006.

Harmon, Nolan B. *The Organization of the Methodist Church.* 2nd rev. ed. Nashville: United Methodist Publishing House, 1962.

Hudson, Hillary T. *The Methodist Armor: Or, A Popular Exposition of the Doctrines, Peculiar Usages, and Ecclesiastical Machinery of the Methodist Episcopal Church, South.* Nashville: Publishing House of the M. E. Church, South, 1882.

Ingersol, Stan. "Methodism and the Theological Identity of the Church of the Nazarene." *Methodist History* 43 (2004) 17–32.

Ingersol, Stan, and Wesley D. Tracy. *Here We Stand: Where Nazarenes Fit in the Religious Marketplace.* Kansas City: Beacon Hill, 1999.

Kirby, James E. *Episcopacy in American Methodism.* Nashville: Kingswood, 2000.

Koskela, Douglas M. "Discipline and Polity." in *The Cambridge Companion to American Methodism,* edited by Jason E. Vickers, 156–70. New York: Cambridge University Press, 2013.

Lakey, Othal Hawthorne. *The History of the CME Church.* Rev. ed. Memphis: CME Publishing House, 1997.

Stevens, Abel. *An Essay on Church Polity: Comprehending an Outline of the Controversy on Ecclesiastical Government, and a Vindication of the Ecclesiastical System of the Methodist Episcopal Church.* New York: Lane & Tippett for the MEC, 1845. 10 revised editions through 1870.

Tigert, John J. *Constitutional History of American Episcopal Methodism.* 6th ed. Nashville: Parthenon, 1996. Reprint of the 1916 edition.

Tuell, Jack M. *The Organization of the United Methodist Church.* Nashville: Abingdon, 2009.

Turner, Henry McNeal. *The Genius and Theory of Methodist Polity; Or, The Machinery of Methodism, Practically Illustrated Through a Series of Questions and Answers.* Philadelphia: Publication Department, A.M.E. Church, 1885.

Woodruff Tait, Jennifer L. "'Everything Arose Just as the Occasion Offered': Defining Methodist History through the History of Methodist Polity." In *American Denominational History,* edited by Keith Harper, 95–119. Tuscaloosa: University of Alabama Press, 2008.

Resisting Race

John Wesley's Championing of Universal Human Dignity

———————— Tamara E. Lewis ————————

O n Thursday evening, March 6, 1788, John Wesley preached a service at the New Room on Broadmead Street in Bristol, England on slavery. Since notice of the sermon topic had been publicized two days earlier, the house was packed. Wesley records,

> I preached on that ancient prophecy, "God shall enlarge Japhet. And he shall dwell in the tents of Shem; and Canaan shall be his servant." About the Middle of the discourse, while there was on every side attention still as night, a vehement noise arose, none could tell why, and shot like lightening through the whole congregation. The terror and confusion were inexpressible. You might have imagined it was a city taken by storm. The people rushed upon each other with the utmost violence; the benches were broke in pieces; and nine-tenths of the congregation appeared to be struck with the same panic. In about six minutes the storm ceased, almost as suddenly as it rose; and, all being calm, I went on without the least interruption.[1]

Why would listeners react in such a dramatic manner? Wesley himself attributed the disturbance to "some preternatural influence." Allowing for

---

1. Diary entry for Monday, March 3, 1788 (Wesley, *Journal*, 7:359).

spiritual forces, what other factors could have stimulated the crowd to react so violently? Did the controversial subject, advertised previously, along with Wesley's unapologetic posture, prick the consciences of some hearers? Bristol was a large slave port, and the coming and goings of shackled human beings bought and sold at auction certainly must have added to the electrically charged setting. Perhaps there were slaves and even owners, sitting in the audience. By the 1780s, Wesley had made a name for himself as the first great antislavery religious leader. Although the slavery question was indeed disputatious, there was biblical warrant for the practice. Why was the existence of the transatlantic slave trade and chattel bondage, both demonstrably lucrative enterprises for Britain's growing eighteenth-century economy, such an explosive matter in this particular setting?

Inherent within the rise of West European transatlantic slavery had been the belief in black African inferiority, used to defend modern chattel human bondage. Propagation of the idea of black inferiority birthed the concept of race, a distinctive element separating the institution of modern slavery from its earlier practices throughout history. The juxtaposition of the race construction as integral to slavery greatly fueled the severe and agonized feelings on both sides of the issue, particularly in religious communities. Wesley's experience reflects this intensity. Further, although Wesley's antislavery position is evident, it is less known that he also specifically attacked racial ideologies used to justify transatlantic slavery. This essay analyzes Wesley's rebuke of the burgeoning dogmatism of race in his antislavery campaign.

Irv Brendlinger's documentary study of John Wesley's antislavery journey provides much needed detailed analysis of the position most historiographers tend to generalize in biographies of Wesley. By describing the evolution of Wesley's stance from the beginning of his ministry to his latter years as an abolitionist, Brendlinger improves upon Warren Thomas Smith's study, which presents a broad biographical treatment related to the theme of slavery. Yet, even closer analysis of the larger part of Wesley's life reveals that while he never actively supported the slave trade or slavery, Wesley remained inactive in the abolitionist cause until his later years. However, Wesley does indicate great sympathy for the plight of slaves and provides resources to many on a number of occasions. Based on his journal notes, Wesley read at least two important publications related to slavery during his younger years in ministry. The first was a play based on the important original work *Oroonoko,* by Aphra Behn.[2] *Oroonoko* is a story about a slave uprising in Surinam, and concentrates on the theme of African nobility rather than the injustice of slavery.[3] Wesley does not specifically record his reactions to this text. Neither does Wesley indicate a detailed response to his reading of another relevant work on slavery, Morgan Godwyn's *The Negro and Indian's Advocate, suing for their admission into the church* (1680). Wesley read this second text during his missionary stay in Georgia.[4] An interesting parallel can be drawn comparing the themes of these two works to Wesley's approach to ministry with slaves. Godwyn, an Anglican pastor, wrote during the seventeenth century and advocated for the inclusion of slaves in the ministry of the newly formed Society for the Propagation of the Gospel in Foreign Parts.[5] Godwyn, however, was not an abolitionist.[6] Similarly, Behn also wrote during the seventeenth century. It is likely that Wesley was swayed by these readings not to challenge slavery directly. Although there is evidence that he, along with his brother Charles protested the campaign to transform Georgia into a slave colony, neither actively promoted the cause of abolition during their stay in America.[7] Instead, John concentrated on the development of a catechetical system for the religious instruction of slaves.[8]

2. The year after his ordination as deacon Wesley read a play entitled *Oroonoko, or the Royal Slave* by Thomas Southerne (1696), based on Aphra Behn's novel, *Oroonoko* (1688) the story of an African prince who started a slave rebellion after being kidnapped and sold into slavery. Aphra Behn is considered to be the first English woman author.

3. See Molineux, *Faces of Perfect Ebony,* 180.

4. Brendlinger, *Social Justice,* 16. See also Wesley, *Works* (Bicentennial), 18:410.

5. Lewis, "'To Wash a Blackamoor White,'" 64. John and Charles Wesley would later travel under the auspices of the SPG in their ministry to Georgia.

6. This was due to a widespread fear of manumission that was later addressed by colonial statutes that specified that conversion to Christianity did not result in freedom. Christian ministers often had to deemphasize that their work with slaves was to obtain their physical liberation.

7. Charles Wesley's journal entry for August 2, 1736 is a detailed account of his growing knowledge of the cruelty and practices of slave masters as well as the overall injustice of slavery. See C. Wesley, *Journal,* 1:36–37. At the time of Wesley's stay in America, since Georgia was not yet a slave colony, his encounters with blacks took place during his visits to nearby South Carolina. See also Wesley, *Works* (Bicentennial), 18:169. John and Charles Wesley vigorously opposed the Georgia trustees in favor of changing the colony to a slave-holding area. They supported General James Oglethorpe, who initially enforced the policy of not allowing slavery in Georgia. See Wesley, *Journal,* 7:244, 255. In 1740, two years after John left America, slavery became permitted in Georgia.

8. See Smith, *John Wesley,* 47.

After his return to England, Wesley did not actively fight against slavery or the slave trade during the next thirty-four years. He did however, demonstrate general disgust for the slave trade as well as sympathy for and support of blacks in slavery. In his diary dated Sunday, June 29, 1740, at Moorfields, Wesley records that he "collected for the Negro school."[9] Most likely this was the Virginia school led by Samuel Davies, Presbyterian preacher, leader of the First Great Awakening, and later president of Princeton.[10] Davies, like Jonathan Edwards, was not opposed to slavery, but did support the evangelism of slaves. Wesley corresponded with Davies "between 1755 and 1757 [and]... sent books (hymns and psalms) to be given to slaves."[11] Moreover, in order to make the Methodist preachers knowledgeable about the campaign for slave evangelism, Wesley published Davies' letters in his *Journal*.[12] Wesley's disgust with slavery is evident in his 1756 writing *Explanatory Notes Upon the New* Testament, in which he excoriates the "Traders in Negroes, Procurers of Servants for America."[13] However, his ambivalence is also revealed in 1758. Wesley records having preached a service at the home of Nathaniel Gilbert, a slave owner. Two of Gilbert's slaves were in attendance. After their conversion, Wesley returned several months later to Gilbert's home to baptize them.[14] Surprisingly, Wesley does not express protestation regarding their enslaved condition.[15] Another indication of Wesley's somewhat hesitant position on abolition prior to the 1770s is his relationship with John Newton.[16] From 1765 to 1769, Wesley regularly corresponded with Newton about their respective publications and theology. However, there is no mention of slavery.[17] In fact, Newton did not officially repent for his slave trading past until the publication of

9. *Works* (Bicentennial), 19:435. See also Richards, "Samuel Davies and the Transatlantic Campaign," 111.

10. Brendlinger, *Social Justice*, 18.

11. Ibid.

12. Ibid.

13. Wesley, *Explanatory Notes*, 558.

14. Wesley, *Works* (Jackson), 2:433, 464.

15. In 1790, Wesley quoted in the *Arminian Magazine* the experience of a slave named Samuel Paynter, a slave ironically converted under Nathaniel Gilbert (who himself became a Methodist preacher). Paynter worked to purchase his own freedom, but his family continued to be enslaved. [*The Arminian Magazine* XIII, 307–309].

16. John Newton was the great hymn writer (*Amazing Grace*) and evangelical Anglican priest.

17. Smith, *John Wesley*, 69.

Thoughts Upon the Slave Trade (1788), fourteen years after the dissemination of Wesley's own tract *Thoughts Upon Slavery* (1774). Further, Newton (unlike Wesley) never became a full-fledged abolitionist.[18] Although Newton was influential in the campaign to eradicate the slave trade, in actuality, he never totally opposed slavery itself.[19] This is an important distinction to consider in evaluating contemporary abolitionists. Later Wesley would always oppose the trade as well as slavery itself.[20]

By 1772, Wesley's consciousness had been dramatically intensified regarding slavery. Since he wrote directly to Granville Sharp, the prominent English abolitionist, it is likely that the highly publicized Somerset case attacking slavery had peaked Wesley's interest.[21] Sharp supplied Wesley with pertinent reading materials. These included writings by Anthony Benezet, an antislavery activist Quaker from Philadelphia, and materials from Sharp himself.[22] The tracts, particularly the sources from Benezet and Sharp as well as other legal activists like Francis Hargrave, and possibly William Blackstone, influenced Wesley immensely. From that time on, Wesley began to take a very active and visible role in the antislavery movement. As Robert William Fogel's study demonstrates, Wesley would have a significant impact.[23] The extremely influential antislavery tract *Thoughts Upon Slavery* (1774) solidified Wesley's reputation as a great antislavery activist.

---

18. A common misperception is that John Newton's Christian conversion corresponded with his active renunciation of slave trading. Instead, according to his *Narrative,* Newton worked on slave ships in the trade for several years after his Christian conversion. He even served as captain of slave ships as a converted evangelical Christian. For Newton's views see his "Thoughts Upon the African Slave Trade" bound with his *Journal of a Slave Trader 1750–1754.*

19. Brendlinger, *Social Justice*, 46.

20. Ibid.

21. Granville Sharp was the primary activist in England who influenced the landmark court decisions, which made slavery illegal in the country of England. Sharp led the 1769 Jonathan Strong case, publishing the research as *A Representation of the Injustice and Dangerous Tendency of Tolerating Slavery in England*; Sharp was also active in landmark Somerset case of 1772, the most famous slavery case of England. Francis Hargrave, another litigation activist, wrote *An Argument in the Case of James Sommersett, a Negro.* Wesley read both of these works and editorialized these sources in *Thoughts Upon Slavery* (1774).

22. Wesley probably read Benezet's *Historical Account of Guinea*; *A Caution and Warning to Great Britain*; and *A Short Account of that Part of Africa Inhabited by the Negroes.* See Brendlinger, *To Be Silent.*

23. Fogel, *Without Consent or Contract.*

[24] Moreover, as Wesley increased in age, the more energetically he fought against slavery. His 1775 *A Calm Address to Our American Colonies* goes on to specifically criticize slavery in America, attacking what he perceives as the hypocrisy of the Americans' protests of "slavery" against Britain while at the same time holding Africans and others in bondage.[25] The following year, he wrote *A Seasonable Address to the More Serious Part of the Inhabitants of Great Britain,* which in turn castigates the British for slavery. Wesley would continue to complain bitterly about slavery in the 1778 *Serious Address to the People of England with Regard to the State of the Nation.* He even used the *Arminian Magazine* as a platform to promote the antislavery cause, publishing liberation stories of slaves as well as background histories of the slave trade.[26] Wesley also went on to endorse and support the 1787 *Society Instituted for Effecting the Abolition of the Slave Trade,* which was organized to influence Parliament to end slavery.[27] And since the mid-1770s, John had been working along with brother Charles to help liberate various Africans from slavery in England.[28] Of course, the last letter of Wesley's life, written from his deathbed, encouraged William Wilberforce, the Member of Parliament who had emerged as a tireless fighter of the slave trade in the House of Commons.[29]

Wesley continually stressed the equality of Africans in his antislavery campaign. This indicates his awareness that a contributing factor to the growth of slavery was the burgeoning racist perception of blacks in mainstream society. As Wesley writes, "Certainly the African is in no respect inferior to the European."[30] While many were advocating the inferior spiritual and physical natures of Africans, Wesley continually stressed their

24. See Baker, "The Origins," 79.

25. Ibid., 34

26. *The Arminian Magazine* for July and August of 1788 carried Wesley's "A summary View of the Slave Trade."

27. Granville Sharp refused to join the Society because it decided to concentrate on ending the slave trade, not slavery. Sharp felt this was a compromise.

28. From 1773 to 1774 John along with his brother Charles ministered to two captured slaves in England and helped them gain their freedom through a warrant from Lord Mansfield (the same judge in the Somerset case). Their story was shared in *The Arminian Magazine* VI (1783), 98–99, 151–53, 211–12.

29. Wilberforce repeatedly brought resolutions to Parliament in order to suspend the trade for over twenty years beginning in the 1790s until the passage of the Slave Trade Act of 1807. See Furneaux, *William Wilberforce.*

30. Wesley, *Works* (Jackson), 11:70.

humanity and dignity. His journal notes indicate that Africans were regular members of the Methodist societies in England.[31] He writes in particular of a May 7, 1780 encounter with a black woman at the Whitehaven society who "semed [sic] to be fuller of love than any of the rest . . . [with] words . . . chosen and utter with a peculiar prosperity."[32] Wesley also used print media to showcase the superior gifts and talents of Africans. In 1781, *The Arminian Magazine* began publishing extracts of the work of the celebrated American poet Phyllis Wheatley. Thus, Wesley directly assailed the racism used against Africans to justify slavery during the eighteenth century.[33] Contrary to the view that "racism was not yet part of the English or American culture when Wesley was first exposed to slavery" and that only at the end of Wesley's life were "physical characteristics of people. . . associated with their way of life and culture," Wesley's intellectual confrontations with black prejudice indicates the pervasiveness of racist ideology.[34] Ideas of black inferiority, based on "the belief that Africans [are] not really men," were disseminated as early as the sixteenth century. These views were simply less evolved manifestations of the Enlightenment-era biological and scientific taxonomies used in subsequent centuries to supposedly prove racial difference.[35] The following analyzes aspects of Wesley's confrontation with ideologies of racial difference.

The origins of the English version of Hamitic curse can be traced to the sixteenth century. In 1577, the sea captain George Best wanted to encourage English settlement and habitation in North America. Therefore, he wrote a fictive story based on Gen 9. In the biblical text, Noah is naked and passed out from wine. After being disrespected by his son Ham, Noah wakes and curses Ham's son Canaan, saying, "Cursed be Canaan, lowest of slaves shall he be to his brothers" (Gen 9:25). According to Best's rendition of the story, Noah commanded that he, his sons, and their wives remain continent on the Ark. When Noah's son Ham disobeyed, "God would a sonne shuld be borne, whose name was Chus."[36] According to the Table of Nations, Chus is the old-

---

31. On Sunday, May 7, 1780, Wesley talks about a meeting a black woman at the Whitehaven society who had faith stronger than he had ever discerned in England or America. On Friday March 10, 1786, Wesley also records that he baptized a "young negro" in the Bristol area who was part of the congregation. Wesley, *Journal*, 7:144.

32. Wesley, *Journal*, 6:277–78.

33. Brendlinger, *Social Justice*, 64.

34. Ibid. See Long, *The History of Jamaica*.

35. Cf. Fryer, *Staying Power*, 143.

36. Best, *A true discourse of the late voyages of discouerie*, 31.

est son of Ham.[37] Best's version declares that Chus and "all his posteritie after him, should be so blacke & loathsome, that it might remain a spectacle of disobedience to all the World."[38] Thus, a tale is created to explain the origins of blackness through a curse.[39] A century later, the Hamitic Myth was used as a justification for slavery. This is evident in the writings of the seventeenth century Anglican missionary Morgan Godwyn who encountered frequent recourse to interpretations of the curse based on "certain impertinent and blasphemous distortions of Scripture."[40] In *The Negro and Indian's Advocate, suing for their admission into the church* (1680), Godwyn describes his interviews with English slave owners on the colonies of Barbados and Virginia. He writes, "[slavers] make [Negroes] the posterity of that unhappy son of Noah, who, they say, was, together with his whole family and race, cursed by his father."[41] Similar to Best's earlier version, Godwyn finds the slave owners believe the effects of the curse are "perpetual, even to the last generation" and are "extended to their very souls" as "a kind of reprobation."[42] However, Africans are not only penalized with interminable slavery. There is an ontological change in their beings, resulting in "a kind of transubstantiating of [Africans] into beasts."[43] Thus, the Hamitic curse, although an ideology of black inferiority or subordination, is a form of racism because it denigrates Africans as subhuman.

Wesley challenged racist ideologies that dehumanized Africans. Writing in 1757, Wesley deconstructs the Hamitic myth by reformulating the interpretation of Gen 9.[44] Instead of using the text to justify slavery, Wesley postulates that the narrative is a metaphor signifying the origins of sin. He argues that the drama of Noah and his Sons serves as an analogy of how ALL people "suffer . . . by the sentence inflicted on our first parents."[45] Whereas Best's sixteenth century version of the Hamitic Myth locates sin in

---

37. Gen 10:6 reads, "The descendants of Ham: Cush, Egypt, Put, and Canaan." Chus is the early modern English spelling for Cush, associated in Gen 10, the Table of Nations, with Ethiopia.

38. Best, *Discourse*, 30–31.

39. Fryer, *Staying Power*, 123.

40. Molineux, *Faces of Perfect Ebony*, 14.

41. Godwyn, *The Negro and Indian's Advocate*, 14.

42. Fryer. *Staying Power*, 50.

43. Ibid.

44. Wesley, *Works* (Jackson), 9:243.

45. Ibid.

blackness, dehumanizing Africans, Wesley's view places the origins of sin in humankind. Relatedly, Wesley protests the brutal treatment of African slaves in methods that undermine their humanity. In his sermon LXIX *The Imperfections of Human Knowledge,* Wesley asks, "And who cares for thousands, myriads, if not millions, of the wretched Africans? Are not whole droves of these poor sheep (human, if not rational beings), continually driven to market, and sold, like cattle, into the vilest bondage, without any hope of deliverance but by death?"[46]

In stressing their humanity, Wesley rejects the myths that animalize Africans, thus critiquing practices of the trade and slavery that reinforced those conceptions. Wesley was striking at the root of racist ideas. For example, he attacked the social and cultural propaganda that claimed all West African societies were barbaric. A frequent justification for placing Africans in bondage was that they lived in an extremely uncivilized environment. In *Thoughts Upon Slavery,* Wesley embarks upon a description of the areas and kingdoms from which the majority of slaves originated in Africa in order to challenge this assumption.[47] He asks, "What kind of country is that from whence they are brought? Is it so remarkably horrid, dreary, and barren, that it is a kindness to deliver them out of it?"[48] Stating that it is best not to form an opinion based on unconfirmed disinformation, Wesley resolves "to take our account from eye and ear witnesses."[49] Wesley utilizes sources in order to depict the broader expanse of the West African territory from which slaves are procured.[50] This includes a description of Guinea, a land encompassing the Grain Coast, the Ivory Coast, the Gold Coast, and the Slave Coast, areas quite enticing to European traders. Within the interior, the provinces constituted the royal kingdom of Benin, Congo, and Angola. Wesley describes the general organization of these centralized domains as well as their specialized bureaucracies including monarchical, administrative, and juridical systems of various tribal jurisdictions. By accentuating the complex, regulatory hierarchies as well as the developed agriculture

46. Wesley, *Works* (Jackson), 6:277–78. This reference is from a sermon, dated Bristol, March 5, 1784, and published in the *Arminian Magazine,* June and July, 1784.

47. Wesley incorporates data directly from Anthony Benezet's *Historical Account of Guinea* (1771) and *A Short Account of that Part of Africa Inhabited by the Negroes* (1762). Benezet's material is a compilation of commentaries and journal notes from multiple travelers in Africa.

48. Wesley, *Thoughts Upon Slavery,* 5.

49. Ibid.

50. Ibid., 8.

and trade industries of the societies, Wesley stresses not only the high quality of life but also the potential for further development. Although he is not
the first to disseminate this information on Africa, Wesley incorporates the
data to argue effectively against racist ideologies. He summarizes, "Upon
the whole, therefore, the Negroes who inhabit the coast of Africa, from
the river Senegal to the southern bounds of Angola, are so far from being
the stupid, senseless, brutish, lazy barbarians, the fierce, cruel, perfidious
savages they have been described."[51]

By the eighteenth century, theories such polygenesis were also being
used by racial proponents.[52] Polygenesis, as opposed to monogenesis, is
the separate creation of distinct groups of humanity at different periods.
Inherent in the theory is that certain groups are inferior to others. Different
creation events supposedly explained the physical diversity (and subordination) among humankind. Specifically, Africans were deemed subhuman
as a species, having been created separately from Europeans. In subsection
7 of *Thoughts Upon Slavery,* Wesley rejects this ideology by emphasizing
the divine worth of Africans as children of God, describing them as "works
of thine own hands, the purchase of thy Son's blood." Thus Wesley affirmed
one act of creation producing all races with inherent equality, declaring that
God is the "Father of the spirits of all flesh who hast mingled of one blood
all the nations upon earth." Wesley also responded to the reality of the degradation caused by slavery. Supporters went on to justify slavery because
the debased condition of many slaves. Yet, Wesley responded in kind to this
line of argumentation, asserting that any barbarism on the part of the Africans was a result of the oppressive treatment of the system. Wesley writes,
"You first acted the villain in making them slaves, whether you stole them
or bought them. You kept them stupid and wicked, by cutting them off
from all opportunities of improvement either in knowledge or virtue: And
now you assign their want of wisdom or goodness as the reason for using
them worse than brute beasts."[53]Hence, Wesley sought to counteract those
forces that perpetuated racist myths, which affected public opinion. He
used print media and art to challenge the prevalent assumption that differences in appearance constituted a separate species. In the September 1790
edition of *The Arminian Magazine,* a poem by Charles Wesley is published
which stresses the humanity and suffering of slaves treated like chattel.

51. Ibid., 9.

52. Brendlinger, *Social Justice,* 64. See also Long, *The History of Jamaica.*

53. Wesley, *Thoughts Upon Slavery,* 75.

Forc'd from home and all its pleasures,
Afric's coast I left forlorn;
To increase a stranger's treasures,
O'er the raging billows borne.
Men from England bought and sold me,
Paid my price in paltry gold;
But though their's they have enroll'd me,
Minds are never to be sold.
Still in thought as free as ever,
What are England's rights, I ask,
Me from my delights to sever,
Me to torture, me to task?
Fleecy locks and black complexion
Cannot forfeit nature's claim:
Skins may differ, but affection
Dwells in white and black the same.[54]

Wesley's attention to the racial question is evident in that he consistently published verse that emphasized the innate equality of Africans. A poem by the great religious writer Hannah More also published in *The Arminian* exclaims,

Perish the illiberal thought which debase
The native genius of the sable race!
Perish the proud philosophy, which sought
To rob them of the powers of equal thought!
Does then the immortal principle within
Change with the casual colour of a skin?
Does matter govern spirit! or is mind
Degraded by the form to which 'tis joined?
No: they have heads to think and hearts to feel,
And souls to act, with firm, though erring zeal;
For they have keen affections, kind desires,
Love strong as death, and active patriot fires;
All the rude energy, the fervid flame,
Of high-souled passion, and ingenuous shame:
Strong, but luxuriant virtues boldly shoot

54. *The Arminian Magazine*, XIII, September, 502–503

From the wild vigour of a savage root.[55]

Wesley's antislavery position is directly related to his theology. For Wesley, all humans are intrinsically equal, despite being totally depraved. Since all people are equally evil, no system is justified which allows certain groups to wield total authority over others. The irresistibility of prevenient grace bestows God's covering upon humanity, leveling the playing field, so to speak. Everyone has the potential of someday attaining the image of God lost in the fall. Hence, each person has fundamental worth as a child of God. Wesley believed in God's eternal love for all human creation and thus rejected any theological system that limits the ability of humans to move in the direction of divine power. When divine election is established unilaterally, completely restricting human agency, the genuine gospel freedom in Christ won through the cross is diminished. Therefore, political or social systems that cripple fundamental liberties for any group represent an intolerable unchristian witness.

Ironically, Wesley was influenced by natural rights theory, which was championed by John Locke. The appeal to natural rights holds that all humans are bequeathed with the gift of rationality, which undergirds their innate liberty. Natural rights deny the validity of slavery in any case. As Wesley writes, "I absolutely deny all slave-holding to be consistent with any degree of natural justice." Locke, however, was inconsistent in his application of natural law, holding some humans to have innate superiority over others, thereby supporting African slavery.[56] Despite his insistence on human equality forming the basis of consensual participation in society, Locke, who came from a Calvinist background, subscribed to the notion of a hierarchy of beings.[57] Calvinist thought presupposes divinely ordained preferentiality, making social inequality and division justifiable. The concept of inequity implied by irresistible salvation makes the disinheritance of certain groups (e.g. the non-elect) conceivable.[58] This may explain why George Whitefield (and Jonathan Edwards) cheerfully possessed African

55. *The Arminian Magazine*, XI (1788), 558–560 (October), 612–616 (November).

56. Locke was a major investor in the seventeenth century "Company of Royal Adventurers Trading to Africa," a business devoted to West African slave trading.

57. Some eighteenth-century thinkers for example held to the idea of polygenesis, the separate hierarchical creations of different races.

58. See Gal 4:30: "But what does the scripture say? 'Drive out the slave and her child; for the child of the slave will not share the inheritance with the child of the free woman.'"

slaves and encouraged others to do so.[59] Wesley maintained no such inconsistencies in the application of natural law through his emphasis on universal prevenient grace. Further, ideological systems that establish the notion of ontological inferiority among certain people are impossible to reconcile with this religious understanding. Thus, Wesley consistently fought against arbitrary racial constructions of human difference used to justify societal inequity. As Wesley writes, "God did never give authority to any man, or number of men, to deprive any child of man thereof under any color or pretense whatever."[60] Indeed, Wesley's uncompromising approach to the incompatibility of racial constructs with the gospel is a spiritual and political stance all true Wesleyans and Christians are encouraged to reclaim.

Bibliography

Antsey, Roger. *The Atlantic Slave Trade and British Abolition, 1760–1810.* London: Macmillan, 1975.

Ayling, Stanley. *John Wesley.* London: Collins, 1979.

Bready, J. Wesley. *England: Before, and After Wesley; The Evangelical Revival and Social Reform.* New York: Harper, 1938.

Brendlinger, Irv A. *Social Justice Through the Eyes of Wesley: John Wesley's Theological Challenge to Slavery.* Guelph, ON: Joshua, 2006.

————. *To Be Silent . . . Would Be Criminal: The Antislavery Influence and Writings of Anthony Benezet.* Lanham, MD: Scarecrow, 2007.

Clarkson, Thomas. *History of the Rise, Progress and Accomplishment of the Abolition of the African Slave-Trade by the British Parliament.* London: Longman, Hurst, Reese, and Orme, 1808.

Curtin, Philip D. *The Image of Africa, British Ideas and Action, 1780-1850.* Madison: University of Wisconsin Press, 1964.

Davis, David Brion. *The Problem of Slavery in Western Culture.* Ithaca: Cornell University Press, 1966.

59. Whitefield fought for the colony of Georgia to become slaveholding in 1740. He eventually bought land and slaves there. See Letter to Whitefield to Wesley on March 22, 1751 in Thompson, *John Wesley as a Social Reformer,* 43–45; and Dallimore, *George Whitefield.* In a famous letter written to Wesley, Whitefield justifies the practice of slavery through appeal to scripture. (This may be one reason why Wesley did not appeal to scriptural proof texting in his argument against slavery). In the letter, Whitefield argues that the "Gideonites were doomed to perpetual slavery," as biblical justification. He also uses the argument from necessity that it is impossible to cultivate farms in the new world without African workers (a position that Wesley strenuously rejects based on his own experience in America). Finally, Whitefield uses the appeal to providence that God's design may include slavery as a tool to bring heathen to Christ.

60. Wesley, *Works* (Jackson), 6:461.

Drescher, Seymour. *From Slavery to Freedom: Comparative Studies in the Rise and Fall of Atlantic Slavery*. New York: New York University Press, 1999.

Fogel, Robert William. *Without Consent or Contract: The Rise and Fall of American Slavery*. New York: Norton, 1989.

Furneaux, Robin. *William Wilberforce*. London: Hamish Hamilton, 1974.

Fryer, Peter. *Staying Power: Black People in Britain since 1504*. Atlantic Highlands, NJ: Humanities, 1984.

Gossett, Thomas F. *Race: The History of an Idea in America*. New York: Schocken, 1965.

Hall, Kim F. *Things of Darkness: Economies of Race and Gender in Early Modern England*. Ithaca: Cornell University Press, 1995.

Hendricks, Margo and Patricia Parker, eds. *Women, "Race," and Writing in the Early Modern Period*. New York: Routledge, 1994.

Molineux, Catherine. *Faces of Perfect Ebony: Encountering Atlantic Slavery in Imperial Britain*. Cambridge, MA: Harvard University Press, 2012.

Pritchard, Elizabeth. *Religion in Public: Locke's Political Theology: Cultural Memory in the Present*. Stanford: Stanford University Press, 2013.

Rice, C. Duncan. *The Rise and Fall of Black Slavery*. London: Macmillan, 1975.

Smith, Warren Thomas. *John Wesley & Slavery*. Nashville: Abingdon, 1986.

Thompson, Edgar. *Nathaniel Gilbert, Lawyer and Evangelist*. London: Epworth, 1960.

Wesley, Charles. *The Journal of the Rev. Charles Wesley, M.A.* Edited by Thomas Jackson. 2 vols. London: Wesleyan Methodist Book Room, 1849.

Wesley, John. *The Bicentennial Edition of the Works of John Wesley*. Edited by Frank Baker and Richard P. Heitzenrater. Nashville: Abingdon, 1976–.

———. *Explanatory Notes Upon the New Testament*. London: William Bowyer, 1765.

———. *The Journal of John Wesley*. Edited by Nehemiah Curnock. Charleston, SC: Nabu.

———. *The Letters of the Rev. John Wesley, A. M.* 8 vols. Edited by John Telford. London: Epworth, 1931.

———. *Thoughts Upon Slavery*. Charleston, SC: Nabu, 2014.

———. *The Works of John Wesley*. Edited by Thomas Jackson. 3rd ed. 14 vols. London: Wesleyan Conference Office, 1872.

Williams, Eric. *Capitalism and Slavery*. London: Epworth, 1960.

John Wesley the Faithful Arminian

—————— Rusty E. Brian ——————

I t is difficult indeed to understand John Wesley (1703–91), his life, and his theology, as well as Wesleyanism, broadly defined, if one does not attempt to understand the work of the Dutch theologian Jacob Arminius (1559–1609). In many ways, Arminius's theology provides the doctrinal framework for Wesley's works. Lack of knowledge of Arminius's theology, I would argue, makes it quite difficult for one to truly understand Wesley therefore. Unfortunately, it is all too common for those of a Wesleyan persuasion to have little, if any, knowledge of Arminius. I cannot help but think that this lack of knowledge renders our understanding of Wesley somewhat inadequate. Personally, I can attest to having never been required to read anything by or about Arminius in school. This despite completing a BA, MDiv, and a PhD all at self-identified Wesleyan institutions. In fact, the most I ever heard about and discussed Arminius was during a year spent at a staunchly Reformed program in Scotland. The result of these discussions with my wonderful Reformed colleagues was the realization that I needed to read and understand Arminius, and help other Wesleyans to do so as well. Having discussed these experiences with colleagues, I would argue that my experiences are not anomalous. This is surely a detriment to what is often called "Wesleyan-Arminian theology." And yet, John Wesley himself, who does not appear to have been especially well read in the works of

Arminius, likely shared this detriment.[1] His theology, though, possessed an uncanny connection and similarity to the works of the Dutch reformer. It would seem, therefore, that as Wesleyan theology continues to develop, and seeks to engage with difficult theological and philosophical issues that are both novel and ancient, a robust discovery of, and engagement with, the works of Arminius is in order.

Wesleyan theology, therefore, is dependent upon, and yet, strangely uninformed about the life and theology of Jacob Arminius. I contend that that this is a problem. Arminius's theology provides the soil, within which the seeds of Wesleyan theology grow and flourish. Simply put, a good understanding of Arminius's theology will help in understanding Wesley's theology. This brief dialogical examination of Arminius and Wesley seeks to aid Wesleyan pastors and scholars in this important endeavor. A general understanding of Wesley's theology is assumed in this brief examination. By focusing our attention in this chapter primarily on Arminius's theology, it will be seen that Wesley was, both intentionally and unintentionally, thoroughly Arminian, and that, moreover, Wesleyan theology is the practical result and development of Arminian theology.

To this end, we will begin with a brief biography of Arminius. This might be review for some, but experience tells me that those familiar with his life and work are few in number. We will then examine the relationship between these two great churchmen, focusing primarily upon their theology. This will lead to a brief examination of the doctrines of sin, grace, and predestination, particularly as set forth by Arminius. With this [albeit brief] doctrinal foundation in place, we will conclude with a look at the missionary zeal that is prominent in Wesleyan theology. It will be argued

---

1. It is clear that Wesley knew of Arminius and was fond of his theology. See his "Arminian Magazine" for example. W. Stephen Gunter has addressed this subject in a most helpful manner in, Gunter, "John Wesley, a Faithful Representative of Jacobus Arminius," 65–82. See also, Pask, "The Influence of Arminius on John Wesley," 258–262. Similarly, Herbert McGonigle states that, "it can be shown that John Wesley had read Arminius' *Declaration of Sentiments* as early as 1731," but "he did not describe himself as an Arminian until 1770." See McGonigle, "Arminius and Wesley on Original Sin," 106. Curiously, Keith Stanglin and Thomas McCall state on the contrary, that, "Wesley never cited Arminius or claimed to have read him, but he encouraged others to do so, he read other Anglican theologians who read Arminius, and he probably was directly influenced by *Declaration of Sentiments.*" Stanglin and McCall, *Jacob Arminius*, 193. Thus, though Wesley was aware of Arminius's work, the extent to which he read Arminius's works is anything but clear. I do not think that this negates the argument, though, for even a cursory read of Wesley, for those who have ready Arminius, will reveal just how indebted Wesley was to the great Dutch Reformer.

that Wesley's such missionary zeal necessarily assumes, and even depends upon, a distinctly Arminian theology.

Arminius's Lasting Influence

Great caution should be exercised when hiring workers to drain your swamps. Such might have been a welcomed proverb by King Charles I of England. Of course, for Charles I, who ruled England, Scotland, and Ireland during a time of particularly troublesome political and religious turmoil, including civil war, such a proverb may have been ill received as well. Nevertheless, as Geoffrey F. Nuttall stated in his 1960 address to the Arminius Symposium in Holland, such a small issue may indeed be a large factor in the Arminianism of John Wesley. Nuttall notes that roughly 200 Dutch families migrated to the vicinity of Epworth, in Lincolnshire, England. Under the leadership of Cornelius Vermuyden, they took up the task of draining around 60,000 acres of swampland. "It is at least suggestive that the greatest English Arminian was reared in a village and neighborhood to which active and self-confessed Arminianism had long been no stranger . . . "[2] Of course, this is circumstantial logic at best, but such is the case with the direct connection between Arminius and Wesley. Dredged swamps, journal titles, and correlative examinations, are about all we have to go on. Some have called the Arminian influence upon John Wesley an "anonymous impact."[3] Whether this is true or not, though, need not discount the thesis that Wesley was thoroughly Arminian, and that Wesleyan theology, therefore, is the practical development of Arminian theology. To examine this further, we will briefly examine the life and work of Arminius.

Arminius was born in 1559 in Oudewater, Holland. His father Harmen Jacobsz died the same year, leaving his wife Elborch to raise the children.[4] Fortunately for Elborch, a local priest named Theodore Aemilius offered his financial support and assumed responsibility for young Arminius's edu-

2. Nuttall, "The Influence of Arminianism in England." 46–63.

3. Stanglin and McCall, *Jacob Arminius*, 5.

4. Arminius was born "Jacob Harmenszoon." Following the custom of his day, he later Latinized his name, adopting the name Jacobus, or Jacob, Arminius. Carl Bangs notes that while it is clear that Elborch was Jacob's mother's name, some records indicate that the wife of Harmen Jacobsz was named Elgeltje. Bangs suggests that the name Elborch fell out of use with the rise of Protestantism in Holland, and that Elgetje (Angelica in English) was the preferred substitute for this previously common name. Bangs, *Arminius*, 26.

cation. Arminius had two or three siblings, all of whom were raised by their mother Elborch.[5] Jacob left home in 1572 to begin his university education at Utrecht. He continued on to Marburg in 1575, but his studies were almost immediately cut short by news of the bloody and terrible massacre in Jacob's hometown of Oudewater. Spanish Catholics invaded Oudewater and brutally massacred every single man, woman, and child that did not have the good fortune to flee from the town. The brutality committed by the Spanish Catholics against this newly converted Reformed Protestant town was meant to send an example to the rest of the region. Arminius left Marburg as soon as possible, only to discover that reports were all too true. He would eventually return to Marburg on foot, only to leave again for the newly opened University of Leiden in 1576.

> After Leiden, Arminius would go on to study at Basel and Geneva, before returning to Holland to assume a pastorate in Amsterdam. At Geneva, he studied under the successor to the great John Calvin himself, Theodore Beza. His theological convictions truly took shape and began to flourish in Geneva. His views on sin and grace—predestination in particular—involved Arminius in many heated debates at Marburg. These trials would only increase over time and in proportion to Arminius's influence. In 1588 Arminius took up pastoral duties in Amsterdam, a position he would hold until accepting an invitation to return to Leiden University as a professor, in 1603. The 16 years that Arminius spent in parish ministry deeply influenced his academic writing and teaching at Leiden. Arminius remained at Leiden until his untimely death in 1609. Arminius's good friend and colleague Peter Bertius concluded his eulogy with these oft-repeated words, "There lived a man, whom it was not possible, for those who knew him, sufficiently to esteem; those who entertained no esteem for him, are such as never knew him well enough to appreciate his merits."[6]

5. The precise number of Arminius' siblings is somewhat unclear. Bangs notes that records show that Jacob likely had three siblings, one brothers and one sister. This is supported by Bertius' funeral oration. (Bangs, 29) Contrarily, Bangs also shows that Casper Brandt, who wrote the primary English biography of Arminius that circulated for roughly 200 years, states in his *Historie der Reformatie* that Jacob had a sister and two brothers. Curiously, though, in Brandt's aforementioned *Life of Arminius*, Brandt states about Jacob, "He lost his father in infancy; and his mother, thus prematurely deprived of her partner, was left, with the three children she had by him, to pass her widowed days in somewhat straitened circumstances." Brandt, *The Life of James Arminius*, 13.

6. Bertius, "An Oration on the Life and Death," 47.

Arminius's somewhat short life and career proved to be long enough to leave a legacy. His powerful opposition to the teachings of Calvin's followers (Beza in particular) on sin, grace, and predestination in particular, provided shape and substance to the Remonstrants, a movement that still exists today. While remaining in line with Calvin in many areas, the significance of Arminius's work lies in its ability to carve out theological and ecclesial space that is at once both contra Calvin and Reformed theology, and yet quite thoroughly Reformed at the same time. In many ways, Arminius's theology can be said to be a *via media* of sorts between Reformed theology and Roman Catholicism. Indeed, Arminius's theology was neither truly Reformed, nor Roman Catholic, and yet in many ways it united the best of both sensibilities while eschewing some of the more problematic holdings of each. Primarily, Arminius rejected the Reformed doctrine of predestination known as supralapsarianism (or supralapsarian double-predestination) as well as the Roman Catholic tendency towards works righteousness of the Pelagian persuasion, along with Mariology and all forms of "Popishness."[7] Arminian theology is characterized by an extremely high account of God's sovereignty, which is nevertheless unchallenged by a strongly articulated doctrine of the free will of humanity—free will to accept, but especially to reject God's grace. Several centuries later, a young English preacher named John Wesley would advocate for very similar positions as he worked for reform within the Church of England.

---

7. In regard to Roman Catholicism, it should be noted that the very fact that the Church deemed Pelagianism heretical long ago, stands as a strong challenge to such a straw man version of Catholicism. Nevertheless, this was the view held by most Protestants at the time, and in some cases for good reason. The real issue lies in the Reformation cry of salvation by grace alone through faith. Though both sides have now come to agree on the doctrine of salvation by *Sola Gratia, Sola Fide*, for several hundred years each sought to be identified as not the other. Each, therefore, moved further and further apart on the spectrum of soteriology. Thus whereas Roman Catholicism did not officially teach anything like "works righteousness," such became an easy caricature. The inverse can also said to be true, that the theology of the Reformed Church came to be caricatured by such high views of God's sovereignty and the sin of humanity, that only the very arbitrary will of God resulted in salvation. It might be said, then, that the medieval and, indeed, modern temptations of the Roman Catholic and Protestant churches are Pelagianism and Nominalism, respectively.

Sin, Grace, and Election in Arminius & Wesley

Arminius's teachings on predestination remain one of his central contributions to the theological landscape of the Church. Indeed, Arminius's insistence upon the universality of predestination [not salvation] has helped to provide theological shape and substance to both his followers and his critics alike. In order to put forward such a position, Arminius embraced a very deep and mysterious tension or paradox within God. Namely, the absolute sovereignty of God was held in tension with the freedom of humanity. Such a tension was difficult to maintain, to say the least, and it certainly brought Arminius his fair share of critics. It also allowed him to unequivocally affirm that God was sovereign and yet was not the author of evil. As we will see, then, God's sovereignty is unchecked by humanity's freedom—freedom of the will to reject salvation, in particular.

Sin

Humans are sinners: originally by choice, and in perpetuity by punishment. Sin is thus both original and ongoing. Sin is the opposite of the love of God and others. It is destructive, or literally de-creative. Sin divides, alienates, stains, and destroys. Sin is necessarily accompanied by death, the latter becoming the necessary end of all humans as a result of the former. Sin was not original to creation, however. God did not create it, nor does God authorize it. Creation was only good; there was no harmony between good and evil for evil did not, as such, exist.[8] "Creation," for Arminius, "is a communication of good according to the intrinsic property of its nature."[9] Creation is and was good. The creation accounts in Genesis document this. God was pleased with the goodness of creation. In creation there was goodness with no hint of destruction, disease, or disorder. To affirm anything else is to affirm that God is the author of evil. "In that case," states Arminius, "creation would not have been a communication of any good, but a

---

8. We could certainly add "does not" as well, as sin, for Arminius, along with the catholic tradition before him, is a *privatio* and not a *quod est*. Denying "thing" status to sin, though, does not deny its very real and ongoing effects. Quiddity comes from God, and sin does not come from God. Sin's reality, therefore, is a parasitic shadow life which God allows but neither ordains nor sustains.

9. Arminius, *Declaration of Sentiments*, 562.

preparation for the greatest evil both according to the very intention of the Creator and the actual issue of the matter . . . ."[10]

According to the mysterious love of God, though, human beings were created with creativity, intellect, and freedom. The goal for creation was and is that it would exist in a loving relationship, or covenant, with its Creator. God would not force this issue though. Instead, God created human beings as God's crowning achievement, and deemed to woo them into such a relationship. Herein lies the chink in the proverbial armor, for God's grace, as nearly overwhelming as it is, is resistible, according to Arminius. Our first parents, Adam and Eve, did just that by rejecting God's command to not eat from the tree of the knowledge of good and evil, desiring that they might be "like God." Their rebellion creates sin, something that is allowed by God. Sin's effects, it turns out, are thoroughly pervasive. Thus, the sins of Adam and Eve stained all. This has come to be known, particularly after Augustine, as Original Sin. Arminius affirmed both the original deed and the ongoing effects of sin. "Two points are crucial for grasping Arminius's thoughts on original sin. First, he defines it primarily as a lack of original righteousness. Second, he further describes original sin as punishment, but not as guilt."[11]

For Arminius, therefore, sin is both original and ongoing, it is pervasive or total, and it does not derive from God. In this, Arminius is in full accord with Calvin as well as the traditional teachings of the Church prior to the Reformation. John Wesley would also affirm this traditional understanding of the pervasiveness of sin.

> Original sin standeth not in the following of Adam (as the Pelagians do vainly talk), but it is the fault and corruption of the Nature of every man, that naturally is engendered of the offspring of Adam; whereby man is very far gone from original righteousness, and is of his own nature inclined to evil . . . and therefore in every person born into this world, it deserveth God's wrath and damnation.[12]

---

10. Ibid., 562–3.

11. Stanglin and McCall, *Jacob Arminius*, 145.

12. Quoted in McGonigle, "Arminius and Wesley on Original Sin," 102. Originally found in Wesley's *The Doctrine of Original Sin According to Scripture, Reason, and Experience* (1757). Though I strive to utilize gender inclusive language in my work, when quoting an author's original words, I have opted to keep the author's words intact, including gender exclusive pronouns.

Whether intentionally, or coincidentally, Wesley's view of sin is nearly identical to that of Arminius. Both would agree, likewise, that stronger than their doctrine of sin, is their doctrine of God's grace.

Grace

While none are free from sin, it is equally and more forcefully asserted that none are removed from God's grace, lest they choose to remove themselves, which is itself a divine act of grace towards rebellious creatures.

> If then sinful men find favour with God, it is "grace upon grace!" If God vouchsafe still to pour fresh blessings upon us, yea, the greatest of all blessings, salvation; what can we say to these things, but, "Thanks be unto God for his unspeakable gift!" And thus it is. Herein "God commendeth his love toward us, in that, while we were yet sinners, Christ died" to save us "By grace" then "are ye saved through faith." Grace is the source, faith the condition, of salvation.[13]

So Wesley says in introducing a sermon on Ephesians 2:8, "For by grace you have been saved through faith, and this is not your own doing; it is the gift of God." (NRSV) Grace is the foundation of Creation, and it is God's continual mode of relating to Creation. Arminius described grace as the very vocation of God.

> We define vocation, a gracious act of God in Christ, by which, through his word and Spirit, He calls forth sinful men, who are liable to condemnation and placed under the dominion of sin, from the condition of the animal life, and from the pollutions and corruptions of this world . . . unto "the fellowship of Jesus Christ," and of his kingdom and its benefits; that, being united unto Him as their Head, they may derive from Him life, [*sensum*] sensation, motion, and a plentitude of every spiritual blessing, to the glory of God and their own salvation.[14]

Salvation comes by faith in Christ Jesus, which is itself only possible by the free and unmerited grace of God.

Sin, therefore, is the result of human volition. Grace, on the other hand, is the work and result of the divine will to redeem all things. The

---

13. John Wesley, "Salvation by Faith," 3.

14. Arminius, *Public Disputation XVI.II,* 231–2.

first "step" of grace, then, is taken by God, allowing for the human, itself, to respond. This first step, which necessarily originates in God, is often called prevenient grace. Subsequent steps, then, are made, cooperatively, by free humans in response to, and in cooperation with, God. "The initial contact of prevenient grace is wholly divine, but the subsequent grace entails a co-operative relationship."[15] As was the case with the view of sin espoused by both Arminius and Wesley, such a view of grace is in keeping with the bulk of Christian tradition. Prevenient grace, for example, is rightfully traced back to Augustine's attempts to combat the heretical teachings of Pelagius. The novelty of this view of grace, is the universal role it plays for Arminius, and later for Wesley. Grace is available for all: none are exempt. Rooted as it is in the work of Christ, specifically his death and resurrection, grace, and therefore salvation, are truly possible for all. The centrality of this claim for both Arminius and Wesley cannot be understated. As strongly as can be affirmed, therefore, both are theologians of grace. More than anything else, it is the fundamental disposition of God, as understood by both Arminius and Wesley, to redeem and save sinful humanity by the undeserved gift of grace.[16]

Predestination

Predestination is a valid and biblically derived doctrine. As such, both Arminius and Wesley strongly affirmed predestination. The witness of Scripture on this most complex subject is anything but simple, though, and has led to much debate. The issue, therefore, is not whether Arminius and Wesley affirmed predestination, but how each understood the matter, and thus how each affirmed this doctrine. In fact, one of the key issues for all theologians is how to understand predestination, and thus where to place it in the *ordo salutis*, or order of salvation. According to the theological schema of the Calvinism that developed after Calvin, all are predestined, but only some are predestined for beatitude. Sin's effects were so pervasive, humanity's rebellion was so total, that most were predestined for damnation. This two-fold view of predestination would be even more strongly parsed out by Calvin's heir at Geneva, Theodore Beza, and by Calvin's theological progeny at the Synod of Dort (1618–1619). For those who hold to this view, known as supralapsarianism (or prior to the fall), God's absolute

15. Stanglin and McCall, *Jacob Arminius*, 153.

16. Gunter, *Arminius and His Declaration of Sentiments*, 7–8.

sovereignty must be maintained above all else. As a result, predestination is not a response by God to the rebellion of humanity, but rather it was always a part of the *ordo salutis* prior even to the rebellion of humanity. Salvation and damnation are completely derived from God and not from human volition or works in any way.

Arminius, however, while completely affirming God's absolute sovereignty, equally affirmed God's decision to create humanity and bestow upon them freedom of will.[17] Indeed, the free will of humanity, for Arminius, is one of the greatest testimonies to God's utter sovereignty, for only a truly benevolent God would make creatures that could rebel against their creator, in order to love them unconditionally and woo them towards God's very self. Arminius's thoughts on this subject comprise his *Declaration of Sentiments*, which is surely the most important and helpful of his writings. In that work, he attempts to combat the views of the "Supralapsarians" by defending what he claims to be a biblical view of predestination as compared to the less biblical version put forth by the Supralapsarians.[18] More than anything else, Arminius's arguments in this work hinge on the notion that God cannot be said to be the author of evil, something that he believes is unavoidably affirmed if one maintains that God predestines even one person for perdition prior to the offense of sin. "God, therefore, has not,

---

17. While human freedom truly is absolute, for both Arminius and Wesley, it is a dependent or derivative quality in that it is created. Thus, God's sovereignty is always supreme, and any development of human freedom is necessarily an advancement of God's sovereignty as well.

18. Arminius's doctrine of predestination is strongly grounded in Christology, whereas the same doctrine as put forth by Calvin's followers is primarily grounded in the doctrine of the Divine Decrees, and only secondarily, in Christology. For example, in his *Declaration of* Sentiments, Arminius identifies the foundational decree (first of four) of God in regard to predestination as primarily Christological in nature. "God decreed to appoint for humanity, his Son, Jesus Christ, to be the "Mediator, Redeemer, Saviour, Priest, and King, who might destroy sin by his own death, and who might by his obedience obtain the salvation which had been lost, and might communicate it by his own virtue" (589–90). This is a very different starting point from that of the Supralapsarians, who begin, according to Arminius, not with Christology but with the Divine Decrees. "That God has absolutely and precisely decreed to save certain particular men by his mercy or grace, but to condemn others by his justice. And to do all of this without having any regard in such decree to righteousness or sin, obedience or disobedience, which could possibly exist on the part of one class of men or the other." (554) Arminius, *Declaration of Sentiments* in *The Works of Arminius*.

by any absolute decree without respect to sin and disobedience, prepared eternal death for any person."[19]

> For Arminius, God is absolutely good—the *summum bonum*— and as such God wills no evil but rather tolerates it as a part of the creation of free beings.[20] Over two centuries later, John Wesley would clearly affirm Arminius's primary theological motif by founding a publication called "The Arminian Magazine," the first volume of which included a hymn written by his father Samuel Wesley, containing these words, "No evil can from Thee proceed: 'Tis only suffer'd, not decreed."[21]

Wesley's "Practical" Arminian Theology

John Wesley was a religious reformer within the Church of England. His central teaching was that the followers of Christ needed to know, love, and serve God with all of their heart, mind, and soul and to love their neighbors as themselves. This message can be described as the message of Christian holiness, and ultimately, Christian perfection—the latter being possible in this life solely by the grace of God. Wesley was concerned that Christianity had become a dead or stale set of propositions, and that accordingly, faith was merely mental assent to such propositions. The goal of Wesley's Methodist bands was to affect deep and personal change of one's heart and soul that would effectively call one out of religious slumber into the passionate and complete love of God and others. As such Wesley was a prophet and a missionary first to England, and then to all of the world. Likewise, Wesleyan theology, by necessity, possesses a distinctly missionary (or missional) and evangelical zeal.

---

19. Arminius, *Declaration of Sentiments XI*, 564.

20. Arminius's doctrine of Middle Knowledge is especially helpful in parsing out such a position. Basically, Arminius affirms both Divine sovereignty and human freedom and believes that the latter does not negate or qualify the former. To do this, Arminius affirms 1) God's necessary knowledge, or knowledge of all necessary truths, 2) God's free knowledge, or knowledge of all that will be (dependent upon God's will), and 3) God's middle knowledge, according to which God knows all that could be or contingent possibilities based not upon God's will, but in this case, the will of creatures. Stanglin and McCall provide a wonderful and succinct account of Arminius' doctrine of Middle Knowledge in Stanglin and McCall, *Jacob Arminius*, 63–69.

21. Quoted in Nuttall, "The Influence of Arminianism in England."

> Among the Puritans of seventeenth-century England not only was any missionary enterprise almost entirely absent but also there was little or no missionary concern. This is apt to surprise us, but our surprise is a measure of the triumph of Arminianism .... Speaking historically, the missionary overspill of Christianity during the last 170 years would hardly have been made possible psychologically but for the Arminianism of the Wesleyan Methodist movement ... [22]

This missional and evangelical zeal could not exist apart from Wesley's thoroughly Arminian theology, focused as it was on the free and universal grace of God made possible by Christ Jesus the Son, through the Holy Spirit. According to Geoffrey Nuttall, "The theology of Calvinism arises, naturally and properly, as a theology of the people of God within the household of God. An Arminian theology arises equally naturally and properly as a theology of mission to the unbeliever."[23] Indeed, fundamental to Wesley's religious reforms, and to subsequent Wesleyan theology, is that all humans are sinners and thus stand in need of redemption, that such redemption has been wrought, once and for all, by the work of Christ, and is freely available to all persons, and that faith in and obedience to Jesus results in the transformation of persons from sinners to those in whom dwells the whole mind of Christ.

Wesleyan theology, therefore, is aimed not only at faith, but living, active, and transformative faith. Such faith draws deeply from the well of Arminius's theological work contra the Calvinistic Supralapsarians. Gunter has already concluded that Wesley's soteriology is "a faithful representation of original Arminianism."[24] I would put it even more strongly, and state that Wesley's theology was thoroughly Arminian as a whole, and that Wesleyanism is the practical flourishing of Arminian theology. Moreover, Wesley's theology, in many ways, is a development of the theology of Arminius. It is, therefore, imperative that Wesleyans return to, or discover for the first time, the works of Jacob Arminius, for in these works the theological grounding for Wesley's religious reforms can be found. Arminius's theology is more than simply compatible with Wesley's. In fact, it is the bedrock for Wesley's practical work towards religious renewal as well as one of the

22. Ibid.

23. Ibid.

24. Gunter, "John Wesley, a Faithful Representative," 77. Here Gunter states that Wesley desired to distinguish his efforts at revival from the work of the so-called "Calvinian Methodists."

primary sources for Wesleyanism's missionary and evangelical zeal. Surely, then, as Wesleyans place more and more emphasis on questions of mission and what it means to be "evangelical," a return to one of the primary sources of our theology—the theology of Jacob Arminius—would significantly aid this process.

Bibliography

Arminius, James. "Declaration of Sentiments." In vol. 1 of *The Works of James Arminius*. Translated by James Nichols and William Nichols. Grand Rapids: Baker, 1986.

———. "Public Disputation XVI.II." In vol. 1 of *The Works of James Arminius*. Translated by James Nichols and William Nichols. Grand Rapids: Baker, 1986.

Bangs, Carl. *Arminius: A Study in the Dutch Reformation*. Nashville: Abingdon, 1971.

Bertius, Peter. "An Oration on the Life and Death of that Reverend and Very Famous Man James Arminius D.D." In vol. 1 of *The Works of James Arminius*. London: James Nichols, 1825.

Brandt, Caspar. *The Life of James Arminius, D.D.* Translated by John Guthrie. London: Ward, 1854.

Gunter, W. Stephen. *Arminius and His Declaration of Sentiments: An Annotated Translation with Introduction and Theological Commentary*. Waco: Baylor University Press, 2012.

———. "John Wesley, a Faithful Representative of Jacobus Arminius." *Wesleyan Theological Journal* 42 (2007) 65–82.

Lodahl, Michael. "'Looking for the End without Using the Means': John Wesley's 'Practical Divinity' and Today's Local Church." In *The Wise Shepherd: Biblical and Theological Resources for the Pastoral Task*, edited by Brad E. Kelle, 111–22. San Diego: Point Loma Press, 2006.

Maddox, Randy. "Reconnecting the Means to the End." *The Wesleyan Theological Journal* 32 (1998) 29–66.

Nuttall, Geoffrey F. "The Influence of Arminianism in England." An address presented to the Arminius Symposium, Holland, 1960. http://evangelicalarminians.org/the-influence-of-arminianism-in-england.

Pask, Alfred H. "The Influence of Arminius on John Wesley." *London Quarterly and Holborn Review* 185 (1960) 258–62.

Stanglin, Keith D., and Thomas H. McCall. *Jacob Arminius: Theologian of Grace*. New York: Oxford University Press, 2012.

Wesley, John. "Sermon 1: Salvation by Faith." http://wesley.nnu.edu/john-wesley/the-sermons-of-john-wesley-1872-edition/sermon-1-salvation-by-faith/.

Afterword

——————— Michael Lodahl ———————

The nine primary essays in this book, written by young and promising Wesleyan scholars, betoken a rich, diverse and stimulating future for theological scholarship in the Methodist and holiness traditions for the good of the Church universal. There is much to rejoice over—along with much to mull over!—in the preceding pages.

Of course these nine authors' chapters represent only a sprinkling of the kinds of thinking, and the sorts of issues, that this next generation of scholars will engage in its teaching, writing and preaching. But even taking just these nine essayists as representative, we might be tempted to wonder about exactly what shared theological commitments, if any, will be able to hold them together. Is there a common vision here? Is there a way to hear and appreciate all of these voices as somehow joining in a chorus that the Wesley brothers' ears would recognize?

In this brief "afterword" I intend to propose just such a vision—or, to utilize the other metaphor, I hope to hum just the barest notes of a tune that I trust all of these authors would themselves recognize as being faithful to the concerns of their particular essays. These notes are: 1) God is love; 2) God has created human beings to be creatures who can receive, be transformed by, and share in love divine; 3) such a transformation by divine love is profoundly experiential; and 4) the love of God is so lavish and unbounded as to include all of creation in its transformative intentions.

God Is Love

I begin to sound this first theme by recalling a statement by contributing essayist Dick Eugenio, a youthful and truly promising theologian teaching in the Philippines. Eugenio alludes to the work of Methodist theologian Albert Outler (1908–1989), who probably more than any other single person has made possible all of our self-conscious reflection upon the idea of a "Wesleyan tradition." In several books titles, Eugenio notes, "Outler speaks of 'the Wesleyan spirit,' although he makes no explanation as to its meaning" (p. xx).[1] Eugenio proceeds then to suggest that Outler is "referring to doctrines," especially the particularly Wesleyan emphases upon "original sin, justification by faith alone, and holiness of heart and life" (p. xx). Without gainsaying this suggestion entirely, I suggest that the most effective way of getting at what Outler means by "theology in the Wesleyan spirit" is to look at the book's cover illustration of a coat-of-arms that includes a banner reading, simply, "God is Love."

I am convinced that this simple Johannine testimony (1 John 4:8, 16) is—and ought to continue to be, long into the future and world without end—both the starting point and the very heart of Wesleyan theological reflection. In that light, I applaud essayist John Bechtold's hope for a renewed focus on the necessity of the church, grounded in a robust, Christologically-rooted ecclesiology, as the basis for "theological discourse which is based on love, not power." As Bechtold convincingly adds, "This, ultimately, is what Wesley aimed for. 'This is the sum of Christian perfection: It is all comprised in that one word, Love'" (p. xx).

Indeed, the critical importance of this starting point— "God is love" —for both the content and the spirit of Wesleyan theological reflection asserts itself throughout this book, even if often only as an unstated implication. For instance, to grapple with the question of a "Wesleyan hermeneutics" in company with essayist Benjamin Boeckel is to recall just how critically this simple declaration of 1 John functioned for Wesley's reading of the Bible; in his classic sermon "Free Grace," for example, Wesley railed against those who espoused a typically Reformed understanding of predestination:

> [This doctrine] . . . is grounded on such an interpretation of some texts (more or fewer it matters not) as flatly contradicts all the other texts, and indeed the whole scope and tenor of Scripture.

1. Eugenio footnotes Outler's *Theology in the Wesleyan Spirit*, and his *Evangelism in the Wesleyan Spirit*.

For instance: the asserters of this doctrine interpret that text of Scripture, "Jacob have I loved, but Esau have I hated," as implying that God in a literal sense hated Esau and all the reprobated from eternity. Now what can possibly be a more flat contradiction than this, not only to the whole scope and tenor of Scripture, but also to all those particular texts which expressly declare, "God is love?" . . . No Scripture can mean that God is not Love, or that his mercy is not over all his works. That is, whatever it prove beside, no Scripture can prove predestination.[2]

I submit that, before anything else, for Wesley the Scriptures bear witness to this root conviction that "God is love," a conviction that is itself grounded in God's ultimate revelation in Jesus Christ. In the words of another passage from 1 John, "We know love" —this love *that God is*— "by this, that he laid down his life for us" (3:16). This provides the vision for "theology in the Wesleyan spirit" such that, to cite Wesley again, *No Scripture can mean that God is not Love.* Or, to put the point more positively, all of Scripture must be read in such a way as to ensure and guard its fundamental testimony that God is love.

The relevance of this conviction to Rustin Brian's chapter on Arminius, and Wesley as an Arminian, is obvious. In his tract "Predestination Calmly [*!*] Considered," Wesley surely waxed Arminian:

It is written, "God is love" [1 Jn. 4:8], love in the abstract, without bounds, and "there is no end of his goodness" [Ps. 52:1]. His love extends even to those who neither love nor fear him. He is good, even to the evil and the unthankful; yea, without any exception or limitation, to all the children of men. . . . And shall [a person supposedly predestined for damnation], for not doing what he never could do, and for doing what he never could avoid, be sentenced to depart into everlasting fire . . .? "Yes," [the classic Protestant predestinarian replies,] "because it is the sovereign will of God." Then you have either found a new God, or made one! This is not the God of the Christians.[3]

While we may not want to replicate Wesley's rhetoric in this regard, we ought to appreciate the theological vision that informs his strong reaction.

---

2. Wesley, "Sermon 110," *71–114.*

3. Wesley, "Predestination Calmly Considered," 227, 234.

God Has Created Us for Love

As briefly mentioned already, 1 John 3:16 provides the Christological content and focus for the fundamental declaration that "God is love" (4:8, 16). But 1 John 3:16 does not end simply with a celebration of Christ's laying down of his life for us; it seamlessly and tellingly continues, "and we ought to lay down our lives for one another" and then expounds upon the implications of such mutually sacrificial living in the concrete terms of sharing material goods with those who experience physical need for food, clothing and shelter (1 Jn 3:17–18). It is noteworthy that this passage includes an appeal to the real agency of its readers—"we *ought* to lay down our lives for one another"—as well as the true contingencies inhering in the possibility of our refusal. This seems to get at the concern for "free will" adumbrated by both Arminius and Wesley.[4] This Johannine call to love one another sacrificially, and in mutually uplifting and concretely material ways, also resonates profoundly, in my judgment, with Nell Becker Sweeden's essay. Her hope that Jesus's disciples in the Wesleyan tradition might be most faithful by developing new forms of Christian community and mutual responsibility, along with fostering greater collaboration and networking across denominational lines in order to more holistically work toward social transformation, flows beautifully out of the Johannine call to love one another as Christ has loved us—which surely does sum up beautifully Wesley's best understanding of Christian perfection.

It is precisely that sort of love, it seems to me, that speaks powerfully toward the ideas voiced in Orlando Serrano's and Andrew Schwartz's essays, which, while certainly different from each other, in their respective ways call us toward a transformed—and hopefully a much more deeply sensitive, respectful and truly loving—engagement with people who dwell in communal forms very different from the Church. We recall again these words of Wesley: "It is written, 'God is love' [1 Jn. 4:8], love in the abstract, without bounds, . . . [God's] love extends . . without any exception or limitation, to all the children of men."[5] Indeed, Wesley grew to understand

---

4. See R. Brian, p. 166. I must confess to a lingering dissatisfaction with Brian's characterization of Arminius's position as upholding an equally absolute free will, i.e., absolute just as God's sovereignty is "absolute." His footnote 17 (on p. 166) eases this dissatisfaction only slightly. As one of his former teachers, I feel sufficiently free (even if not absolutely so!) to offer Rusty this mild chastising even as I thank him for his thoughtful contribution to this book.

5. See note 3, page 148.

that Love Divine such as this must flow to each and every one of God's creatures, and to all of creation as a whole.[6]

These youthful essayists whose work is gathered in this volume are passionately pleading that, somehow, by the grace of God, the Church (especially in its Wesleyan permutations) would become much more faithfully effective in its reflection of such love as this—to all. For, as Wesley himself interpreted 1 John 4:17, "as [God] is, so are we in this world"—and if God is love, then what are we to be?

Transformation by Love Divine Is Profoundly Experiential

But this calling, this invitation, to love as God loves cannot be interpreted as a new form of legalism. Thankfully, we are not left to our own devices. Eugenio in his essay has called us to the Eucharistic table, as indeed Wesley himself did so faithfully,[7] that we might be nourished and nurtured in the practices of love around a common meal hosted by our Lord and Teacher. We approach this Table in faith and hope that the Holy Spirit comes upon those common elements of earth's bounty, and upon us. And Wesley would encourage us to seek and to expect a living and transformative experience of the love of God outpoured into our hearts through the gift of the Spirit (Romans 5:x). Thus, "we love because God first loved us" (1 John 4:19). Further, as Wesley insisted in his two sermons on the Holy Spirit's witness, "[W]e must love God before we can be holy at all, this being the root of all holiness. Now we cannot love God till we know he loves us . . . and we cannot know his pardoning love to us till his Spirit witnesses [that love] to our spirit."[8] To put it once more in the words of 1 John, "By this we know that we abide in him and he in us, because he has given us of his Spirit"

6. See Wesley, Sermon 56, "God's Approbation of His Works," Sermon 118, "On the Omnipresence of God," Sermon 120, "The Unity of the Divine Being," and especially Sermon 60, "The General Deliverance." For the purposes and constraints of this Afterword, reference to these sermons must suffice to make the point regarding the fourth "note" in the Wesleyan tune I'm trying to hum: that the love of God is so lavish and unbounded as to include all of creation in its transformative intentions. This, in my judgment, is the one crucial element lacking in this otherwise fine collection of essays.

7. See Wesley, Sermon 101, 427ff. See also Maddox, "Reconnecting the Means to the End," 29–66, and Lodahl, "'Looking for the End without Using the Means,'" 111–22.

8. Wesley, Sermon 10, 274. Wesley repeats this line of argument word for word in "The Witness of the Spirit, II," ibid., 290.

(4:13). If there are realities we come to know because God actually gifts us with the very Spirit of God, then there is indeed a critical role, as Wesley often insisted, for Christian experience of the Holy Spirit as contoured by the person and ministry of the Incarnate Word (cf. 1 John 4:2).

What these young scholars proclaim, then, is profoundly Wesleyan: this dynamic love of God in Jesus Christ, freely and graciously lavished upon our lives by the very Spirit of God, impels us outward, out of our own narrow and provincial concerns to realities much bigger: to a world of diverse peoples, including especially all those people whose experiences and voices were effectively silenced for centuries—even for millennia—by the colonial and hierarchical rule of the "white man" of Western Europe and North America. If white males such as I will yet have a voice in the Wesleyan theological chorus, it will not and must not ever again be a dominating, "solo" performance; no, the time is now upon us to listen closely, carefully, respectfully, openly and hopefully to the experiences and the voices of women, of once colonized and marginalized peoples, of Southern Hemisphere Christians—and indeed of the groaning creation itself.

83ff - categorisation of Wesleyanism, context

106-107 - hermeneutics, Wesley & Salvation
  (+ 112)
113-114 - theological tradition & ecclesial location

Printed in Great Britain
by Amazon